Performing Life

Performing Life

· THE STORY OF RUTH POSSELT, AMERICAN VIOLINIST ·

Diana Lewis Burgin

Acknowledgments

This book has been a long time in the making, and I owe thanks to the many people who encouraged me along the way and helped to make it possible. First of all, to my dear friend Rosina Persad, who cared for my mother and was there for her till the very end. To Ann Taylor Casadaban, Hiroko Nakahara, Dr. Michael Nieland, Lois Gosa, Malcolm Brannen, and Charles Rex, violinists all, whose memories of Ruth Posselt made an invaluable contribution to this book.

To Nathan Brown, who single-handedly saw to it that Ruth Posselt's legacy was preserved on compact discs. To the late Fred Maroth of West Hill Radio Archives, who produced the three-CD set of Posselt's historic performances, and to Ward Marston, who also did masterful remasterings of seemingly hopelessly broken records. To Wilbur Herrington for making possible my Dukelsky project on YouTube. To Bridget Carr, archivist for the Boston Symphony Orchestra, who was helpful in trying to locate numerous materials and tapes. To my UMass colleagues Pratima Prasad and Claudia Esposito for helping me understand Jacques Thibaud's letters both literally and figuratively. To Jessika Hazelton of The Troy Bookmakers for producing this book, and to Brian Halley of the University of Massachusetts Press for distributing it. Special thanks to Susanna Sturgis for her meticulous and brilliant copyediting of the manuscript and to Kalen Ratzlaff, my first reader, whose comments galvanized me into making much-needed revisions when I thought the book was done. And finally to my cousin Juliusz Burgin, who took me to concert halls in Holland where my mother had played in the thirties and translated into English her Dutch reviews; to my brother, Richard, who lived through Ruth Posselt's performing life with me; and to the other two ladies of Housatonic, dearest Svet, who's been with this opus from start to finish, and Dasha Samsonovna, who listened to its many revisions, occasionally offering a bark or a paw push urging me to go out and play.

To the memory of
Ruth Posselt,
my virtuoso Mom

"It's child abuse, really, isn't it, what he's had to go through.,"[said Rudy.]

"That's a bit extreme, don't you think?"

"Well, look at it. He starts the violin at – what? – four, five years old. That's when most of them start. You think it was his idea, no parental pressure? Then his mama stands over him for three or four hours a day, making him practice. I've seen these kids. . . They're like those tennis prodigies, the teenagers with some big loudmouth bully of a dad hovering over them every minute of the day. They've had their childhoods taken away from them. I'd say that was abuse, wouldn't you?"

"Some kids like it," I said. "You can't generalize."

– Paul Adam, *Paganini's Ghost*

The curse of the artist is to have the best part of one's faculties occupied only with one's craft. Friends and family skim your existence like a fisherman on the Abersee, while your real self is as inaccessible to them as the depths of the lake.

– Matt Rees, *Mozart's Last Aria*

Table of Contents

I am a fiddler and a great musician plays like a devil.
– Ruth Posselt, 1978

Preface

When I heard the Dukelsky, the first thing that came to my mind
was: My GOD! That woman could play!!! Unbelievable still. The
jaws of anyone with ears have to drop when they hear her.
– Ann Taylor Casadaban, June 2010

Ruth Posselt is one of the three greatest violinists playing today,
the other two being Heifetz and Menuhin. The only reason why
she is not known as one of the world's foremost violinists is because she is an *American girl.*
– Serge Koussevitzky, November 1938

Posselt was an important figure in America's music-making life
and if she never quite reached the ranks of the elite the works
written for her, or promoted or premiered by her, were ... hardly
insignificant. She was a splendid, proselytising musician and this
salute [these CDs] will be welcomed by her admirers everywhere.
– Jonathan Woolf, June 2008

The above impressions of Ruth Posselt's violin playing sum up her
story, the story of a twentieth-century virtuoso violinist who was
technically and artistically comparable to the greatest violinists
of her age but was not and still is not known as such because, as
Serge Koussevitzky said, "she was an *American girl.*"[1] Even the few

mentions of Posselt's career that exist in the literature often contain mistakes and misinformation. This first-ever full-length biography of Ruth Posselt, based mainly on materials in her personal archive, seeks first of all to inscribe her performing life and achievements into the history of twentieth-century American music. In a broader context, it also shows how Posselt's personal and professional struggles and experiences both perform and illustrate the career trajectory of many women instrumentalists of her generation.

At the same time, this biography cum remembrance has a narrower, more subjective focus. Like many performers of her day, Posselt fairly stringently separated her public and private lives and stories; she kept certain secrets so well that even those closest to her, including me, her daughter, remained clueless unless and until she chose to reveal them. Her well-rehearsed and -performed anecdotes, and even her more private "spontaneous" revelations, allowed her to control the narrative of her life so closely that although she was part of my life until I was over sixty, I came to know her in some important ways only after her death, when I had the chance to pore over her life as it was reflected in the voluminous collection of papers and memorabilia she left behind.

My mother had a repertoire of favorite stories and reminiscences, which I heard so often that I came to know them by heart, to the point that I could hear her telling them in my head, almost verbatim, as I was writing them into this book. As I wrote them down, they seemed to me virtual quotations from a kind of oral autobiography spoken to me through my memory. I have chosen to quote such stories and comments directly, in quotation marks, rather than put them into the third person. I cannot vouch for the accuracy of what Posselt said to family and friends, or of what she was quoted as saying to the press in the numerous stories about her, and of course, in the process of going through the published and unpublished memorabilia she left behind and organizing her archive, I often wondered how much of the life she regaled public and private listeners with was actually supported by "the facts." The scholar in me was challenged to find out. In the end, I was frankly surprised that, as best I could determine, most of the stories she told were essentially true, making allowances for normal exaggeration and performer's hype.

Most interesting to me, a professor of literature and a trained reader of text, were those parts of Posselt's familiar, familial, yet more or less public narrative that seemed to me to contain hints about her truly untold private life. These struck me as the secret underpinnings, or even the inner content, of some of her performances, both public and private, both onstage and off-.

All of this leads me to speculate: What if the essence of a successful performance, technical considerations aside, is a concerted effort on the performer's part to hide from her listeners the deep-lying feelings she has suppressed in order to express them in controlled and aesthetically pleasing fashion? In this book, I attempt a quasi-daughterly, quasi-scholarly answer to this question by trying to re-create, contextualize, and read Ruth Posselt's performing life on the basis of her own and others' stories, on the one hand, and documentary evidence that she saved and left behind, on the other: photographs, newspaper accounts and clippings, concert programs, business and personal letters, publicity material, diaries, interviews, contracts, and various public documents.

I have organized this heterogeneous material into a continuous, more or less chronological narrative that presents my reconstruction of Ruth Posselt's *performing* life in nine parts: a Prelude that provides some family history, seven chapters that follow the trajectory of her career from the twenties through the seventies of the last century and that contain an inner narrative called "Performing Premieres," and finally, a Postlude. For the most part, I have resisted the temptation to comment on Posselt's story, and have generally allowed the material to speak for itself, even when it seems to beg for interpretation. In the remainder of this preface, I sketch out the broader historical, cultural, and musical contexts which frame my rendition of Ruth Posselt's life in music, as I heard it in her own voice and read about it in the words of others.

♩♩♩

Dubbed at different times both "the female Heifetz" and "the female Menuhin," Ruth Posselt (1911–2007)[2] was about a decade younger than Jascha Heifetz and five years older than Yehudi Menuhin, whom Bruno Monsaingeon has called the last of the great twentieth-century virtuosi.[3] In terms of her female coevals, Posselt was a close contemporary of another largely forgotten American violinist, Joan Field (1915–1988), whose career in some ways paralleled hers, and she has been compared (as many female fiddlers are) to the Jewish-Austrian virtuosa Erica Morini (1904–1995). Morini's career was bigger than Posselt's, but like Posselt, she became disappointed by the way managers treated her because she was female. There is no small irony in the fact that Morini's last notoriety came not for her playing, but for the theft of her Stradivarius.

At the beginning, Posselt's story reads like that of many virtuosos, male and female. She shared with her peers exceptional talent that manifested very early, personalized instruction, musical sensitivity, and love of the attention her playing brought her. Billed as a "prodigy," Posselt made her debut in New York's Carnegie Hall at the age of eleven, and her concert debut, with the New York Philharmonic, at eighteen. She had an excellent, if not world-renowned, and dedicated teacher. Like many concert violinists as well, she had at least one parent who single-mindedly pushed her toward stardom, so that she sacrificed part of her childhood, youth, and formal education to practicing the violin. She also shared with other great violinists a desire for perfection in her art, which perhaps was a source as much of self-torment as of joy.

More ironically, Posselt was typical of the majority of outstanding violinists in that she did not make it to superstar status. In the relatively small field of virtuosi, there were and are always too many prodigious talents for the number of highest-status engagements available. As in other brutally competitive professions, to make it to the top, a virtuoso needed and still needs (in addition to exceptional talent, long hours of practice, and mastery of a supremely difficult instrument) important musical contacts, successful management, and just plain good luck – having the right people hear her in the right place at the right time. When Posselt finally did reach her high, but less than celestial, peak, it was due in large part to the active support of leading musicians such as Jacques Thibaud, Serge Koussevitzsky, Eugene Goossens, and Richard Burgin.

At the same time, Posselt's beginnings as a violin prodigy also differed in some important ways from the childhoods of the biggest prodigies of her day. First of all, she was a native-born and -educated American violinist, while most of the others were Europeans. Posselt's nationality unexpectedly proved somewhat of a disadvantage for making a big-time career because when she was starting to perform in public in the early 1920s, America was still considered at best a poor relation to Europe in serious classical music. American audiences wanted to hear European virtuosi. In addition, there were sociocultural and family factors that combined to isolate Posselt, both geographically and musically, from her older and younger peers, and that forced her into a more interrupted career trajectory than the Heifetzes, Menuhins, and Morinis, to all of whom she was frequently compared.

Although Posselt had an ambitious parent pushing her, that parent was not dominant in her life until Ruth was past the prodigy stage, nor did she have any important connections in the music world. As a result, she got a comparatively late and halting start even in the major concert venues of her home country, let alone those of Europe, which at that time was still the center of violin virtuosity. Finally, Posselt's German immigrant father insisted that his exceptionally talented youngest daughter grow up as a typical American girl, a life in which a professional career was not a priority. This attitude kept her out of the prodigy mill while she was still young enough to seem prodigious, and it developed in her a center or focus not restricted to the violin. She grew up with "normal" American-girl dreams – for love, fame, fortune, and, most of all, the movies.

Nevertheless, the most important factor that set Posselt apart from most of her young-virtuoso peers appears to have been her gender. Emil Posselt, himself a violinist and music teacher, encouraged musical training for his daughters and approved of their becoming musicians, especially teachers, but he was adamant about their not leaving home in pursuit of a career. There was nothing unusual about such attitudes. Teaching music, particularly voice or piano, was not only a perfectly respectable career for a woman in the United States by the latter part of the nineteenth century, it was actually a female-dominated field, so much so that from about 1910 cries were increasingly heard that classical music had become excessively "feminized."

The prejudice against female instrumentalists, other than pianists, however, goes back to the Middle Ages. By the age of the great violin virtuosi, from Paganini onward, the violin was widely perceived as a man's instrument, in part, perhaps, according to one theory, because of its shape and the names of its parts,[4] and in part because of the widely held opinion that women did not look good or "feminine" when playing instruments.[5] In a woman's hands, the violin even acquired phallic symbolism. (Posselt herself claimed a psychiatrist had told her that her violin was her penis.) No matter how attenuated or absurd such theories may strike many people now, until very recently they were not without influence on how women violinists were perceived.

In more practical terms, the notion that the violin was for men to play was a reality that dictated which soloists were hired in American concert venues in the 1920s and 1930s. When Posselt negotiated her first contract with Haensel & Jones, an independent concert bureau, her manager would only sign the agreement after pointing out to her "the general difficulty in the past which we have experienced in endeavoring to book a woman violinist." They took her on "only because of our faith in your ability and artistic standing."[6]

Throughout Posselt's career, American music critics, from the most to the least knowledgeable and prestigious, revealed in their highly positive reviews of Posselt's playing their collective conviction that women, especially attractive ones, are usually not up to the challenge of virtuoso fiddling, a man's job. Critics repeatedly underscored how Posselt's playing could not have been predicted from her appearance: she seemed too "fragile" a girl "to undertake the performance of Tchaikovsky's formidable concerto";[7] "look[ed] too young and beautiful to be so talented";[8] and "she ha[d] the slender, blond, fragile prettiness that no one expects to show up with mature talent."[9] Her "deceptive appearance" (which she certainly cultivated, not intending it to be deceptive) bewildered a Cincinnati critic in 1939 when Posselt "took the Dvorak Concerto in hand with a forthrightness that was anything but dainty or feminine."[10] Six years later a Houston critic summed up a widely held perception: "The chances are very small that a young and attractive blonde in red velvet can do anything that displeases an audience. Miss Posselt, however, needed little dependence on her good looks to put her listeners in a mood of enthusiasm. She is a very graceful and eloquent musician, and she proved a good master of all the hazards of the Tchaikovsky score."[11]

In short, Posselt was hailed as the exception that proved the sexist rule – she was judged "far superior to anything in the feminine line of violinists we have heard in several years,"[12] she "displayed a virtuosity with this instrument seldom found in women artists,"[13] and she "played with utter abandon rarely displayed by women violinists."[14]

Being perceived as a woman who looks like a woman but plays like a man is obviously a double-edged compliment; it reinforces the stereotypes it seems to disprove, and draws too much attention to those stereotypes rather than remarking on the genuinely exceptional things Posselt did accomplish in American music and on which this book will focus. She premiered and popularized a number of major works for the violin by contemporary composers, with whom she enjoyed collegial relations, among them Edward Burlingame Hill, Walter Piston, Samuel Barber, Paul Hindemith, Bohuslav Martinů, Aaron Copland, and Vladimir Dukelsky (Vernon Duke). She toured Europe several times in the 1930s, causing a sensation, ironically, as an *American* virtuosa. In 1934 she was one of the first American violinists to tour the recently recognized Soviet Union; in 1937 she was invited to play at the White House. From 1935 to 1964, she appeared sixty-four times with the world-renowned Boston Symphony Orchestra under four different conductors; she also played with most of the major U.S. symphony orchestras and with numerous less prominent ones. Not only did she have a distinguished teaching career, but, exceptionally for a female virtuoso of her generation, she managed both to have a forty-year-long career in music performance and to be a full-time wife and mother.

On a personal note, I imagine the very first piece I heard my mother perform was the Dukelsky Violin Concerto. I was in utero at the time since my mother was pregnant with me when she gave the world premiere. I think that from the beginning of my post-birth life I heard and saw my mother mainly as a violinist and a performer. I absorbed a fairly large amount of music that I knew only from hearing her practice – I learned the names of the composers only much, much later: Bach, Mozart, Nardini, Hindemith, Copland, Kabalevsky, Fauré, Franck, Achron, Manén, Dvořák, Vitali. However, I didn't recognize the Dukelsky when I finally heard it on a digitally remastered CD of the original performance.[15] Evidently, she hadn't played it enough, which in itself says something about the "sacrificial" aspect of performing (but never getting the chance to record) new music.

And Ruth Posselt was, above all, a performer, a performer for live audiences. By all accounts, from musicians, colleagues, friends, fans, critics both knowledgeable and not, even naysayers, she performed superbly. A brief selection from about two hundred reviews of Posselt's playing by American and European music critics testifies to the general response of audiences to her playing over the years: Her performance of the Goldmark Concerto with the New York Philharmonic in 1929 "aroused real enthusiasm"; she was "cheered wildly" for her Tchaikovsky at her 1931 Denver debut; she "electrified an unusually large audience" in Jordan Hall, Boston, in 1932; she was hailed as "one of the few elect" in Amsterdam (1932); she "brought the hall to ecstasy, stormy and long applause, flowers too," in The Hague (1934); at her first New York Town Hall recital, "the audience showed its appreciation in a demonstrative manner" (1935); in Richmond, Virginia, in 1936, "she was recalled time after time until one ceased to count"; "Applause reigned supreme" after the 1940 world premiere of the Piston First Violin Concerto in New York; at the conclusion of the Dvořák in Pittsburgh, 1943, "the audience, orchestra players and conductor recalled Miss Posselt seven times"; and finally, at Tanglewood in 1956, "Miss Posselt's execution of the Hindemith was a tour de force . . . an unsurpassed performance."

An "unsurpassed performance" – but at what cost? And from a totally different angle, with critical acclaim and audience appeal, not to mention violin playing that was demonstrably second to none, why were there so relatively few performances over a career of forty years? The easy answer was suggested by one of my mother's students: "Too bad she performed at a time when women violinists were not appreciated." That answer is certainly correct, but in a more complex way than I had originally thought. More important, it is not the whole answer.

My mother's diaries, which she kept sporadically in the early 1940s and the late 1960s, give telegraphic accounts of her daily life, performances, and activities. A clue to their contents is provided by my discovery that the five most frequently occurring words were *practice, rehearse, concert, love,* and *swim/beach.* This underscored my impression that performing and performances permeated about sixty percent of my mother's life. As for her remarks on her actual concert and recital performances, they confirmed what I had gathered from overhearing her concert postmortems when I was older, that every performance, regardless of venue, was a kind of test: Would she come through against the odds (nerves, sleepless nights, occupational aches and pains)? Would she succeed despite the threat of failure? Was she really as great in her own ears as most people said she sounded? And after she married and had children, could she have it all? When she liked what she heard – and most of the time she apparently did – she seemed to feel unabashedly triumphant, powerful, and sometimes even godlike. That kind of payoff must have been worth whatever it cost. And yet . . .

Life is multi-focused and diverse, but for performers, the performance is all; it requires total absorption in every detail of what one is doing as one is doing it, and always with the goal of convincing a

crowd of strangers that what one is doing is totally natural, spontaneous, and costing no effort at all. To me, this is the real gift of virtuosity.
The successful, and yet hazardous, expression of this gift is the story
of Ruth Posselt's performing life, both from her own and from other
people's point of view. I shall record it, as accurately as possible, in
this book.

A Musical Family in Medford, Massachusetts

Born on September 6, 1911, at her family's home on Sheridan Avenue in Medford, Massachusetts, Ruth Pierce Posselt was the last of the seven children of Emil August Posselt, a music educator and freelance union musician, and Ida Lewis Pierce, homemaker and voice teacher.

Emil Posselt came from a branch of a widely dispersed German family that had its roots in Upper Lusitania and had produced several generations of musicians. Ruth's paternal great-grandfather, Tobias Josef Posselt, a smallholder and tailor in Rusdorf, near Königshain, was also an amateur musician. Two of the nine children he had with his Bohemian-born wife, Theresia Czidiel, took up music as a profession: the oldest son, Josef, born in 1830, eventually became municipal conductor in Dresden, and the next oldest, August Bernhard Conrad Posselt (Ruth's paternal grandfather), became municipal conductor and band oboist in the First Pioneer Battalion Band in the same city. August Posselt's marriage to Juliane Böhmer produced nine children, of whom the oldest was Emil August Posselt, Ruth's father. As a boy, Emil learned to play all the band instruments as well as the violin and viola; when he was in his late teens, his father died, of throat cancer or TB, and his mother remarried.

Emil Posselt emigrated to the United States in 1885, as part of a German orchestra, and for his first several years in this country, he was the director of several popular bands, most notably the Our Star Orchestra, with which he toured widely in America and Canada. Around 1890, he settled in Middleborough, Massachusetts, as a boarder in the home of Thomas W. Pierce, a local hardware dealer, whose ancestors, through his mother's line, had come over on the *Mayflower*. Thomas was a six-times-great-grandson of Myles Standish.

Thomas Pierce and his wife, Mary Besse, of Ware, Massachusetts, had seven children, six girls and one boy. The Pierces were music lovers who enjoyed family singing and amateur music making. All five Pierce daughters – Cora, Dora, Ida, Maude, and Grace – turned to music as a profession. After studying voice in Boston, Cora established herself in Maine as a voice teacher. Dora was an organist and organ teacher in Connecticut, and Grace Gordon Pierce, who never married, became supervisor of music in the Arlington, Massachusetts, public schools. Maude Pierce Allen had a professional stage career and appeared on Broadway and in various Hollywood movies in the thirties and forties.

Like her sisters, the third Pierce daughter, Ida, had a fine voice and aspired to a career in music or on the stage. She studied both voice and piano in Boston and appeared now and again in semiprofessional and amateur musical productions. She may have sung for a time in an opera company in Albany, New York. For a young woman of her time, she also possessed a good formal education, having graduated in 1888 from Middleborough High School, a member of a class of only five – all women. Ultimately, young Ida decided to go into teaching and matriculated at the Bridgewater State Normal School, from which she graduated in 1892. By that time, however, she had fallen in love with the handsome young German musician living at her father's home on Courtland Street in Middleborough, Emil Posselt, who would shortly file his final application for American citizenship.

By this time, like all freelance musicians of all times, Emil had numerous jobs. He was a jack of all musical trades: he played cornet, baritone, saxophone, and other winds in various touring bands; he conducted various groups (like the Bay State Band of ninety men, based in Middleborough, of which he became director in 1891); he apparently even composed – one of his works, "Wedding on the Plantation," was said to be a "descriptive piece of much merit and beauty" after a performance in Frederick, Maryland, in January 1891. Emil traveled a lot, too, not only as a member of touring bands and opera orchestras, but between part-time teaching jobs in Middleborough, Boston, and Albany. He had established a professional base in Albany by the beginning of the nineties, serving as director of music at the First Lutheran Church until 1895, as a member of the opera orchestra and the Albany String Quartette, and as a music teacher.

Emil and Ida were a handsome and passionate young couple. As a middle-aged woman Ida Posselt loved to repeat to her daughters how her husband had told her that if she didn't marry him, he was "going to kill 'er." This might have been a cover story for a shotgun wedding, however. The records show that the couple was married in Middleborough on June 7, 1893, then moved to Albany, and a little less than six months later, on November 29, 1893, their first child, Gladys, was born. Yet all her life my aunt Gladys believed what her mother told her, that she had been born in March 1894.

The young family moved back to Middleborough a couple of years later, when little Gladys could easily pass for three months younger than she was. Two years later, and one (almost two) daughters larger, the Posselt family moved to Medford, where they would live for the rest of Emil's relatively short life and Ida's long one.

"My mother used to joke," Ruth would often recall, "that she had only to hang up my father's pants and she would get pregnant." But she always added that Ida loved her children and never complained, continuing: "She worked at home her whole life, washed all the linen by hand, gardened, cooked, gave voice and piano lessons, substitute taught – she was very strong. Once she fell down the cellar stairs and broke her hip, but she refused to go to the doctor. She just lay there, for six weeks, on a bed my brother made for her. My brother brought her food, and my sister washed her, and eventually the hip healed itself. She was a remarkable woman. But once she started having all those children, that was the end of her dreams of becoming a singer – and she had such a beautiful voice! Later, I realized that my mother was ambitious for me and wanted me to become what she had failed to be herself."

After the Posselts settled in Medford, Emil rented a studio in Boston and advertised himself as a private teacher of violin, mandolin, guitar, and banjo. He became instructor and director of music for the Boston Elevated Railway Band, founded in 1898; for over twenty years he served as a music instructor at the Leopold Morse Home for Jewish Orphans in Dorchester and as the director of its Juvenile Band, which he had founded in 1902. Later, he gave instrumental classes in the public schools of Arlington, Watertown, and Milton. He joined the Boston Musicians' Protective Association when it was founded in 1911 and according to Ruth was "very proud of his union membership." He also played for many years in the Tremont Theater Orchestra in Boston and the Boston Opera Orchestra.

Due to Emil's strong work ethic, his love of manual labor, Ida's thrifty household management, and contributions to the family finances from the older girls – Gladys, Molly, and Marjorie – once they became young adults, the Posselts maintained a middle-class, middle-brow lifestyle until the Great Depression. By today's standards, they were certainly not well-off, but by the living standards of the era before the social safety net, neither were they poor.

Ruth shared very few memories of her father, except to say that he was a strict, straitlaced man who would not allow a playing card or any alcohol in the house. The difficulties of supporting a family on a musician's salary seem to have embittered him about music as a profession in his adopted country; he became convinced that America was commercial and did not need any more starving musicians, and he apparently refused to allow his only son, Emil Lockhart, to learn to play an instrument despite the boy's obvious musical talent and love for music.

On the other hand, Emil Posselt encouraged his daughters in developing their musical talents with the predictable result that they almost all became musicians and music teachers, like many of their aunts. Gladys, a pianist and violinist, went on to graduate in piano from the New England Conservatory, eventually becoming a prominent piano teacher in Boston. Molly was a cellist in her youth, though she gave up any career aspirations when she got married. Marjorie studied violin from a very young age and was, in a sense, Ruth's precursor as well as her first teacher. She became an accomplished violinist but had to give up her dream of a concert career due to "nerves." In the twenties, Marjorie formed a popular all-women jazz band, the Friendly Maids of WEEI, which had a significant following. Later, she eked out a living as a violin and piano teacher. Grace was also a violinist and violin teacher before severe depression began to afflict her in midlife.

In the teens and early twenties, Emil and Ida Posselt in fact presided over a kind of family cottage music industry. Emil encouraged his daughters to play in various local venues. He would include Marjorie, Gladys, and Molly in violin recitals of his pupils at his church in Medford; in one of them the Posselt girls appeared in nine of the thirteen numbers. In their teens, the older sisters played as the Posselt Trio, as a string quartet, and as soloists. Gladys and Marjorie were proficient on several instruments, and everyone in the family sang.

The Posselt Trio went semiprofessional in the teens with Ida Posselt serving as self-appointed manager and director of the group, and sometimes playing herself. Billing themselves as "sisters who had been coached by their father, a prominent musician in Boston," they played gigs at concerts, weddings, churches, and private socials, both as a group and separately as soloists. Emil Posselt occasionally joined his daughters in a group called the Posselts, in which the versatility of the various members was stressed: Emil Posselt (violin, viola, cello, mandolin, guitar, trumpet, drums); Gladys Posselt (piano, violin, soprano); Marjorie Posselt (violin, piano, soprano); and Molly Posselt (cello, contralto). Finally, both Emil and Ida gave private lessons – Emil in violin, mandolin, guitar, cornet, and trombone, and Ida in piano, voice culture, elocution, Latin, French, and English.

So this was the "musical family" into which Ruth Pierce Posselt was born, coincidentally in the same month and on the same day, September 6, as her father had been born in 1865. Looking back, she noted to a newspaperman, "We had a lot in common in my home, with Marjorie and Grace and myself playing the violin, Gladys the piano, and Molly the cello, but as time went on, the family became broken up." In fact, not all the Posselt children left home. For four of them, and for various reasons, 60 Sheridan Avenue remained their actual or "official" address for a large portion of their lives. Even for those who established their own homes as adults, the Medford house, with its permanent residents, Ida, Emil Jr., and Grace, retained its aura of home, for better or for worse. The Posselt family tentacles embraced all the children, psychologically and emotionally.

CHAPTER ONE

A Wonder-Child's Normal American Girlhood: 1914–1925

What an angel you were, and what a soldier to practice so diligently as a mere infant!

– Marjorie Posselt

On Ruth Posselt's thirty-fifth birthday, her mother waxed poetical on her youngest daughter's birth: "Greetings, with oceans of love on this, the greatest of all days, your 'Birthday.' I would that I had something to send as sweet as you, but do you know I haven't been to the stores for months, not even to the car line, for Emil [her son] has bought everything. But then, that would only be material and not to be compared to the love of the little gentle spirit that was ushered into the world thirty odd years ago with the tiny little fists held so tight together to your chin and seemed quite immovable. I cannot forget it!"[16]

Ida Posselt's first five children came one after the other in the first ten years of her marriage, but after Grace was born in 1903, she had a break from childbearing, so that her last two girls, Naomi and Ruth, were relatively late-in-life babies. Like their biblical prototypes, they were constant companions (at least in childhood), but contrary to those prototypes, Ruth was the leader and Naomi her devoted follower, in every area where she could follow. Both baby sisters seem to have been mothered as much by their older sister Marjorie as by their biological mother. Marjorie later remembered with elation "our happy times when you were a beautiful baby and I used to imagine you and Naomi were my own – remember? I have repeated so often what an angel you always were and what a soldier to practice so diligently when a mere infant."[17]

The stories of violin virtuosi are a genre in themselves, related to hagiography, in which the subject's musical destiny is usually revealed by a special sign in earliest childhood. In reality, most virtuosi cannot remember *choosing* to become concert violinists. They have to begin study at such a young age that they often can't recall exactly when they started playing the violin. That "memory" is imparted to them by others when they get older and becomes the central event of their official biographies – the revelation of their gift.

Ruth Posselt was no exception. Her mother's story, widely reported in the press when the child first appeared onstage, invariably stressed the musical family in which Ruth grew up and her own special role in it. With so many in her family playing the violin, Ida would explain, it was not strange that Ruthie would too. And she would add that when Ruth was an infant, she used to lay the sleeping baby on her lap two or three hours a day while she played and sang.

The revelatory moment came when, as a toddler of three, Ruthie went (in some variants, "crawled") into her father's music room (or, in some variants, "the attic"), which was filled with instruments and musical memorabilia from his touring days. There she discovered a toy violin; she would climb up on an old trunk that had belonged to Nellie Melba and attempt to play it. Her father finally bought her a real, child-sized violin. Then her sister Marjorie taught her some tunes, and shortly thereafter Ruth gave her first impromptu "concert" – very possibly the only unrehearsed performance of her life. At a church festival with her parents, the four-year-old was put on a table and played the popular song "Tipperary," so fervently that her listeners made her play it several times over before they would let her go. Marjorie, already a professional violinist, was sure they had a genius in the family and started teaching Ruth scales.

This story may have some truth in it. After months of research, I was able to confirm that Emil Posselt had played in Melba's orchestra when it toured in the mid-1890s, so it's not beyond the realm of possibility that the trunk in question had once belonged to the great diva. "Tipperary" was a big hit song in 1914, shortly before the time when Ruth began playing violin, and it's not hard to imagine her learning to play it and performing it at a church festival. Most important, Marjorie Posselt was Ruth's first teacher and a lifelong admirer of her talent. Ruth always gave the lion's share of credit for her success to the daily lessons she had for three years with Marjorie. Because of those lessons, she stressed, she never had to practice by herself and "therefore, I never practiced mistakes. I had that distinct advantage."

Ruth claimed that as a young child, she wanted to play the violin very much. Music, she appeared to feel, echoing her mother, was just part of her home environment: everyone was playing and singing, to her and to each other. She wanted to be part of the closely knit family group, and so she later concluded it was natural she would start playing, too. In addition to perfect pitch, innate musicality, and talent, she possessed both a strong desire to perform and a desire for the special attention her playing attracted, and, later, the competitive urge to outperform others.

In Bruno Monsaingeon's film *The Art of the Violin*, the great Russian-born, American violinist Nathan Milstein makes a delightfully ironic comment about his profession: "When you come to think of it, there's something sort of ridiculous about an adult standing up in front of a crowd and playing the violin." Posselt, who was down-to-earth and not given to waxing ironic or otherwise about her profession, often said that when she was a child, playing the violin seemed like a game to her. When she got older, playing became more serious and fraught, even nerve-wracking at times, but it was still what she had been doing since she was a very little girl. Her performing life began before she knew it had; she did not consciously choose it.

Maybe, though, it was all in the stars? A curious document lay buried in a heap of moldy papers hidden in a carton, one of many in my mother's voluminous and chaotic collection of forgotten memorabilia. It is a copy, written on notebook paper in her own youthful hand, of a commercially produced natal horoscope for a Virgo whose destiny was controlled by Mercury. As confirmed by teenage Ruth's own 20/20 hindsight (which is probably why she copied it), this piece of mass-produced pop astrology revealed, almost uncannily, as these things sometimes do, some salient aspects of her personality and offered several spot-on predictions, which I have italicized in the representation given below.

Planet that controls your destiny is <u>MERCURY</u>

<u>VIRGO</u> House the VI

Disposition – *Affectionate. Methodical.*

Vocation – *You will excel in Music.*

You are good at keeping Secrets, your own, and others'.
You have some false pride.
Do not try to domineer over other people, this is your weakest point
and will not work.

Diseases – *Legs.*
You will imagine you are sick when you are not.

Travels – *you are going sometime on some*
Important Mission.
Look out for obstacles in
Love Making

☋☋☋

After three years of Marjorie's teaching, little Ruth had progressed so quickly, and shown such promise, that her mother arranged for her to play for a wider public. Ruth's performing life started on May 21, 1918, in Steinert Hall, Boston, after which a newspaper headline announced above the prodigy's picture, "Six-Year-Old Violinist Has Great Talent."[18]

Many aspects of this first, non-professional performance served as harbingers of more serious performances to come. From the very start, Ruth's father had resolved not to commercialize her. Unlike the classic ambitious stage parents, Emil and Ida (as long as her husband was alive) steadfastly insisted that little Ruthie should have a normal American childhood, and they carried through on their intention. At the same time, they did organize a small number of "debuts" for Ruth which ensured that she got a measure of attention from Boston and, later, New York audiences and critics as a "child prodigy."

Ida Posselt took on the managerial role from the get-go. Since she was the wife of a musician, had been a semiprofessional singer herself, and was also the sister of the New York artiste Maude Allen, she did have some contacts in the musical and theater world. She also was a member of the Republican Woman's Club and cultivated the acquaintance of a few wealthy Boston patronesses of music.

One of Boston's prominent voice teachers and singers in the first decades of the twentieth century was Helen Allen Hunt, who had been born in Melrose in 1870 and was a graduate of Braintree High School. Madame Hunt studied voice in Europe and enjoyed a career as a recitalist and vocal soloist in Boston and New York before turning to teaching. She was Ida Posselt's coeval and, like Ida's sister Maude, an ardent Christian Scientist. The two women were almost certainly acquaintances, and Ida somehow arranged for her youngest daughter to make her first "debut" as an "Assisting Artist" in a recital by Madame Hunt's voice students. With Marjorie as her accompanist, six-year-old Ruth played short pieces by de Bériot, Allard, Massenet, and Seitz. Marjorie recalled a quarter of a century later: "I am still raving over you as the dearest child . . . when you played Seitz G minor."[19]

Even this amateur first debut ran into problems due to Boston's strict child labor laws. The mayor of the city apparently objected to Ruth's appearance because of her "tender age." "But he was awfully nice," she told an interviewer many years later when she was recalling her childhood as a young concert artist. "He agreed that I could play after Mother assured him that I was not appearing for money."[20] A description of this first performance reported that while Miss Hunt's pupils performed, Ruth waited close to her mother and sisters, sucking her thumb. When she was told it was her turn to play, her mother put the tiny fiddle and bow in her hands, and she went up on the stage.

In an interview after the concert, Ruth gave a seemingly unrehearsed, unselfconscious comment on her first performance: "Mother and the girls were all afraid for me, but I wasn't a bit scared. I love to play and a thousand people couldn't frighten me when I have my violin. I did forget at first when they clapped, though – I bowed right at my music stand instead of to my audience. I was glad when they called me back for flowers because then, I could show everyone that I really did know how to bow."[21] Ruth must have been unaware of her unintentional pun on bow/bow, but Marjorie, who appreciated such wordplay, may have noted it. What strikes me is the typical little girl's concern over having at first forgotten not her notes, or correct bowing, but the right protocol for bowing to her audience, and then her unfeigned satisfaction that she got the chance to correct her mistake. Once Ruth outgrew her child-size violin, it was put in a special display case that she kept for the rest of her life. It is still in her last home, where she was living at the time of her death almost ninety years after her Steinert Hall debut.

After that first performance, Marjorie took Ruth to play for her own teacher, the well-known Czech virtuoso Emanuel Ondříček. Born in Plzen, Bohemia, in 1880, Ondříček had begun his life as a child prodigy like his three brothers, all of whom were taught by their father. His brother Carl played in the Boston Symphony Orchestra for several years, and his brother Franz gave the world premiere of the Dvořák Violin Concerto. At the age of fourteen, Emanuel entered the Prague Conservatory as a student of Otakar Sevčik and graduated with the first prize in 1899. His career as a concert violinist took him to all the capitals of Europe, Russia, and America, but after settling in the United States, he gave up concertizing and devoted himself to teaching and composing. In 1915, he opened a studio in Boston, which five years later became the Ondricek School of Violin Art, with a New York branch on Madison Avenue. As a pedagogue, Ondříček was the author of two important violin manuals still in use today, *Superior Finger Exercises* and *The Mastery of Tone-Production and Expression on the Violin*. He also discovered and edited many forgotten compositions, including a concerto by Tartini and several pieces by the Italian Baroque virtuoso Geminiani.

Posselt studied with Ondříček for twelve years and became his star pupil. In 1926, he became her brother-in-law, marrying her oldest sister and favorite accompanist, Gladys, who by then had established herself as a piano teacher in Boston. Ondříček had a long and distinguished teaching career and taught a number of talented violinists, including, at the end of his life, Charles Castleman, but Ruth Posselt was his first big success.

Ondříček's first step in bringing his protégée before the wider public was to arrange a noncommercial (at her father's insistence) "debut" for her in Jordan Hall on May 26, 1920, by including the eight-year-old in the annual concert of the students in his school. The event was called "An Evening of Czechoslovak Music," and "Little Ruth Pierce Posselt" played one number, Wieniawski's Russian Fantasy. Boston critics did not attend, of course, but the coverage in *The Medford Mercury* for May 28, 1920, stressed the local prodigy's *American* talent and training, comparing her to "the well-known Sammy Kramar, the so-called prodigy violinist who comes of Russian parentage," and claiming (on the opinion of unnamed "musical authorities" and "members of the Boston Symphony") that "she could take the palm of being the real American prodigy of which Boston could be proud."

Her first public appearances notwithstanding, Posselt actually did seem to have had a normal childhood, filled with school, household chores, weeding the garden, outdoor sports, summer camp, the beach, games of hopscotch and jacks, and a minimum of practice. She loved her dolls as much as her violin, adored the movies like her mother and sisters, and, most of all, wanted "to have fun." Several of Ruth's favorite past-times in childhood remained favorites her whole life, especially having fun, sports, the movies, and the beach.

Posselt attended the Medford public schools and was a conscientious, even ideal student, liked reading and arithmetic best, and wanted to be like the other kids. Most of all, she hated when the teacher singled her out and asked her to tell the other students about her concerts. "I was so embarrassed when that happened, I wanted to disappear," she would often recall to me.

Ondříček, however, was eager for her to appear as soon as possible and in a big-time concert venue, of which there was only one in those days: Carnegie Hall in New York City. By the summer of 1922, *en plein air*, with her dolls as an audience, Ruth was already practicing much more than a half hour a day in preparation.

Positive reinforcement came from her sister Marjorie, who was traveling with Ondříček in Germany, ostensibly as his fiancée: "Ondi says for you to be sure & practice every day as you are going to play the concert in New York. Besides, if you practice nice I promise to bring you a beautiful doll, the one you said you wanted, about two feet long, glass, with big brown eyes." In making this request, Ruth had feared she was asking too much, but Marjorie assured her, "No, you are not asking too much provided you practice nicely every day.

I trust you will be a nice sweet little girl so when I come back, you can show me all you accomplished. I couldn't believe you played the whole of Wieniawski [Concerto in D Minor] & it pleased me to hear it. I am reviewing it again so I think of you every note I play." Marjorie also encouraged Ruth "to practice the scales by Sevčik [both with] separate bows and sautille, a wonderful exercise. I do it 20 minutes daily – improves technic."[22]

On March 6, 1923, "the amazing eight-year old American violinist, Little Ruth Pierce Posselt," made her New York debut in Carnegie Hall, as the protegée of Emanuel Ondříček, director of the Ondricek School of Violin Art of New York and Boston.[23] Posselt was actually eleven years old at the time, a perfectly respectable age for a child prodigy to make her debut, yet Ida Posselt and Ondříček insisted on shaving three years off her age, in order to make their prodigy seem even more prodigious, a practice which was very common at the time. This is probably why most sources give Posselt's birth year as 1914.

There was a blizzard on the day of the concert, but Carnegie Hall reportedly had a good-sized audience. In the green room as she was about to go onstage, Ruth was her ebullient, insouciant self: instead of warming up, she recalled that she danced around the room playing with some ribbons that came off a box of candy sent her by Margaret Matzenauer, an opera singer who was an acquaintance of her mother's. With her oldest sister, Gladys, as accompanist (probably Ida Posselt's professionally unsound choice made in order to save money), Ruth played the Vitali Chaconne, the Wieniawski D Minor Concerto and Fantasy on Russian Themes, Sarasate's Spanish Dance Op. 21, No. 1, and her favorite piece at the time, Rimsky-Korsakov's Hymn to the Sun.

The papers reported that an enthusiastic public thronged the stage at the end of the program, demanding encores. Ruth played several. After it was all over and friends crowded into the green room, the young recitalist was overheard pleading with her sister, "Oh, Marjorie, aren't we going to stay in New York for a little fun?" And they did. They went to see Charlie Chaplin in *The Pilgrim.* This proved for eleven-year-old Ruth the best part of going to New York, as she later reported to her class at school.[24]

For her mother and Ondříček, the best part of Posselt's Carnegie Hall debut must have been the glowing review given her performance by the noted New York critic Max Smith. After the usual caveats about "not looking with favor on the exploitation of youthful prodigies," Smith wrote that as a reviewer, "in all his experience he could not recall an instance of early development that seemed so remarkable as the case of Ruth Pierce Posselt of Medford, Mass. Remarkable not so much because of the technical skill [she] disclosed as because of the God given musicianship that characterized her playing and the warm, pulsating life, the heartthrob that vitalized her tone. With eyes closed you might have supposed you were listening to a grown up woman, yes, more than that, indeed, a man accomplished in the mechanics of his art."[25]

Ida Posselt told her child's story for local readers in an article about her daughter's New York debut that appeared in *The Boston Sunday Globe* under the long headline "Tiny Medford Girl Violinist Has Won Acclaim of New York Critics. Eleven-Year-Old Ruth Posselt, Seventh Daughter of Musical Family Is Just a Shy Little Mite, Who Likes Charlie Chaplin and Arithmetic and Hates to Practice. Gave First 'Concert' at Age of 3."[26] Mrs. Posselt, the article noted, "speaks heatedly. Her story of making something of her children and making home homelike on a musician's salary is a tale of conquest." At the very end, her ambitions for her youngest daughter come through loud and clear: "Mrs. Posselt has decided Ruth shall get ahead on her own merits. She has made all arrangements for Symphony Hall and goes staunchly on shouldering responsibility. Mrs. Posselt speaks with a gleam in her eye. 'Mother is going to do something for her baby.'"

In an April interview before her Symphony Hall debut, that was now in the offing, Ruth had a chance to speak for herself a bit. She "impressed the interviewer not as a child prodigy, but as a sweet sensible little schoolgirl." She reiterated that she liked to play very much, and when asked whether she wasn't frightened sometimes when she went out on the stage and saw a crowd looking at her, she replied: "Why, I

Medford Girl Violinist
Read Music at 4 Years

Little Ruth Pierce Posselt, child violinist, whose recent New York concert caused critics to proclaim her a genius. Ruth will play in Boston April 15.

Ruth Posselt Impresses Interviewer Not as a Child Prodigy, but as Sweet, Sensible Little Schoolgirl

SYMPHONY HALL

Sunday, April 15, 1923
at 8 P. M.

MR. EMANUEL ONDRICEK
Director of the
ONDRICEK SCHOOL OF VIOLIN ART
of New York and Boston

Presents His Protegee

LITTLE RUTH PIERCE POSSELT

The Phenomenal Child Violinist

PROGRAMME

I. CHACONNE . . . . Vitali

II. CONCERTO IN D-MINOR . . . . . . Wieniawski
    a. ALLEGRO MODERATO
    b. ROMANCE
    c. ALLA ZINGARA

III. a. HYMN TO THE SUN . . . . Rimsky-Korsakoff-Franko
    b. SPANISH DANCE, Op. 21, No. 1 . . . . . Sarasate
    c. FANTASIE ON RUSSIAN THEMES . . . Wieniawski

Miss Gladys Posselt, Accompanist

The Mason & Hamlin Pianoforte.

TICKETS: 50c, 75c, $1.00, 1.50, 2.00, 2.50.
    War Tax, 10 per cent additional.
    On sale at Box Office, Symphony Hall.

don't think about the people. I just think of my music, and I play and play and that's all."27

Ruth's Symphony Hall recital, on Sunday afternoon, April 15, repeated both her Carnegie Hall program and its success. The *Boston Globe* critic wrote, almost paraphrasing a comparison made earlier by Max Smith, that Ruth's "playing would be extraordinary for a grown man. From a little girl of 11 it is phenomenal." He noted her poise and "a platform manner that would be an asset to very many grown-up concert givers"; she "struck the spectator as a normal child of her years, with unusually good manners, and not a trace of the freakishness often miscalled 'artistic temperament.' She played . . . with a beauty of tone and a mastery of the resources of her instrument that many concert violinists never attain. There was no sense of effort in her performance. Her double stopping, harmonics, and other tricks of the fiddler's trade, proved that she had been an apt pupil with remarkable natural gifts. . . . One could not tell how much of last night's performance was astonishingly faithful mimicry of other violinists and how much of her interpretation was her own. . . . Until she is ten years older nobody can be sure that Ruth Pierce Posselt is a genius. But in her case there seems a far greater probability than in the case of most 'infant prodigies' that she will grow up into a world-famous violinist."28

On the same occasion, Chance offered another, unnoticed but wholly accurate portent of Ruth's future. After her performance, two prominent young violinists came backstage to congratulate the little girl. Both of them were destined to figure importantly in her later life. One was the already world-famous Jascha Heifetz, who would shortly and unwittingly catalyze a major family row about Ruth's future; the other was Heifetz's friend and slightly older colleague Richard Burgin, the newly named concertmaster of the Boston Symphony Orchestra, who would, a couple of decades down the road, become Ruth Posselt's almost entire future.

Burgin and Posselt had begun their lives about as far apart as could be in time, place, and culture. When she, daughter of a Yankee mother and a German immigrant father, was born in Medford, Massachusetts, he, a Russian Jew from Warsaw, was beginning his last year of study in Professor Leopold Auer's class at the St. Petersburg Conservatory of Music in Russia. When he arrived in America to take up his duties as concertmaster of the BSO, she was a nine-year-old schoolgirl starting the fifth grade. However, we see that in meeting backstage after Ruth's Symphony Hall violin recital, Burgin and Posselt, despite their many degrees of separation, had already moved significantly closer. The instrument of their rapprochement was the violin.

After her Symphony Hall recital, Ruth returned to family life, practicing, and the beach at Manomet, where her father was building a large cottage. She always liked the outdoors, particularly at Manomet, where she practiced in the fresh air. Ruth and Marjorie loved to pack a lunch, take their violins, and head to Manomet Point to spend the day playing together.

In September 1923, Ruth entered the eighth grade at Swann Junior High School in Medford. Answering questions for a school assignment aimed, apparently, at a self-assessment of one's strengths, weaknesses, and aspirations, she provided a straightforward and uncoached portrait of herself at twelve. She expressed pride in her physical strength, skill at gardening, and bravery when suffering pain, and rated herself as "equal in strength, endurance and courage to other children her age." She wrote that she was a reader of Horatio Alger, her grades were nearly the same in all her subjects, and she liked "paintings, music, books, animals, and all out-door sports." The last question asked what she would do if a million dollars were left to her next week. Her answer: "If I had a million dollars left me next week I would support my father so that he would not have to work as he is very ill with heart asthma. I would also go to Europe to see the country and to give concerts. The rest of the money I would put into a large car big enough for our family of nine and the remaining money I would deposit in the bank."[29] Except for "going to Europe to give concerts," Ruth sounds like the typical American schoolgirl her father wanted her to be.

Ruth did often say about her father that he was a versatile and hardworking musician, very proud of his union membership, and very

European and strict in his character and outlook. She also would recall that during the First World War, her father's German roots made him and his family potential targets for what one historian has called "the wave of anti-German feeling that swept Karl Muck [conductor of the Boston Symphony Orchestra] off his Boston podium [and] infiltrated lives public and private throughout the United States."[30] Emil Posselt felt the need to downplay his German origins: his wife encouraged him to Frenchify his surname by accenting it on the last syllable and by writing his given name as Emile.

No doubt the tensions of the time, and the fear of losing or not getting work, only enhanced Emil Posselt's belief that America was commercial and Europe was the only place for a serious musician, especially a violinist. Indeed, American virtuosos were few and far between during Ruth Posselt's childhood. Ondříček, too, realized that his star pupil would face huge obstacles getting the audience she deserved in America.

Ida Posselt eventually saw the virtues of Europe, but her ambition in 1923, after Ruth's debuts, was "to do something for her baby" in America. In the narrative she had constructed for Ruth, Ida stressed that her daughter was an *American* prodigy born and bred. She showed more managerial acumen in her equally determined attempts to find a patron for Ruth among the greatest violinists of the day, men like Fritz Kreisler, Mischa Elman, and the greatest of the great, for her as for many others, Jascha Heifetz. Encouraged by the fact that Heifetz had introduced himself to Ruth after her Symphony Hall recital, Ida decided to take her twelve-year old daughter to Heifetz's next recital in Boston, at the end of February 1924. After the concert they went backstage, reintroduced themselves, and then Ida asked Heifetz if he would have time to hear Ruth play before he left Boston. Heifetz said he would be happy to.[31]

After this audition, at which Posselt recalled she "had the nerve to play the same Rondo Capriccioso Heifetz had just performed at his recital," the world-famous violinist apparently suggested to Ruth's parents that she be taken to New York to study, and he offered to help find her a teacher and himself keep tabs on her progress. Ida Posselt was convinced this was the best course to take; she felt Heifetz had "offered Ruth everything." When Ondříček heard about it, however, Posselt later remembered that he "blew his top. 'I do all the work,' he ranted, 'and now she's going to go to him and he'll get all the credit. He's not a teacher. He's a great artist, but he doesn't teach.'"

Heifetz's suggestion "caused a big row in the family." Her mother wanted to take Ruth to live in New York and have her continue her studies with the teacher Heifetz recommended, but her father did not. Perhaps he agreed with Ondříček, or perhaps he had personal reasons of his own, but to have his twelve-year-old daughter living away from home, even with her mother, was not acceptable to him. He just did not want her to leave home at that time to pursue a concert career.

At this point, Emil Posselt was seriously ill and almost unable to work. His last months must have been difficult for him and the family. Ruth continued with school and started earning some money, giving mandolin, banjo, and ukulele lessons – all instruments her father had taught her. She worked in the garden, helped her mother with the cooking, and continued practicing the violin. By the beginning of December 1924, her father was bedridden, terminally ill with chronic endocarditis and nephritis.

For the rest of her life my mother reiterated the trauma of her father's death: "I'll never forget the night my father died – it was just after Christmas and it happened at night. His room was next to mine, and I could hear him gasping for breath, it got worse and worse. Everyone was running around, in and out of his room, crying and nearly hysterical – I was the only one who was calm enough to call the doctor to come. But I was so scared, and after it was over, and he was dead, I felt so guilty. While he was bedridden I used to rub his legs in the evening – they were very painful and the massage gave him some relief, but that evening, I was too tired and when he asked me, I said, 'Papa, I just can't tonight, I'm too tired.' And that was the night he died."

Funeral services were held for Emil Posselt on Wednesday morning, December 31, at his home and were attended by a large number of friends, colleagues, and former students. Appropriately, the funeral was a family affair. The music was furnished by Marjorie Posselt, who played Schubert's "Ave Maria" on the violin with Gladys Posselt at the piano, and Emil Posselt's favorite hymn, "My Jesus, If Ever I Love Thee, 'Tis Now," was sung by Gladys, Marjorie, Grace, and Ruth and their aunt, Grace Gordon Pierce. George M. Butler, former pastor of the Mystic Congregational Church, officiated. Emil Posselt was buried in Central Cemetery, Middleborough, Massachusetts, in the Pierce family plot.

Ida Posselt had turned fifty-five a month before her husband died. She was left the care of her two youngest daughters, both teenagers, and the houses Emil had built for his family in Medford and Manomet. She had been the official owner of 60 Sheridan Avenue since 1914. She never remarried and never left Medford, living there longer as a widow than she had as a wife. After a year of mourning, she plunged into "doing something for her baby" in earnest. Only ten years down the road would she relinquish her backstage managerial role.

CHAPTER TWO

A Struggling Young Artist: 1926–1931

I am playing the violin, that's all I know, nothing else, no education, no nothing. You just practice every day.

– Itzhak Perlman

When Posselt reappeared as a young virtuoso on the stages of New York and Boston, she was already fifteen years old, no longer a child prodigy, and almost unknown to audiences. Despite her talent, training, and early debuts, she had fallen behind in the race to the virtuoso top, a situation which caused her mother a good deal of anxiety, as one of her early supporters wrote to Ruth nostalgically many years later: "How nice it would have been to recapture those days when you were really a struggling artist, wondering whether anybody really would accept you and how anxious your mother was for you."[32] Her late father's conviction that she could wait to start her career until she graduated from high school had proved commercially unwise.

How did teenage Ruth feel about this late start? It's hard to tell. Like the "good soldier" she was, she never publicly questioned the commands and plans of her superiors, or the story of her life constructed for her by her mother. She supported her parents' decision not to commercialize her as a youngster and believed that she gained from it in the long run, convinced as she became that gifted violinists also need to lead a normal, balanced life. As for the option of going to New York at the age of twelve, that did ultimately strike her as a missed opportunity. When asked in a 1969 Florida radio interview whether she would do anything differently if she were just starting out, she suggested that her father's belief that young girls should not be traveling in pursuit of a career, and should be educated in the domestic virtues as well as music, did reflect the thinking of another generation. She felt that as a result she had carried quite a heavy burden in her early years, what with school, practicing, and domestic duties, learning to cook and help her mother. "It was a very big and full schedule for a child to carry," she concluded, "and I think if it had been in this day and age, I probably would have concentrated more on my music."[33]

What Posselt most lacked when she started her career in earnest was exposure to a musical culture outside her family, and contact with her musical peers. She also might have benefitted from a teacher who had more extensive connections in the big-time music world. Ondříček was one of the foremost violin teachers in Boston, and he did do everything he could to help his most gifted student, but he just didn't have the contacts and clout young Ruth Posselt needed, especially in view of her gender, to make it into the upper echelon of artists. Ondříček was also, perhaps, too much a member of the Posselt family to act effectively as a professional advocate. It was probably his desire to enhance his own professional standing as a "producer of prodigies" that finally convinced him several years down the road that young Posselt had to go out into the world, in fact to Europe, if she was to have a chance of fulfilling his and her aspirations. The headline of a publicity article in *The Boston Traveler* (October 21, 1935) certainly conveys Ondříček's attitude: "Producer of Child Prodigies Seeks for 'Soul' in his Pupils."[34]

Posselt's early *musical* education, not unlike that of many virtuosos, seems to have been focused on incessant practice, on learning how to play the violin "perfectly," which meant exactly in the way she was taught. As a child, like all violin prodigies, she was able to achieve this goal without knowing quite what she was doing or why she was doing it. As she often said, she just "played and played and that's all."

In June 1925, Ruth graduated from Swann Junior High School, playing violin solos at the graduation exercises, and in the fall, she entered Medford High School. She had completed her freshman year, and two years of intensive work with Ondříček, before her professional

BOSTON TRAVELER, MONDAY, OCTOBER 21, 1935

Producer of Child Prodigies Seeks for 'Soul' in His Pupils

Miss Ruth Posselt, famed Medford violinist, and her teacher and brother-in-law, Boston's famed maestro, Emanuel Ondricek.

manager, Haensel & Jones, succeeded in setting up a second New York recital in Aeolian Hall. It was billed as her "first appearance since her phenomenal debut in Carnegie Hall four years ago," and she was presented as "the Young American Violinist," Ruth Pierce Posselt. The picture on the program showed a tall, willowy, young woman of fourteen or fifteen with a fashionable flapper's haircut.

The program, in which Ondříček's name appeared prominently, included the Vitali Chaconne and the Paganini First Concerto, with a cadenza by Ondříček, followed by a slew of short pieces, including an arrangement by Ondříček of one of Dvořák's Silhouettes, and concluding with Wieniawski's Scherzo-Tarantelle. Gladys Posselt was again Ruth's accompanist. The audience response was described as "very enthusiastic," and the reviews were again highly complimentary, citing

Posselt's impeccable ear, perfect intonation, beautiful and warm tone, marked progress in technical ability, and rich endowment of musical talent. "She brings to her work a freshness which, harnessed to her industry and enthusiasm will go far toward placing her some day in the foremost rank of her profession."[35] Unfortunately, Posselt's own industry and enthusiasm alone did not have enough horsepower to pull her to that "foremost rank." She needed patron power and money.

As it happened, a former voice student of Ida Posselt's, Viola Davenport, had grown up to marry Alvan T. Fuller, one of the wealthiest men in America and governor of Massachusetts from 1925 to 1929. Ida set to work on her former pupil, who was now an important patroness of the arts in Boston. She was successful in garnering Viola Fuller's support and, through her, the sponsorship of the governor, lieutenant governor, mayor, and many prominent Boston musicians and critics (including George Chadwick, Mabel Daniels, Philip Hale, and Serge Koussevitzky) for a recital in Symphony Hall, Boston, following Ruth's appearance at Aeolian Hall. Ida Posselt had seen to it that the Boston papers heard about her daughter's second New York triumph. She and Ruth were featured in a *Boston Traveler* preview for the Symphony Hall recital, the headline of which must have pleased

Ida greatly: "First Gained Fame at Steinert Hall When Only Six, at 10 She Played in Carnegie Hall, at 14 She Is Acclaimed as the Feminine Heifitz [*sic*] of the World."[36] An article with a picture of the "feminine Heifitz" was reprinted in the Sydney, Australia *Daily Mail*, where a distant Posselt relative saw it and sent it back to 60 Sheridan Avenue. Ida pasted the original photo, taken by Keystone View Co. of New York City, into Ruth's scrapbook.

Although Ida Posselt had created the public narrative of her "baby's" life story, by the time Ruth reached adolescence she clearly had opinions of her own. Generally, she followed her mother's script, quickly learning to speak of herself in a well-rehearsed manner that was persuasive in its naturalness. Occasionally, however, she would make a spontaneous comment that was not in the script and appeared to express how she really felt. This seems to have happened in the *Traveler* article. At first, the interviewer's impression conforms to Ida Posselt's Ruth, the normal American all-around wonder child: "She came back" from New York, comments the reporter, "a little girl, submissive to her mother, in spite of her success at Aeolian Hall. Ruth isn't the affected young miss one would expect to meet after hearing of her unusual talent. She is a normal, healthy girl, full of life and a great athlete. Swimming, tennis, riding, she likes them all. And the Charleston? – she's an expert. She obeys her mother's wishes without a murmur, even when it means giving up one of her life's cherished dreams."

Then suddenly we hear Ruth telling us something we haven't heard before, as well as the reason why we haven't: "I always wanted to be a movie actress," she is quoted as saying. "But mother doesn't want me to be. So that's that." This comment bowled me over when I first came across it in a fragile yellow-brown clipping which had lain in a box for almost one hundred years. It was so immediately recognizable as the authentic voice of my mother, who loved the movies and who when I was growing up always seemed to know almost as much about Hollywood as she did about anything else.

Ruth never openly rebelled against her mother's ambitions and overprotectiveness – she let her mother, her managers, and her teachers "guide" her, and she worked tirelessly to achieve what they (and maybe she, too) wanted. Just because inwardly she dreamed of being Gloria Swanson or Mary Pickford, not the "feminine Heifetz," or the "feminine Menuhin," or, later, the "Adelina Patti of the violin," did not mean that she wasn't ambitious or competitive. She was. Instead of bucking her mother, she joined her, at least as far as her mother or anyone else could see, but as happens with so many child prodigies when they reach adolescence, Ruth nurtured her own rebellious dreams in secret. Often enough, she was able to give expression to her own tastes and dreams in her external self-presentation, especially her hairdos and makeup. In her teens, she also began "having and keeping secrets, her own and others," just as the stars seem to have predicted. Perhaps she was pleased that the incessant comments about her appearance in the press included occasional comparisons with film stars.

As luck would have it, a storm beat down on Boston on December 5, the day of Posselt's well-publicized recital, and the audience in Symphony Hall was very small, filling no more than a quarter of the floor. Those loyal friends who did come were invited to leave their seats and take new ones nearer to the stage. While Ida Posselt bemoaned the meteorological disaster – she remembered it to her dying day as one of the terrible obstacles that her "poor little rich girl" had to overcome – Ruth herself calmly soldiered on. She "stood on the stage in the soft light, and as she played," wrote one critic, "she was strangely absorbed in the music which she and her violin seemed to send out together in a message of euphony. Detached though she appeared in a visible way, she nevertheless wove a web of tone as sympathetic bond between herself and her listeners."[37]

Acknowledging the "Medford girl's phenomenal skill," another critic highlighted her stage presence and good looks: "Ruth Posselt is very definitely a personality, with natural grace and ease of manner as well as unmistakable individuality and energy. She gives promise of becoming a very pretty girl. Best of all she seems unspoilt by the fuss made over her playing."[38]

What fuss? young Ruth may have wondered. Despite her prodigious talent, splendid reviews by critics in Boston and New York, and a major New York management company (Haensel & Jones), no offers came her way, no engagements ensued, no orchestras hired her. She went back to Medford High School and daily practice.

Ruth had now reached puberty, and while continuing to be a dutiful student and daughter, she was equally drawn to movies, fun, clothes, shopping, and boys. She had a lot of friends, loved to dance, and craved excitement. Many commentators on the careers of child prodigies on the violin agree that puberty is the critical moment in determining whether or not a gifted youngster will progress beyond the prodigy stage and develop into a mature artist. Ruth's adolescence may also have been complicated by her father's death when she was thirteen. She seemed to have felt ambivalent about her father's and her own attitudes to her career on one hand, and her beloved mother's ambitions for her to become the American female Heifetz on the other. To some extent she had made her mother's ambitions her own, but she probably wasn't as wholeheartedly dedicated to them as she led her mother to believe.

Ida was beset by her own increasing worries about the bad influence "the other girls" Ruth knew in high school might have on her – they, after all, were allowed to go on dates and wear lipstick while she wasn't. Such concerns may have been one reason why she decided Ruth should leave high school at the end of her junior year in order to concentrate on her music. She tried to compensate for Ruth's lack of a senior year by tutoring her in English and French. Gladys, the most musically educated member of the family, was called upon to give her lessons in harmony. In the summer, Ruth worked with Ondříček in Manomet towards the immediate goal of preparing for her first concert appearances, hopefully with first-rung orchestras. She set about learning the Tchaikovsky Violin Concerto, a piece she would play more often than any other concerto over the course of her career and use for a number of debuts at home and abroad.

Ida Posselt's and Emanuel Ondříček's plans were moving along well. And then Ruth "met Arthur on the beach at Manomet and fell madly in love with him. He was very handsome, a college boy who'd attended the University of Chicago, interested in sports, and tone deaf."[39]

Arthur Newcomb reciprocated Ruth Posselt's young love. He had already left college, joined his father's business, and was living in Newton, Massachusetts, with his family. Ruth and Arthur started a secret romance, at least "secret" from Ruth's point of view. She went to some lengths to keep her love for Arthur and meetings with him secret from her mother.

Her sister Naomi was a go-between at first; later on, Grace assisted in this role. Her correspondence with Arthur was secret: she sent him letters in envelopes addressed to someone else to give to him, so that no one in Arthur's family would say, she explained, "Oh! Heavens! Another letter from that Posselt girl!" Ruth also proved adept in setting up rendezvous and advising Arthur of a "plan B" in case they couldn't happen: "Your letter came this morning and we'll let our date stand as it is but – if it rains too hard don't bother to come in [to Medford] because my ma won't want me to go out in the pouring rain. . . . Na and I will leave here at one o'clock because we have several errands to do in town, so if it is not raining at one o'clock I'll certainly see you at three."[40]

Friends played their role. Arthur had his Christmas gift to Ruth that year delivered secretly through one of their friends; when Ruth went to New York in the spring under her mother's watchful eye, her friend "Vi" passed Arthur's letters on to her, and she sent her letters to a friend of Arthur's. Ida Posselt surely knew that Arthur existed, but she had no inkling of the depth of Ruth's feelings for him or of their eventual secret "engagement" and plans to marry, which provided the emotional center of Ruth's life for the next two years while her mother was making a major effort to push her into the national spotlight.

Both mother and daughter knew that Ruth could not even dream of a national career as a concert violinist until she had the imprimatur of the New York critics. Yet getting an engagement with a New York orchestra was almost impossible for a comparatively unknown American girl with no concert experience and no heavyweight and deep-pocketed musical backers. Ida Posselt had tried to get the Boston Symphony Orchestra interested in Ruth at the time of her Symphony Hall recital, but Pierre Monteux, the conductor at that time, would not even listen to her. She later learned that the Boston critics were tired of infant prodigies, and audiences wanted to hear newcomers who had proved themselves in New York.

By 1928, Ondříček had decided to aim lower, in a venue which he controlled. Invited to guest-conduct the People's Symphony Orchestra of Boston, Ondříček decided on a program of Slavic music (Smetana,

Dvořák, Suk, Tchaikovsky) that featured "Young American Violinist" Ruth Pierce Posselt as "Assisting Artist" in Tchaikovsky's Violin Concerto. The concert took place on Sunday afternoon, January 29, 1928, in Jordan Hall. According to the *Boston Globe* review, Ruth's performance revealed not only her "remarkable technical facility," but "a genuine and spontaneous feeling for the characteristic beauty of each phrase, a delicate command of tone quality with which to express that feeling, an irresistably strong and elastic rhythm and an engagingly unaffected personality."[41]

With Ondříček's encouragement, Ida took her daughter to New York that spring, hoping to have her audition for various conductors. Entrée into the New York musical elite was provided by Max Smith, the noted music critic, who had heard Ruth at Carnegie Hall five years earlier and acclaimed her "the most remarkable case on record." Smith facilitated a series of auditions, starting with the manager of Roxy's Theater, the virtuoso pianist Ernö Rapée (1891–1945), one of the most prolific American conductors of photoplay music. After that audition, Ruth wrote Arthur, "I played well through sheer force, for I thought I would sink thru the floor any minute. However I must have made a wonderful impression for he immediately engaged me for a Sunday concert anytime I desired in April in the Roxy Theater before an audience of 6200." Ida sat on this offer for about three weeks and apparently decided against it; she considered appearances in picture theaters too lowbrow for her feminine Heifetz.

Max Smith took Ruth Posselt out on the town, introducing her to theater and musical celebrities. Her ingenue head was spinning from the attention, and from the glitter of the big-time concert world: "I sat in a box with all the notables and swells. Such wonderful gowns and jewels! Oh! My!" On March 15, Smith escorted his protégée to an Arturo Toscanini concert at Carnegie Hall, took her backstage, and introduced her to the maestro, who was a close friend of his. Toscanini agreed to give Ruth a hearing the following week. The next day, she played for Albert Stoessel (1894–1943), composer and violinist, who had been assistant conductor of the Oratorio Society of New York under the eminent conductor Walter Damrosch. Stoessel helped set up an audition with Damrosch himself, which would take place three days after the one with Toscanini. "I must tell you how wonderful certain people have been to me here," Ruth wrote Arthur excitedly. "They seem to be just crazy about me! Last nite I met Clarence McKay, the father-in-law of Irving Berlin, and he raved all evening about the sweet and dear little face I had. Hot! Soup!"[42]

Playing for the stars of the musical firmament was not a wholly fun experience for Ruth by that time in her development, however. She later explained: "Children don't have nerves. They think it's all a game. It's only later, when they realize how serious it is that they get nervous." She obviously was thinking of her own experience, for from the time of her New York auditions in the late twenties, she began to manifest those symptoms of "nerves" that would often precede her performances for the rest of her life: chronic insomnia, hypochondria ("thinking she was sick when she wasn't," as her horoscope had predicted), nervousness (what she called "nerve strain"), and excitability.

She confided to Arthur: "I had a very sore throat and a severe cold, but it didn't seem to be either of these disturbances that affected me so, it seems to be my nerves. I can't sleep well any more and all I seem to do is think & think. My Ma says I'm on the verge of a nervous breakdown and that I've got to watch my step. My throat is still very sore today but that isn't what bothers me. I feel like dropping and sleeping, never to wake up again. I'm going to see a Dr. today and ask him what I can do to sleep nights. I know I'm too excitable and all that but then, isn't it my nature?"[43]

Before Ruth played for Toscanini, her Christian Scientist aunt, Maude Allen, who was acting in a play in New York, phoned her and told her niece "to repeat over and over, 'Mind is directing' – 'Love is protecting' – and the 'Spirit is operating.'"[44] Ruth found that her aunt's mantra helped her a lot. She played the Paganini Violin Concerto No. 1, and reported that after hearing her, Toscanini shouted "Bravo! Bravo!" then rose and came over and patted her on the cheek. Nothing came of this audition, however.

She had better luck with Walter Damrosch, though her pre-audition sufferings were more intense. When she awoke the day before this audition, she "just couldn't seem to move. I had terrific pains in my back and neck and a splitting headache. Right then and there I cried because I felt so weak." Despite a long and taxing day, she didn't sleep well that night either. What gave her energy was a letter from Arthur: "Was I happy when I recognized your script? I'll say! It seemed as though I could go through the day without a whimper!"[45]

Her Monday morning "ordeal" of playing for Damrosch turned out just wonderfully. She felt she could not have played more perfectly – and he engaged her to play with the New York Philharmonic in the fall. Ida Posselt treasured the moment. Shortly before her death, more than two decades later, she reminisced to Ruth: "I note the big musicians will not read circulars, they want to hear you because so many criticisms are paid for – Max Smith said they were always trying to bribe him. I know when I took you to Walter Damrosch and handed him your circular, he said, 'I don't want that. I want to hear the lady.' After he heard and engaged you, he said, 'Now I will take the circular.'"[46]

Damrosch included Ruth Pierce Posselt as soloist on the fourth of his Young People's Concerts on Saturday afternoon, December 1, 1928. Carnegie Hall had a capacity audience "who were thrilled at Posselt's playing," said the *New York Telegram,* "and she was recalled again and again."[47] That evening Max Smith held a dinner party for Posselt, who later thanked him: "I had such a dandy time with you when in N.Y. and I shall never forget it. You are always so good to me, and I appreciate your kindnesses more than I can say."[48]

By the end of the twenties, Ruth began taking a more active role in trying to get engagements. Her mother, who, as we know, considered herself her daughter's personal representative and distrusted Haensel & Jones, as well as resenting having to pay commissions, encouraged her in this endeavor. Unfortunately, neither mother nor daughter really knew anything about the music business. Ida Posselt relied on her restricted social and family network and a few Boston society people who patronized classical music and had shown an interest in Ruth. In early spring, Ruth wrote to her brother-in-law, Kenneth Teele, a businessman, asking him for information about the concert venues in Richmond, Virginia, where he and her older sister, Molly, happened to be living at the time, and whether he could not put her in touch with a venue that might engage her. Ken did his homework, but informed her that the 1928–29 concert schedule for Richmond was already arranged and had been for some time. His letter gives insight into classical music life in America outside of New York at the time: "Every year there are three series of concerts given here. One series is sponsored by a Mrs. Wilson-Greene in collaboration with . . . a music company, here. The second is sponsored by *The News Leader*, the evening paper. The third is under the auspices of the Musicians Club of Richmond. The Corley Company, another music company, occasionally joins with the *News Leader* in putting on opera or concerts." He enclosed circulars for the first two series and recommended that Ruth write to a prominent society woman who "arranges concerts there, in Baltimore and elsewhere."[49]

In trying to make a career in the United States, Posselt was disadvantaged not only by her lack of wealth and musical connections, but by two other factors, her nationality and her gender, that had been working against even wealthy American-born female instrumentalists since the late nineteenth century, when such artists first tried in numbers to crack the glass ceiling of the classical music world. No one knew this better than Texas-born pianist Lucy Hickenlooper (1880–1948), who, despairing of getting anywhere on the American concert stage, paid her way to Europe, enrolled at the Paris Conservatory, changed her name to Olga Samaroff, and returned to America. There, she rented Carnegie Hall and made her debut in 1905 under Walter Damrosch and the New York Philharmonic. Masquerading as a Russian, Samaroff-Hickenlooper went on to become one of America's most famous international female concert artists of the early twentieth century. In 1911, the year Ruth

Posselt was born, Samaroff married the famed conductor Leopold Stokowski. They were divorced in 1923, but by then, Madame Samaroff was a leading figure in American classical music, and also a famous piano pedagogue who launched the careers of the first generation of American-born and -trained concert pianists.[50]

Samaroff did not forget her early struggles as gifted Lucy Hickenlooper from Texas. She wrote about the problem of nationality in making a career in music for the *New York Evening Post* (she was the first woman music critic for a New York paper). On her live radio show, she attacked gender bias in music by having pianists on the show play behind a screen – one of the female pianists was thought to be a male by ninety-two percent of the studio audience.

The year 1928 saw worldwide commemorations of the centennial of Franz Schubert's death. At the American celebrations in New York, Samaroff, then a faculty member at both the new Juilliard School and the Philadelphia Conservatory, used the occasion to launch the first national competition for American musicians only, the Schubert Memorial. Its aim was to introduce young American artists to audiences of musicians and music lovers. It sought to address the near impossibility in the classical music world for a native-born and locally educated American musician to obtain a hearing before the musical public of the United States without first securing a European reputation. In the Schubert Memorial's brochure and mission statement, Olga Samaroff wrote: "Although for a time within the last decade it seemed as if the United States would achieve musical independence, present conditions indicate a tendency toward the pre-war basis. The question is, shall we definitely and finally assume the responsibility of recognizing our own young talents, or shall we resume our former provincial status which means letting Europe do it for us. The answer to this question will be found in the attendance at the concerts of the Schubert Memorial."[51] Ossip Gabrilowitsch became the national president and Samaroff the secretary of the Schubert Memorial. Stokowski was chairman of the Artist Advisory Board, which included such musical notables as Bodansky, Damrosch, Goossens, Koussevitzky, Reiner, Rodzinski, Stock, Sokoloff, and Toscanini – most of whom were foreign-born, and all of whom were male.

The Schubert Memorial consisted of about twenty-five groups of musicians and patrons in the chief music centers of the country. Candidates for the annual prize, which was given to two new artists every year, applied to the local committees, which vetted them according to stated admissions standards and by auditions. Candidates who passed the initial tests earned the right to participate in the preliminary national auditions held in New York, Chicago, Los Angeles, and San Francisco. From these preliminary auditions, nine finalists were chosen to compete in New York. The prize consisted of an appearance with orchestra in Carnegie Hall, the opportunity for appearances in cities across the country where the Schubert Memorial had extension chapters, and a chance to make a record for Victor Records.

Ida Posselt thought the Schubert Memorial Prize seemed tailor-made for Ruth, who was struggling to gain both national recognition and management that would really work for her. So in 1929, only the competition's second year, she entered her daughter. Ruth initially had little confidence in her chances of winning against the more than 150 contestants, most of whom were older and far more experienced than she. She remembered the months-long competition as "a frightfully hard grind" which demanded much of the serious contenders, playing two full recital programs and preparing six concertos with orchestra.

In a telling juxtaposition of Ruth Posselt the serious musician and Ruth Posselt the all-American girl, while the first and second rounds of the Schubert competition were in progress, Ruth's oldest sister, Gladys, now Mrs. E. Ondříček, nominated her for the *Boston Evening American's* quest for a "Typical American Girl" and sent in a recent publicity picture: In support of her sister's nomination, Gladys wrote: "She is five feet, five inches in height, and weighs 115 pounds, has light hair and brown velvet eyes brimful of expression, a very fair skin, and is 18 years of age. She has a high school education and is a very unusual violinist, starting her career at the tender age of three years."[52]

Part of what sustained Posselt through the arduous Schubert competition was her love for Arthur Newcomb. By the time she reached the preliminary national audition in New York at the end of March, the couple was planning to marry in September as soon as Ruth turned eighteen. Posselt's auditioner for the preliminaries was Nikolai Sokoloff (1886–1965), Russian-American violinist and conductor. As music director of the San Francisco People's Philharmonic, he made a point of hiring women for the orchestra and paying them the same wages as men. In 1918, he founded the Cleveland Orchestra, for which he was music director till 1932. Ruth's audition for Sokoloff was a "success," she reported to Arthur, and she moved on to the finals in New York at the end of April.

After arriving in New York on April 21, Ruth telegraphed Arthur that she was so nervous over the auditions she couldn't sleep nights. Nevertheless, she passed the first round successfully after playing for three judges, Harold Bauer, Louis Persinger (the teacher of Menuhin), and Stokowski, who were uniform in their praise. Said the violinist Persinger: "You certainly have the real stuff!"[53]

Ruth's most dangerous competition among the violinists in the final round came from Bernard Ocko, a twenty-six-year-old New York fiddler and winner of the prestigious Naumberg Foundation Competition. Ocko was well connected and known in New York music circles, and had graduated summa cum laude and with a silver medal from the Institute of Musical Art, which soon became part of the Juilliard School of Music, where Schubert competition founder Olga Samaroff was on the faculty.

Moreover, Ocko had been a student of the near-legendary Franz Kneisel and played second violin in the Musical Arts Quartet, three of whose members were pupils of Kneisel. In their first appearance in Aeolian Hall on January 10, 1927, the Musical Arts Quartet gained notice not only for their playing, but for the instruments they played: all of them were Strads loaned to them by Felix Warburg, who had recently purchased them. Ocko played a Strad for the Schubert competition, a fact that *The Medford Mercury* made much of in its report: "At the completion of the week, two [violin] contestants were left, Bernard Ocko, prominent New York violinist, playing on a $6000 violin, and Ruth Posselt playing on her $200 instrument. Among the judges were Harold Bauer, famous pianist, Ernest Schelling, noted conductor, Louis Persinger, prominent teacher of the violin, and Ernest Hutchinson, famous pianist."[54]

Ocko's superior qualifications on paper were unassailable, and he had every right to consider himself the favorite for one of the Schubert prizes. In contrast, Ruth Posselt from Medford knew she was a dark horse. As she confided to Arthur: "I don't know how I'm ever going to get through it all. There is too much prejudice already. Heavens! I'm so nervous."[55]

But the dark horse won, and Ruth took unabashed pride in her victory over such a worthy competitor as Ocko, who, she wrote Arthur, had "accomplished so much in the music world." After her victory, Armour and Company, a well-known dealer in violin strings and accessories, asked her for a testimonial to include in their advertising booklet, and she noted to Arthur that she would "be the only woman violinist in their Ad."[56] In closing, Ruth told her fiancé to tell his family about her victory. "Let them laugh if they will," she wrote, which suggests that Arthur's family did not take Ruth's career aspirations seriously.

Ruth's attitude of simultaneous pride and disbelief in her success, her sheer joy that she had won, respect for the competition, gender awareness, and desire to be vindicated in the eyes of those who hadn't taken her seriously – all this inner excitement over her triumph against the odds seemed to set a pattern for how she would approach many important performances for the rest of her life. In recalling her performing life, she usually mentioned winning the Schubert competition as a turning point. And it was, although it proved more a catalyst for her transformation into a truly engaged and committed performing artist than a catapult to national exposure.

After all the excitement, it was back to Manomet for the summer, back to practicing and expanding her repertoire: she fell in love with Bach that summer, working very hard on the famous Chaconne from the D Minor Partita for Unaccompanied Violin. Her other love, for Arthur, came to its long-awaited climax that fall, a month after her eighteenth birthday. After filing marriage intentions at the beginning of October, the couple eloped to Marion, Massachusetts, and were married on October 20, 1929, four days before the stock market crashed and the Great Depression began. On her marriage certificate, Ruth gave her name as Yvonne Ruth Posselt, her residence as New Hampshire, and her profession as housewife. She also gave her age as nineteen. Since her mother had entered her into the Schubert contest as an eighteen-year-old, Posselt may have feared revealing (to whom?) that she was not her putative official age, nine months older than her real one. Meanwhile, the press and public were making her out to be at least two years younger.

For several months, Ruth did not tell her mother she was married, and her husband kept their secret from his family, as well. The newlyweds would meet, my mother once confided to me, and "go to the woods or any place to make love." When Ida finally found out, she apparently accepted it with equanimity, but she also convinced her daughter and son-in-law that for the sake of Ruth's career the marriage had to remain secret to everyone outside their immediate families. And, remarkably, it did.

The astrological prediction that Ruth would keep secrets, her own and others', uncannily came true. For the next ten years, she convincingly masqueraded as a virgin virtuoso while enjoying life in private as a married woman. Newcomb attended most of his wife's concerts, followed her to Europe more than once, and apparently was content to play in public the role of his wife's fiancé. Rather than allow her secret marriage to distract her from the career that was just beginning for her, Ruth convinced her husband, at least at first, that he was crucially needed for her to be successful in that career.

The stated aim of the Schubert Memorial Prize was to introduce young American artists to American audiences of musicians and music lovers and help them gain recognition without benefit of a European musical education and fame. Did it succeed in Posselt's case? The answer is yes and no. Considering that during the period 1929–1934, seventy percent of America's musicians were unemployed, and many wealthy patrons of classical music were no longer able to support young talent to the degree they had formerly, the Schubert prize helped Posselt through the bleakest of economic times. However, it did not help enough to keep her from becoming a struggling young artist who increasingly despaired of getting the broad recognition she deserved. And it did not make European success any less important than it had ever been.

The first part of the Schubert prize was an appearance for the 1929 co-winners, Ruth and violoncellist Phyllis Kraeuter, in Carnegie Hall with the New York Philharmonic, conducted by Arthur Bodanzky. Posselt chose to perform the Goldmark Concerto. The capacity audience included the elite of the musical world, and all the New York critics reviewed the concert in detail. New York critics had (and still have) a reputation for not being easily impressed and for not sparing anyone's feelings. Bad reviews were even their stock in trade, and Posselt's reviews for this concert were some of the most ambivalent she ever received. There was disagreement about her tone, which appealed to H. J. Henderson, who called it "a real joy," but repelled Olin Downes as "unnaturally disagreeable." On the other hand, Downes praised her "brilliant left hand," while Henderson wrote that "her technical resources revealed no great brilliance of execution." All the critics agreed, however, on her "platform poise" and audience appeal: her playing "aroused real enthusiasm," had "no lack of spirit and élan," and demonstrated "the poise and assurance of one who is not new to the public."[57]

Next, Ruth made her first recording for Victor Records: Wieniawski's "Sielanka" and Fibich's "Poem," with Gladys Ondříček as accompanist. Then, in the spring of 1930 she started her appearances on the Schubert circuit, which constituted the "transcontinental tour" promised the winners of the Schubert prize. She did appear (mainly in recital, sometimes sharing the program with her co-winner) and was reviewed in cities across the United States: Baltimore, Washington, Denver, Santa Barbara, Atlanta, Providence, Nashville, Philadelphia, Detroit, and St. Louis. These concerts were not part of a continuous tour, however, and most of them took place in private homes of wealthy patrons or at private colleges. Such venues did not provide opportunities to be heard by large classical music audiences in any of these cities except Denver, where her sole appearance as soloist with orchestra was "wildly cheered by an unusually large and most enthusiastic audience."[58]

In fact, her performance of the Tchaikovsky Violin Concerto made a truly indelible impression on one member of the Denver orchestra, who recalled it in a letter he was moved to write to Posselt over forty years later, after hearing a performance of hers on the radio: "One of my unforgettable moments was the time you played the Tchaikowsky Concerto with the Denver Civic Symphony. I was in the cello section. The moment came when one of your strings broke: was it just before the cadenza? You calmly inserted another string while we were all overcome with emotion, went on, and gave an outstanding performance. One of our violinists was so swept off his feet (as indeed we all were) that he didn't look at another girl for years. In fact he is a bachelor to this day."[59]

The newspapers that lauded Posselt's playing everywhere on her Schubert tour also made much of her gender and her appearance: "Blonde, bobbed and bothered by the slipping of an unruly new string, Ruth Posselt played nonetheless one of the best violin recitals heard in town this year" (Baltimore, April 14, 1930). "Ruth Posselt, a slender and very pretty young girl from Massachusetts gave an exhibition of fine violin playing last night in the Social-Religious building of Peabody college" (*The Nashville Tennessean*, April 7, 1931). "An unusual young woman violinist made her Detroit debut Monday afternoon at the Colony Club, discounting the idea that frail-appearing girls cannot make a violin talk. Miss Posselt made her instrument do practically everything" (*The Detroit News*, October 13, 1931).

Certainly, Posselt's appearance and personality were factors in her appeal to audiences and critics alike, factors she herself cultivated, and one could argue that her gender and good looks worked in her favor. Still, it was a mixed blessing to be young, blonde, and pretty in the virtually all-male classical music world of the 1930s, not to mention the prevalence of the "ditzy blonde" stereotype. The astonishment provoked by her virtuosity and artistry was palpably different from the astonishment that greeted a young, blond, and handsome Menuhin, or a young, dark, and temperamental Heifetz – if, indeed, any music critic even remarked on the male soloist's appearance. Listeners were astonished by Menuhin and Heifetz as wonders of nature, by Ruth Posselt as an exception to nature. It's hard to know if such astonishment is a plus or a minus when one seeks to be appreciated as a serious artist or musician.

In any case, by the end of the year, Ruth's Schubert tour was over. Whatever interest it had aroused in her playing had yielded no important future engagements, and her prospects as a performing artist in Depression-struck America were dim indeed. Her husband was doing okay, working for his father in Maine; her unmarried siblings and her mother, like many others, survived from day to day on meager earnings. As far as her work was concerned, Ruth was "a struggling artist, wondering if anybody really would accept her," and her mother was very anxious for her. Ondříček likewise was concerned and increasingly convinced that America was not yet a land of opportunity for his protégée; somehow she had to get to Europe and make a name for herself there. Once again, Ida Posselt approached her wealthy acquaintances, asking them if they would consider sponsoring a trip to Europe. They were open to the idea, but their husbands, who held the purse strings, wanted some professional opinions of Ruth's chances for success. They were wary of supporting a woman who was likely to give up her career for marriage and children. (They did not know, of course, that she was already married.)

By this time, Ruth Posselt had developed a wider professional network in Boston. One of her musical friends and admirers, Boaz Piller, contrabassoonist in the Boston Symphony Orchestra and well connected in American and European musical circles, suggested she audition for Georges Enesco (1881–1955), the world-famous composer, conductor, and violinist, whose opinion of her professional prospects would carry weight. Enesco agreed to hear her and, after an hour's examination in New York, told Piller that the girl's playing merited anything her sponsors might wish to do for her. Fuller and Hobbs were impressed, but wanted to set Ruth up with a European mentor. They thought of the famous French virtuoso Jacques Thibaud, who happened to be giving a benefit recital in Boston for the Morning Musicale Series at the end of February 1932. It was Thibaud's first appearance in Boston since the beginning of the Depression.

Thibaud promised to give Posselt a fifteen-minute hearing after his recital. But when she began to play, he apparently forgot that he had set a time limit. After listening for an hour and a half, he told her sponsors to send her to him in Paris and he would see that she met everyone she should meet. Thibaud promised her an appearance with the Paris Symphony Orchestra and debuts in major European cities. One of Posselt's ardent longtime supporters recalled twenty years later: "For twenty four years I have been a member of the Morning Musicale's Committee and I recall the morning after a concert you played for Mr. Thibaud and he confirmed our belief in your great talent, intelligence, and tenacity."[60]

In March, Posselt gave a benefit recital in Jordan Hall, sponsored by a committee of prominent Boston society patrons, headed by Mrs. Alvan T. Fuller and Mrs. Franklin W. Hobbs. Gladys Ondříček once again served as accompanist, and the main work on the program was the Goldmark Concerto. Warren Storey Smith, a musician and music editor of *The Boston Post*, who had been following Posselt's career since her child-prodigy years, called her performance "flawless" and summed up her progress to date: "The violinist in question was Ruth Posselt who, in the ten years or more since she first appeared as a child 'prodigy' in this, her native city, had been heard here occasionally, always bearing out the promise of her youthful debut. But not before had Miss Posselt played here with the all-around mastery of her instrument, the sensitive musical feeling and the exciting virtuoso flair that she disclosed last evening."[61]

A month later, Posselt wrote to Max Smith, with whom she had been in correspondence for the past several years, to tell him her "exciting news": "Society people of Boston have recently shown great enthusiasm for my future, and through the efforts of Mrs. Alvan T. Fuller and Mrs. Franklin W. Hobbs . . . and with other contributions, I am going to Europe in May. When Jacques Thibaud played here last I met him and played for him and aroused his interest to such an extent that he has promised my debut with the Paris Symphony next October, and I am thrilled."[62]

After a farewell tea at the Hobbses' Commonwealth Avenue residence, with bon voyage gifts and flowers bestowed upon her, the young virtuosa set off for Europe. On a moonlit Saturday night in May, on the afterdeck of the SS *Bremen*, her sister and brother-in-law, Molly and Ken Teele, bid her a tearful and loving good-bye. Ruth Posselt was going out into the Old World.

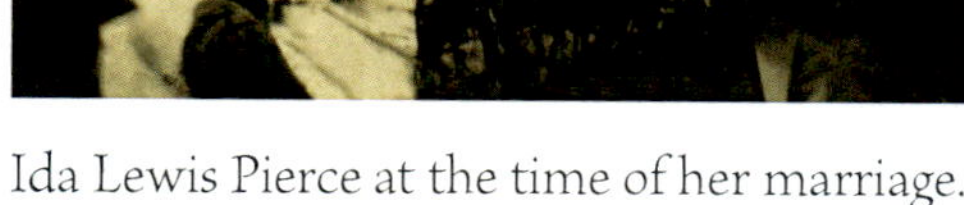

Ida Lewis Pierce at the time of her marriage.　　Emil A. Posselt as a young violinist.

The Friendly Maids of WEEI, left to right: Ethel, Lilian, Marge, Mildred, and Elizabeth. *Green Photo.*

Ruth and Naomi Posselt, ca. 1919.

Arms akimbo. Left to right: Ruth, Ida, Marjorie, and Grace Posselt, in Medford, ca. 1917.

Marjorie Posselt, violinist. *Photo by Roberts, Boston.*

Ruth's first violin in its glass case, with pictures from her first two debuts.

Ruth, the eleven-year-old violinist, poses helping with the dishes, 1923.

Teenage Ruth Posselt going to a lesson at Ondříček's studio in Boston.

Ruth Posselt in 1926, before her recital at Aeolian Hall, New York. *Photo by Horner, Boston.*

Ruth Posselt and Arthur Newcomb, August 1927.

Portrait of Emanuel Ondříček, inscribed "To my dearest Ruth, in remembrance of her phenomenal talent, from her loving teacher, Emanuel Ondricek, Jan. 25th '28.

Playing for her passage: Posselt performs aboard the S.S. *Bremen,* 1932.

FIRST TIME IN HISTORY OF SYMPHONIC MUSIC
IN NEW YORK

CARNEGIE HALL

Wednesday Evening, February 27
at 8:30 o'clock   *1929*

Symphonic Concert

OF

CZECH, SLOVAK AND RUSSIAN
MUSIC

MANHATTAN SYMPHONIC ORCHESTRA
OF NEW YORK CITY
(Full Orchestra)

EMANUEL ONDRICEK
Conductor

RUTH POSSELT
Young American Violinist
Assisting Artist

EMANUEL ONDRICEK
NOTED CZECH VIOLINIST,
COMPOSER AND CONDUCTOR
(Formerly of Prague, Czecho-
slovakia)

PROGRAMME

I. Festival Overture: "Libussa" .... *Smetana*

II. Slovakian Pictures .... *Emanuel Ondricek*
    (a) Tatra
    (b) Slovakian Lullaby
    (c) In the Village (A Dance)
(First time in New York)

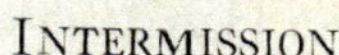

INTERMISSION

III. Concerto in D major for
    Violin and Orchestra
Tschaikowsky
    (a) Allegro Moderato
    (b) Canzonetta
    (c) Allegro Vivacissimo
RUTH POSSELT, *Soloist*

IV. Symphonic Poem: "The
    Golden Spinning Wheel"
Dvorak
(First time in New York)

Tickets: $1.00, $1.50, $2.00, $2.50

On Sale at Box-Office

RUTH POSSELT
VIOLINIST
"Phenomenal violinist."—*Boston
Globe.*
"God-given musicianship."—*New
York American.*
"Brilliantly executed—Surprising
talent."—*N. Y. Times.*

Management:
Haensel & Jones, Steinway Hall, New York

Program of Ondricek–Posselt Concert, 1929.

Schubert Memorial Concert

CARNEGIE HALL

Wednesday

DECEMBER 4, 1929

At 8:45 P. M.

Only Concert this Season

with

80 Members of

The PHILHARMONIC-SYMPHONY ORCHESTRA

ARTUR BODANZKY, Conducting

Soloists

PHYLLIS KRAEUTER
'Cellist
and
RUTH POSSELT
Violinist

Price of tickets and application form on last page

Recital Management Arthur Judson, Steinway Hall, 113 West 57th Street, New York

Program for the Schubert Memorial Concert, December 1929.

Double-dating in the 1920s: Arthur and Ruth in front; Naomi and her boyfriend in back.

Boaz Piller and Ruth Posselt, n.d.

An American Virtuosa in Europe: 1932–1935

The Dutch critics called her appearance a real St. Nicholas surprise.
America may be proud, they say, of being able to send out such an artist.
— *The New York Herald*, Paris, December 24, 1932

For the first time in her life, twenty-year old Posselt, a married woman of three years presenting herself as an ingenue in her teens, and an acclaimed but little-known American concert violinist, left home for the Europe she had dreamed of seeing as a schoolgirl in Medford. Although she had visited several U.S. cities, she had never lived alone for any length of time, and certainly not in a foreign country. So this trip represented a giant leap into the big, exciting world, and she was on her own. Of course, she had a small American social network abroad, made up of her patronesses' socialite friends; she knew a little French; and most of all, she was under the watchful eye of Thibaud and his family, who, like everyone in the music world, thought Posselt was somewhat younger than she was. Thibaud, while sincerely admiring her talent, treated her as his protégée, his American discovery.

Jacques Thibaud (1880–1953) is considered the foremost representative of the modern French school of violin playing.[63] He studied with his father and with the Belgian violinist Martin Pierre Marsick, and began his professional life by playing gigs in nightclubs, cafés, and brothels in Paris. In the Café Rouge there, he got his first break when the famous conductor Edouard Colonne heard him and invited him to join his orchestra, where he eventually became the concertmaster.

Appearing as soloist with the orchestra, Thibaud established himself in Paris, then toured Europe to critical acclaim and made his first American appearances in 1903, eight years before Posselt was born. Thibaud served in the French army during World War I, was wounded, and was decorated for bravery. As physical therapy, he took up golf, which remained his favorite pastime for the rest of his life.

In the opinion of the violinist Albert Spalding, "Thibaud exemplified the adventurous spirit of Gascony; the sun-shot warmth of Southern France illuminated his smile. He could tell tales with enthralling zest. The same grace and charm that individualized his violin playing was evident in everything else he undertook. He was irresistible to women, young and old, and was as proud of this power as he was modest about his musical genius."[64]

Thibaud married a wealthy pianist, Marguerite Long, and the couple had two sons, Phillip and Roger. Mme Thibaud tolerated her husband's legendary infidelities, which he went to almost farcical efforts to conceal. The Thibauds had a long and close professional collaboration. As committed teachers, they operated a school in Paris, and during the summer, Thibaud taught exceptional students at his St. Jean de Luz estate near Biarritz, eventually founding a school there where young virtuosos were lodged, fed, and offered free master classes.

Thibaud's recent French biographer, Christian Goubault, surmises that the plan for this school came to Thibaud during the summer of 1932, when he was working with "his three prodigies: Ruth Posselt, Grisha Goluboff, Paul Makanowitzky, young, exceptionally talented violinists to whom he gave a white donkey to amuse themselves with on his estate."[65] Goubault mistakenly assumes that Posselt was a young child like the two boys, Goluboff and Makanowitzky, and that, like them, she had been a student of the world famous violin teacher, Ivan Galamian.

Posselt warmly recalled her summers in St. Jean de Luz, saying she valued the opportunity of daily interaction and exchange of ideas with other violinists. In private, she would tell story after story about both Thibaud's and his son Phillip's amorous pursuit of her, and her successful, if flirtatious, thwarting of their advances. One of her favorite exchanges with Thibaud took place when they were taking a rest from work and had sat down on a couch in his studio. Thibaud began to move closer and make advances, at which point Ruth said, "I think we need an intermission," and Thibaud retorted, "And I was hoping for an act!"

Thibaud sent periodic reports on Ruth's progress to Mrs. Fuller. In one of them, he wrote fulsomely, "Everybody here loves her, she is a true little dignified American and an artist of genius. I am mad about her talent and I want her to be a Queen of the Art. . . . I am certain that her triumph will begin in Paris. She works like a little Chinese and I am proud of her!"[66]

In the thirties, Thibaud was nearing the end of his forty-year-long performing career. His popularity with audiences had not waned, and he was touring all over the world with undiminished energy. Posselt quickly realized, however, that her teacher, as she confessed to her husband, was an "awful golf fiend who play[ed] all day long rather than practicing his violin!"[67] And Thibaud, who had the unusual quality among virtuosi of not taking himself too seriously, would probably have agreed with his "little dignified American's" assessment. On the other hand, Thibaud did take his teaching seriously. He viewed his main teacherly goal as the development of each individual's capabilities within that person's own norm. "A violinist's natural manner of playing," he wrote, "is the one he should cultivate; since it is individual, it really represents him. And a teacher or a colleague of greater fame does him no kindness if he encourages him to distrust his own powers by too good naturedly 'showing' him how to do this, that or the other. . . . All really good violinists are good artists."[68]

Thibaud's teaching approach differed significantly from Ondříček's. The latter was a product and exponent of the Sevčik school of violin playing that Thibaud, perhaps predictably, despised: "Sevčik's purely soulless and mechanical system has undoubtedly produced a number of excellent mechanicians of the violin. But it has just as unquestionably killed real talent!"[69] Ondříček had certainly not killed Posselt's talent, but neither had he encouraged her to break free of the ideal-student mold that may initially have constrained her individualism.

Thibaud was the right mentor and coach for Posselt at the right time. He let her flawless left-hand technique and bowing alone and focused instead on broadening her repertoire, introducing her to French works, notably the sonatas of Franck, Fauré, and Lekeu, all of which became staples of her repertoire. He also suggested she "calm her vibrato." Most of all, Thibaud worked tirelessly to bolster Posselt's confidence in her own playing and artistry. Despite the teacherly self-interest in his cheer-leading efforts, which accompanied her every European debut, they also enabled Posselt to grow both musically and artistically.

Posselt enjoyed her first sojourn in Europe, but she was homesick, missed her husband and encouraged him to come over and join her. She wrote him long letters daily, telling him every detail of her life, and tried to soothe his understandable worries over her "men friends," especially Thibaud's son: "Please do not worry over my men friends! . . . Phil Thibaud does not even kid himself that he should be so lucky as to be the object of my affec-tions. As far as being near people with romance in their heart did you ever see a man that didn't have romance in his heart – at least for someone? But it would affect me not in the slight-est! More or less disgusts me!"[70] Arthur apparently believed and trusted his wife, but he did grow increasingly jealous, not so much of Thibaud *fils* as of Thibaud *père*.

The only direct testimony of Thibaud's feelings for Posselt are the twenty letters she saved that he wrote her over seven years from October 21, 1932, to January 7, 1939. These letters, three in English, the rest in French, are varied in terms of tone, intent, degree of intimacy, and sincerity. Overall, their tone is fatherly, teacherly, and always af-fectionate, sometimes suggestive of something more. However, there is no way of determining, out of context, whether the "something more" reflected an actual or a wished-for reality. A good example is the letter he wrote Posselt after she left Paris for her Berlin debut in 1932. After bolstering her confidence, assuring her that his heart will be with her, that she must play for him, "be *la grande Ruth,*" and telegraph him afterward about her big success, because no one in the world is prouder of her than he, his teacherly concern and encouragement seems to transition smoothly into a tentatively amorous key: "And no one in the world loves you as I do! Do you know that? – And you? Do you have the same feelings for me? I think, maybe a little . . ."[71]

Similar letters and telegrams accompanied Posselt's debuts in several European capitals in late 1932. With the exception of Paris, these debuts were recitals, which was common practice for introducing unknowns at that time, and recital programs often included at least one full-length concerto played with piano rather than orchestral accompaniment. Thibaud wanted Posselt to play the Paganini Violin Concerto at all her debuts, but Dr. G. De Koos, her European manager and Dutch mentor, discouraged her from playing Paganini in any of her Holland concerts, on the grounds that it would not go over well with the Dutch public. Thibaud deferred to De Koos's judgment, and so Posselt played the Goldmark Concerto not only for her debuts in The Hague and Amsterdam, but also for those in Berlin, Vienna, and Brussels.[72]

Her success everywhere was remarkable: "a very gifted young lady of whom more will assuredly be heard" (London); "She is the Adelina Patti of the violin, her tone cannot be compared with any other one. Ruth Posselt must be placed among the greatest artists of her instrument" (Amsterdam); "One need not be a prophet to be able to foretell that this young lady will have a successful career. She has a rare talent. A splendid tone, the violin is singing in her hands" (Berlin); "Her recital was something of a sensation by virtue of her big, brilliant tone, her impeccable technical equipment and a truly dashing temperament" (Vienna); "America may be proud of being able to send out such an artist" (The Hague).

Ruth was euphoric as she shared her success in The Hague with her "beloved mother": "Just a line. Your baby is so busy. Either traveling, practicing, rehearsing, or playing! Honestly, I've been having a sensational success . . . Let me tell you about last nite! My concert was in the biggest hall here "Diligentia" in The Hague. It was full. A marvelous audience!!! This a.m. De Koos came to see me & was so excited because I had received such a <u>marvelous criticism by the leading critic & newspaper here!</u> He said it's a page long. The critic is mad over me!!! He says I'm in line with Kreisler, Heifetz, Elman & Menuhin!! De Koos said he <u>never read</u> such a sensational criticism in all his life! It even surpassed my Amsterdam criticism in superlatives if you can imagine such a thing! Well, as a result, De Koos is giving me a <u>big return concert in the same hall on the 21st of this month.</u> De Koos nearly cried he's so happy. And me too."[73]

In December, Thibaud and his accompanist took Posselt to Spain to audition for music directors and conductors in Barcelona and other cities. In Barcelona, Thibaud personally presented her to an auditorium of maestros: Casals, Millet, Costa, Toldra, Ponsa, and others. She made such an impression that the Associació de Música da Camera hired her for two concerts the following season in the Palau de la Música Catalana. Posselt always remembered playing for hours for Casals, his brother, and Francesca Costa at the conservatory in Barcelona. The result of this foray was a Spanish tour for the 1933–34 season.

As soon as Posselt had arrived in Paris back in June, she had encouraged her husband to join her in Europe, which at some point he did. When he arrived she introduced him to everyone as her fiancé. She clearly felt it prudent to keep up her unmarried persona since, once Thibaud met his protégée's "fiancé," he told her in private, halfjokingly, "If you get married, I kill you." Arthur managed to persuade his wife to come home with him in early 1933 during a short break in her concert schedule. They sailed for New York on the SS *Champlain*, traveling as two single persons under separate names. As soon as they arrived in Boston, Arthur Newcomb disappeared, and Ruth Posselt, "luminous eyes flashing from beneath a modish Paris hat,"[74] walked down the gangplank to be greeted by Mrs. Fuller and Mrs. Hobbs as well as Boaz Piller of the BSO. At such times, it could not have been easy to be Arthur Newcomb, and it's clear that after Posselt's first European tour, Arthur began at least a half court press to make "coming home" – and staying there to pursue her career – an attractive possibility for his errant, though faithful wife.

It would not be an easy sell. In six weeks, Posselt would be off to Europe again, to complete her engagements and then work with Thibaud over the summer in preparation for the fall. Although touring Europe was expensive (her manager, De Koos, took a whopping thirty-five percent of her fees), Posselt gained in prestige what her pocketbook lost, and she was thrilled by the European audiences and their enthusiasm for her. "Those audiences," she exclaimed to a Boston reporter, "are so different, especially in Italy. At Milano they yelled and clapped and stamped their feet for what seemed hours. I played seven encores."[75] During the short time she was stateside, she played a few concerts, also to enthusiastic audiences, the most important of which was a recital at the Fuller mansion, another benefit to raise money to go back to Europe.

The ballroom, library, and reception rooms in the Fuller residence were crowded with debutantes and their escorts. Mrs. Fuller hosted the event, which was sponsored by the Boston branch of the Schubert Memorial. Among the by-invitation-only audience were "Boston's music luminaries": Serge Koussevitzky, Arthur Fiedler, Gregor and Jacqueline Piatigorsky, the composer Mabel Daniels, and the composer and music critic Warren Storey Smith, who had written so appreciatively of Posselt's playing the year before. After the concert, the soloist met Koussevitzky, who was destined to become one of her most ardent supporters.

The *Boston Traveler* reporter who covered this society musical event provided a detailed description of Posselt at twenty-one: "Her hair is very blonde and she wears it curled up tight, and very short, and parts it in the middle. Her eyes are very expressive and large and brown. Since her face is beautifully rounded, it gives her the look of a cherub. You can't help a start of surprise when she picks up her violin and starts in on some particularly difficult classic. She really looks too young and beautiful to be so talented. All of which is altogether enough praise for any young lady to receive for one evening. But you should have seen the crowd of admirers around her the minute she finished playing!"[76]

Posselt's second tour in Europe was an extension of the first. She was still finishing her work with Thibaud and in the midst of launching what they hoped would be a career in Europe. After leaving the States in early April, she made a return appearance in Berlin, then played three concerts in Holland. In the summer, she had three more concert engagements in Holland, and completed her tour in late fall. Arthur did not join his wife this time. After she left in the spring he planned a surprise for her homecoming, building her a house in Maine on Hermon Pond; in his letters he enclosed pictures of their love nest, "Ruth's House," in the process of construction. (Posselt would later recall how much she loved the house and being there with Arthur, but she also admitted to finding life there boring.)

Ruth certainly kept up her end of her long-distance marriage. After playing in Berlin, Rotterdam, and The Hague, she went to her apartment in Paris on the Rue de Square Carpeux. From the balcony, a friend took her picture, which she sent to Arthur, the first of many that summer, with a love note on the back, assuring him she was all his: "Thinking only of you my wonderful husband. I have your picture on my heart (the one you had taken in Chicago) and your cross on my neck, your vision in my eyes, and your love in my soul. I love you so madly precious! July 9, 1933 – Paris."

Later that month, she gave concert performances at the Concertgebouw in Amsterdam and The Hague, while living in Scheveningen, Holland, which throughout the thirties was the site of a major summer music festival. In early August, Thibaud performed the Bach Double Concerto with her at Scheveningen, a concert she often recalled as one of the highlights of her relationship with him. After the concert, Thibaud socialized charmingly and on his best professional behavior with Posselt's mother and the Ondříčeks, who had joined her in Scheveningen. From there, Ruth sent Arthur a veritable, predigital-age album of snapshots of her and her family enjoying their

leisure, all of them conscientiously and lovingly annotated on the back, like this one of herself, her mother, and Gladys on August 10, 1933: "To my precious life, Arthur: Taken after a most strenuous swim – a very tired baby-wife." This was followed the next day by three photos taken on the beach containing a view of the beach chairs, which, Ruth explained, "keep out both sun and wind – there are hundreds of them"; a picture on the beach "with the donkeys, who take children for rides"; and another of the donkeys, with the exclamation, "It quite thrilled me being so close to these animals, even tho they're as calm and harmless as could be." By the end of the month, Posselt was back in St. Jean de Luz, living with her mother in a pension that Thibaud had found for them. From there she sent a picture of herself with the note: "Daddy: This is your little blond apparition. Would you recognize your baby?"

In the fall, Posselt added the Dvořák Violin Concerto to her repertoire, performing it three times in Holland with the Residentie Orchestra under Henri van Goudoever, who became a close colleague of hers and who recommended to the maestro of the Amsterdam Concertgebouw, Willem Mengelberg, that she play the Dvořák concerto with him in the spring. Posselt had originally studied the Czech work with Ondříček, whose brother, František, had given the first performance of the piece in 1883, during Dvořák's lifetime. This concerto would serve Posselt well over the next twenty years as she reintroduced it to audiences in Europe and the United States, where it had not been heard for years. It would also become associated with several adventures and dramatic moments in her performing life as we shall see.

Posselt returned to the United States with her mother in late November for a brief visit home. Shortly before she went back to France in mid-January, her portrait was drawn by the young graphic artist Dwight Shepler and appeared in the *Boston Herald* together with the artist's insightful impressions of her.

"RUTH POSSELT TAKES SALT WITH HER FLATTERY"

Shepler's article conveys just how successful Posselt had become at appearing unaffected while affecting her tried-and-true pose. As his portrait reveals, he works from the outside in: "Ruth Posselt masks a rather sensitive face with a landslide of mascara, lipstick that wanders off the beaten path, and her blonde hair is aided and abetted by whatever they use to aid and abet with. The eyebrows go where the tweezers direct. The result makes one look at least twice, though, and is probably a professional asset. She also pointed out the very interesting phenomenon that the muscles underneath her left jaw bone are developed decidedly more than those on the right, and that there is a worn place on the skin; the result, of course, of her incessant practice.

"In the course of her conversation Miss Posselt revealed herself as something of a philosopheress, having some well ordered ideas about values. She says that it behooves the young lady musician to take flattery with a grain of salt, and her attitude seems to substantiate the statement, although we gave her no provocation to season our remarks. She dislikes the pose of ultra-sophistication and hopes that she never falls into an attitude of blasé boredom. *Marriage to her is a distant thing, but she does believe that the husband of an artist should allow her to pursue her career. Jacques Thibaud, the noted French violinist, who introduced her to Europe, said to her: 'If you get marry, I keel you!'*

". . . Miss Posselt spends six hours a day practicing. On the stage her manner is one of complete confidence and mastery. She says that her musical tastes change with time, but that at present she is more enthusiastic about Bach than any other composer. She has to be careful of her arm, and has had to forego tennis and similar sports, but swims and skates. On the coolest day she says she gets very warm playing, and that it requires a lot of physical exertion.

"'She is the Adeline Patti of the violin,' said De Telegraf in Holland. 'Her tone cannot be compared with any other one. Ruth Posselt must be placed among the greatest artists of her instrument.'

"Her name is accented on the first syllable."[77]

𝄢𝄢𝄢

The year 1934 would prove climactic professionally, personally, and politically. The Stavisky affair in France, sporadic revolts in Spain that were a prelude to that country's civil war, Hitler's assumption of absolute power in Germany, economic crisis throughout Europe, the assassination of Kirov in the Soviet Union: these were some of the major events that played themselves out around Posselt as she toured Holland, Spain, Scandinavia, and the Soviet Union, reaching the peak of her European fame and experiencing for the first time what it was like to be a touring concert violinist. With the typical virtuoso's tunnel vision, she was aware of the turmoil going on around her but was untouched by it. From her Spanish tour, she recalled running through a street to her recital in Bilbao with an evening dress under one arm and her fiddle under the other, while police and soldiers charged into the shouting crowds of a communist workers' demonstration. From the end of the year, in Soviet Russia, she remembered being locked in her Moscow hotel room during the manhunts and demonstrations that followed Kirov's murder.

Her tour of Holland in January (The Hague, Lochem, Middelburg, Rotterdam, Deventer, and Tilburg) yielded new critical accolades, which took her artistry seriously but occasionally made the sort of fulsome comparisons with her male peers that seemed imported from the American press. The Hague greeted her as "the female Menuhin from America," "the blonde fairy," a "gifted genius and young heroine, whose large audience was brought to a high pitch of enthusiasm and charmed in an unforgettable manner." A Rotterdam critic commented: "Two surprises have arrived in the last two years in the violin world: Francescatti and the "blond American doll," Ruth Posselt. Once more she held us dumbfounded under the spell of her wonderful talent. Isn't it gratifying how she makes that violin sing? And the artist's spirit she conveys? . . . At the end of the concert it was impossible for the star to leave until she had played several encores."[78]

Such examples of the way reviewers praised women violinists in a then largely male profession were widespread, and plagued the critical reception of almost all outstanding female performers until relatively recently.

Posselt had already been hailed in America as "a female Heifetz" and "a female Menuhin"; now in Europe she was "a blonde fairy" and a "blond American doll." It would be a while yet before she was hailed simply as a virtuoso violinist, as Zino Francescatti had been from the get-go.

Admittedly, Posselt herself was hardly upset by such praise, and back home in Medford, Ida was thrilled; she had snippets of her "dearest Baby bunnie's" Dutch reviews translated by the manager of the Medford Economy Store, who used to live in Amsterdam, and wrote to her daughter excitedly: "Some small criticisms! I only hope you get them in this country."[79] Perhaps Arthur wished so too, for at some point, he joined his wife in Paris, possibly at her urging.

After her Dutch tour, Ruth returned to Paris and remained there, apparently with Arthur, until she left for Spain on February 10 for a whirlwind two-week traversal of Catalonia, playing recitals in Bilbao, Gijon, Girona, Tarragona, Valencia, Reus, Figueras, Sabadell, Terrassa, and Barcelona, where she appeared twice, giving a recital and playing two concertos, Mozart and Dvořák, with the Orquesta Clásica de Barcelona. The terms of her contract are worth noting: she received a total of 5,000 pesetas (about $681 then, the equivalent of $12,185 in 2016 dollars) for ten concerts, plus all train travel, first class, to and from Paris and within Spain, plus 25 pesetas (about $60 today) per day for expenses. Her European manager did receive a thirty percent commission, but for a young, relatively untried violinist from Depression-starved America, she did quite well.

Throughout her Spanish tour, Posselt was in correspondence with Thibaud, who was on his own tour in southern France. When he arrived in Bordeaux, he received a letter from Posselt, who must have been nervous about not having a chance to see him before her upcoming debut with the Concertgebouw in Amsterdam, which followed hard upon her arrival in Paris from Barcelona. In an unpublished letter of February 26–27, 1934, Thibaud reassured Posselt that "everything was *all* right," for he had come up with a plan to travel back to Paris with her. After his concert in Limoges, which was on the Barcelona–Paris train route, he would board her train when it stopped there, at 1:30 a.m., and they would travel to Paris together. Thibaud advised her to buy a first-class ticket from Barcelona to Paris, but not a sleeper (he would reserve that) and to be on the lookout for him when the train pulled into Limoges because he would be waiting for her on the platform. The tone of his letter conveys both urgency and pleasure that he has found a way to spend a few hours with her as well as to ensure that she would be able to make the rehearsal in Amsterdam on the 27th. He closed, with not a little romantic anticipation, "I love you and kiss your heavenly mouth, Jacques."[80]

So, what happened on the night train to Paris?

Not quite what Thibaud seemed to be hoping for, perhaps. While poring through my mother's memorabilia, I discovered that she, too, left a reminiscence of that train trip to Paris with Thibaud, but in context and tone it was strikingly different from what her mentor anticipated in his personal letter. Her recollection turned up in a story for a press kit, written in the mid-1940s, as one of the adventures she had experienced in her life as a traveling violinist:

"Another interesting experience happened on a train trip from Spain to Paris. I was preparing for a concert in Holland, and Jacques Thibaud was on the train with me. 'What cadenzas are you using now?' he asked. To my reply, he advised impatiently, 'Oh, but the people in Holland will not like those. They are all right for American or English audiences, but you need something different.' 'Maybe,' I reminded him, 'but it takes practically a whole month to learn them and I give my concert in three days. Furthermore I have no music.' 'No matter. I will write them for you from memory.' He had no paper, but on old programs he scribbled his rows and rows of tiny notes. 'Get out your violin and practice them now,' he urged. There was only one man in our compartment who apparently enjoyed the impromptu concert. As for the rest of the train, well, they could hear me but they couldn't see me. I'm still using those same cadenzas, too, and whenever I play them, I think of that stuffy, rickety train and practicing them all the way to Paris."[81]

Professionally composed and correct as it is, Posselt's public story rings at least partially true, if only because the upcoming concert in Amsterdam was a big one, her debut with Mengelberg, and in a letter to De Koos before she left for Spain, she had expressed doubts about playing the Dvořák.

On the other hand, Ruth's arrival in Paris from Barcelona and that important Amsterdam concert seem eventually to have become inextricably linked in her memory with a major rift between her and her first husband. As she recalled to me a half century later, when she returned to Paris, her husband was waiting for her. To celebrate their reunion, they went out on the town, but Arthur had too much to drink. Later in their hotel room, he got sick and they "had a terrific scene. I was due to leave for Amsterdam the next day to play with the Concertgebouw. He said if I left, he was through. We reconciled, but after that we grew increasingly estranged."

The concert was a huge success: "Ruth Posselt was the soloist with the Dvořák Concerto. She was a brilliant soloist, young and warm, with great enthusiasm, superb technique, an ardent tone full of passion; a violinist by the grace of the muses!"[82] Another tour of Holland followed – Enschede, Haarlem, Nijmegen, Apeldoorn, Zeist, Amsterdam, Dordrecht, Breda, and The Hague, after which the Newcombs sailed for New York aboard the SS *Paris,* arriving on April 3; Arthur Newcomb appears on the passenger list as married, Ruth Posselt as single.

Starting in 1934, Posselt had a new manager for her American engagements: Alexander Merovitch, at that time president of Musical Art Management Corporation. A Russian Jew, born in St. Petersburg, Merovitch had left Russia in the early twenties as the self-styled "manager" of three virtual unknowns: the violinist Nathan Milstein, the pianist Vladimir Horowitz, and the cellist Gregor Piatigorsky. All of them eventually came to America and became world-famous. Merovitch probably got involved with Posselt's management through De Koos, with whom he was partnered.

Posselt was eager to launch her career in the United States for professional and personal reasons. More immediately, upon her return to the States, she had to decide about the summer. Thibaud expected her to spend June and July in St. Jean de Luz, as she had done for the past two years, but she felt drawn to stay in Maine with her husband. Thibaud tried to persuade her to come back to Europe: "No, Ruthie, you must come to St. Jean de Luz for the whole month of July; I will be there the whole month, and we shall work together calmly and intensively. I'll be travelling for the first three weeks of August but starting the 20th, as I proposed in my last letter, we will take a car trip with Tasso [Janopoulus] to the lakes of Aix des bains and d'Annecy."[83]

Torn between the demands of her career and her desire not to give up on her marriage, Ruth resolved her dilemma with a compromise weighted in favor of her personal life. She spent the summer with Arthur and returned to Europe with him at the end of August. Throughout the summer, she was in correspondence with Merovitch, who began the conversation by admitting that the work of introducing her in the United States for the 1934–35 season had been handicapped by a late start and the bad economy.

In 1934, the music business was slowly and cautiously beginning to emerge from the Depression, but most local managers and organizations had sustained such heavy losses in recent years that they were more careful than ever about choosing only big box-office artists with firmly established names. Posselt did not fall into this category. She was still considered a "new young artist," which meant she had to be introduced in America – déjà vu all over again – through a New York recital. A way had to be found to finance such a recital, and Merovitch suggested asking Mrs. Fuller to underwrite the cost, approximately $850.

Merovitch had some good news as well: he had booked Posselt in March with the Boston Symphony Orchestra and Koussevitzky, at the admittedly small fee of $150. Nevertheless, he told her that an engagement with the BSO was important enough that even artists with established names accepted whatever fee was offered.[84] The most exciting news was that a member of Merovitch's organization had secured for Posselt a tour of the Soviet Union, including concert appearances in Moscow and Leningrad. She would be one of the first American violinists to perform in Soviet Russia, after Heifetz had made his groundbreaking tour in the spring of 1934.

The one thing that worried her, she explained to Merovitch, was her lack of a good violin. For her European concerts over the past two years, she had played a Guadagnini lent her by the violin dealer Caressa in Paris. She had her heart set on buying it, but making such a purchase before her Soviet tour was out of the question. Merovitch set her mind at ease by promising to have a well-known New York dealer loan her a suitable instrument of her choice. In the end, however, Thibaud came to the rescue, writing her in mid-August that she "would have Caressa's Guadagnini for September."[85]

The Newcombs arrived in France on September 2. Posselt headed to Scheveningen to make an AVRO radio broadcast and then perform the Tchaikovsky at the Kurzaal. Then, she and her husband went to St. Jean de Luz for the rest of the month before she began an extensive tour of Holland with appearances in The Hague, Zuphen, Tilburg, Zeist, Hilverum, Utrecht, and Amsterdam. As she recalled later, something unexpected and totally unrehearsed occurred when she performed in Utrecht, where she played the Dvořák Violin Concerto, a work that was beginning to acquire a tragicomic Macbeth-like aura in her performing life. To begin with, the conductor in Utrecht, Goudoever, told her she would be playing on the second half of the program, at about 9:30 p.m. She arrived forty-five minutes early in order to dress and warm up, only to be told that Goudoever had been mistaken and she was to go on stage in three minutes! She managed to put on her gown and walked out onstage smoothing her hair down. She played the forty-minute concerto, received a wonderful ovation, and was hoping she could make a quick exit and go home to bed since she had a bad cold.

As soon as she entered the wings, however, Goudoever came up to her to ask a favor. The concertmaster had suddenly fallen ill and couldn't play the second half of the concert, the Cesar Franck Symphony in D Minor. Goudoever asked if she would take his place. She objected that she had never played in an orchestra and had never even seen the music. Goudoever said he would show her how the difficult passages went right then and there, she could sight-read the rest; he begged her to do this for him. She couldn't let him down. When she appeared onstage again and sat in the concertmaster's chair, the audience was surprised. Goudoever explained the situation, and Ruth would end her story by saying that she got through the symphony by watching the conductor "the way a cat eyes a strange dog."

At the end of October, Merovitch wired Posselt the good news that he had talked with Mrs. Fuller and she had agreed to underwrite the cost of a Town Hall recital in February. He also reminded her that since the Soviet authorities did not allow any rubles out of the country she would have to pay his ten percent commission to his brother, Adolph Merovitch, a professor at the Leningrad Conservatory.

Posselt's tour of the Soviet Union deserves the overused epithet "historic." In November 1933, the United States had established diplomatic relations with the Soviet Union, and William Bullitt, the first American ambassador to the USSR, arrived in Moscow. Diplomatic relations led to the development of cultural exchanges. The Kremlin began to encourage foreign tourism in Russia with major tourist companies in England, America, and Germany. A ten-story hotel for foreign tourists was built in Leningrad, and in May 1934, the city hosted its first international music festival featuring stars like Leopold Stokowski, Efrem Zimbalist, and Jascha Heifetz. When he arrived in the Soviet Union, Heifetz gave a series of recitals and orchestra concerts in Moscow and Leningrad, visited the conservatories in both cities, and met all the leading musicians.

Posselt was the first native-born American and the first female artist to tour the Soviet Union. Musical Art Management Corporation contracted with GOMETS, the State Organization for Music, Stage and Circus, for Posselt to play fifteen concerts in the USSR, three in Moscow, two in Leningrad, and ten in provincial cities (Kiev, Kharkov, Odessa, and Saratov-Engels). Posselt received seven hundred rubles for each concert, first-class rail transportation from Paris or other European city to Moscow and back, "first-category" sleeping cars within the USSR, automobile transportation from station to hotel, hotel to concert hall, and all hotel accommodations in the USSR. GOMETS provided visas, and Posselt was enjoined to spend all her rubles in Russia.

Newcomb apparently accompanied his wife to Leningrad and then Moscow. From one of his letters to Posselt, it is clear that he got his visa through Intourist, the Soviet tourist agency, in Hamburg, Germany, and planned to be in Leningrad, traveling as a private citizen, when his wife arrived via Finland as an official artist guest.

Posselt entered the Soviet Union on November 26, 1934, and played with the Leningrad Philharmonic the following evening. She made an unforgettable, if slightly mistaken, impression on at least one young student in the audience, who happened to recall her in his memoirs years later: "In my sophomore year [at Leningrad State University] we had the chance to get subscriptions to the concerts of the Leningrad Philharmonic in the famous large hall at a much reduced price. The subscription included forty concerts, five per month. We heard the best musicians of the day, not only our own, but foreigners on tour. Unfortunately, I've forgotten the names of most of them, but I did remember one – Ruth Posselt – an English [*sic*] woman violinist who played with the Philharmonic, which was then under the direction of Fritz Shtidri. She was a tall, slender, interesting woman with blond hair in a luxurious white dress."[86]

Posselt had already moved on to Moscow when, on December 4, Sergei Kirov, the general secretary of the Leningrad region Communist Party, was assassinated in Leningrad. During the ensuing public demonstrations, she recalled being "confined to her hotel in Moscow in a state of high anxiety" since she had no idea what was going on. She managed to make phone contact with "a young American friend" who was in Moscow at the time, and he promised "to skid about town" to her hotel and keep her company.[87] When the commotion died down, funeral parades began and "seemed to go on day and night."After her recital in the Small Hall of the Moscow Conservatory, she left on her tour of Kiev, Odessa, Kharkov, Saratov, and Engels.

For the Soviets, the visits of Western artists were part of an active propaganda campaign whose goal was to show foreigners the achievements of so-called socialist construction. The idea was to send foreign visitors home with a positive view of the Soviet Union that would hopefully make them vocal supporters of its achievements. Posselt, like Heifetz before her, responded exactly as the Soviet authorities hoped she would. In fact, some of Heifetz's and Posselt's comments, in widely separated press venues, bear an eerie resemblance to each other. For example, in the Russian-language paper *Russian Voice,* in May 1934, Heifetz said: "In the USSR a good concert is considered by many people worth making real sacrifices for. . . . There are music lovers there who are ready to sell their prized possessions in order to attend a good concert."[88] A year later, Posselt, who knew no Russian, noted in *The Boston Globe*: "In Russia, even a poor peasant would spend his last cent willingly to hear a great artist or attend a good concert. Almost every street laborer in Russia can talk to you intelligently about music, can discuss Brahms, Beethoven, Schubert."[89]

Posselt took what she saw (and was shown) in Soviet Russia at face value, though with a certain amount of common sense. She admitted that her opinion of Russia had been colored by what she had read or heard in the United States, and found that the Russians she met had equally false notions about America. In Moscow, she recalled, people pictured New York as being full of gangsters and kidnappers.[90] She was most impressed by how large and appreciative the audiences were, including one of five thousand soldiers, and how cold the weather was. "I was freezing all the time," she said, "and had to wear evening dresses which were high enough to cover my woolen undershirts."[91]

She had some interesting encounters, which probably were arranged especially for her, though she took them to be spontaneous. In Kharkov, a committee of six workers came backstage before the concert and asked her to change her program to include compositions by Bach and Beethoven instead of the small pieces by lesser composers she had intended. After a moment of surprise, she told them she would be happy to change her program – she began with a Beethoven sonata and ended with the Bach Chaconne. The audience was one of the most enthusiastic she had had.

On Christmas, Posselt was scheduled to play with the recently founded German State Philharmonic Orchestra[92] in Engels, a city on the Volga River across from Saratov, where her hotel was located. A snowstorm was raging when she was taken across the frozen river by horse and sleigh. The temperature was about minus ten Celsius, and even though she was covered with heavy fur robes, she thought she would freeze before they reached the other side of the river. The blizzard caused them to stray from the sleigh path and they were forced to zigzag to avoid weak spots in the ice, sometimes going a quarter of a mile out of their way. Posselt's hands were aching with the cold and had become numb. Finally, a lantern appeared on shore in the distance. When they arrived at the concert hall Posselt's hands were rubbed with snow. Half an hour later, she was already onstage.

Another time, she had to play in an opera house that was so cold, her hands turned blue, and she said she couldn't play. She blew on her hands and shook them, trying to warm them as everyone laughed good-naturedly. Then she went backstage to her dressing room, put on her fur coat, and gave the recital that night so attired.

On December 28, Posselt played with the State Philharmonic in Moscow, performing the Mozart D Major Concerto. Then came the New Year's Eve party at the American embassy, where she met the cream of the Russian musical world, including the young virtuoso David Oistrakh and the composer Dmitri Shostakovitch. She danced with the latter all evening, finding him "a somewhat timid person, in spite of the violence of much of his music," but, she confided to the American press, "he is no Fred Astaire." Many composers gave her manuscripts, some of which she later performed at one of her Town Hall recitals.

On New Year's Day Posselt gave her last concert in Russia. A member of the audience drew a sketch of her "in remembrance from Moskow," and the reviews, as elsewhere in Russia, were positive, though one critic chided her for her American habit of playing too much light music.

♩♩♩

In remembrance
from Moskow.

Already in Paris at the beginning of January, Posselt wrote Georg Fazer, her Swedish liaison for the tour just concluded, about her desire to plan another tour there for the following season. Fazer replied that he had heard of her "colossal success" in the USSR, and suggested that if she did return to Europe for the 1935–36 season, she should plan on beginning with Denmark and Norway, then go to Stockholm and Helsingfors and travel by sleeper train directly to Leningrad from the Finnish capital. It sounded promising, and Posselt worked hard, both apart from and with her managers for almost two years to make it happen, but it was not to be. Politics, bad economies, Stalinist purges, life, and, finally, love intervened.

Although Posselt did not know it when she and her husband returned to New York in mid-January, her career in Europe had reached its peak. She did make two more short tours before the war, but despite her usual rave reviews, she was essentially forced to let her European career lapse, something Thibaud, who tried to help her mount a European comeback in the late thirties, regretted and chided her about. There were many reasons why after Russia, Posselt refocused her energies on the United States. Initially, and most importantly, giving concerts in Europe, now in a full-blown depression, became financially unremunerative. Nor could she really contemplate living for long periods in Europe; she knew her husband did not want her to, whereas he encouraged her in all her stateside endeavors.

The year 1935 was a turning point in Posselt's professional return to her native land. In early February, Alexander Merovitch's Musical Art Management Corporation launched Posselt in her first Town Hall recital. Accompanied by the well-known pianist Arpad Sandor, who had collaborated with her in Europe, she played the Vitali Chaconne, Mozart's Violin Concerto No. 4 in D major, the Franck Sonata, and a selection of "small pieces." The all-important reviews of the New York critics were very positive. *The New York Tribune* critic noted that she "impressed as a very able musician, with a comprehensive, fleet-fingered technique and notable taste and artistry in her phrasing."[93] *The New York World-Telegram* praised her "well balanced program," writing that "the youthful violinist's playing of the Mozart piece disclosed almost at once a maturity and artistic comprehension beyond her years," and "a large tone of surprising purity, a rapid and unencumbered technic and a delicately shaded legato further distinguished her performance."[94] What is absent from these particular reviews is also noteworthy: there's not a word about her gown, her appearance, and her blondeness; she is hailed simply as who she was, Ruth Posselt, Violinist.

In the fairly intensive Boston press coverage that greeted Posselt's return from the Soviet Union, she seemed to speak and give her opinions with a new confidence and maturity. "Every artist tries to improve with the years," she opined to one reporter, "there is no fixed goal, but each year he aims higher. . . . After a certain point, though, musicians, particularly, tend to retrograde. They lose their grip, their tone becomes feeble, their technique slips. I suppose you can't make a set rule, but some begin to wane at 50, others at 60. Only a very few can continue playing the way they want to play into advanced age."[95]

The large audiences for classical music in Europe had spoiled Posselt, and upon her return home, she was struck by the scantiness of Boston audiences. She commented to one interviewer: "Our America is music minded, yes, but not on so-called classical music. I myself like a symphonic style of jazz such as Paul Whiteman plays. But very few people really want to hear classical music in this country."[96]

Underscoring Ruth's mastery of the art of keeping secrets, the Boston press was also fixated on whether she would ever marry. Rather than avoid such questions, the secretly married virtuosa embraced them with élan, disingenuously commenting in a *Boston Sunday Post* article, "Ease of Russian Divorces Keeps Medford Genius Single": "In Russia they could not understand why I was not married at my age of 19. The girls of Russia marry at a very tender age. In fact, at twenty many of them are divorced. Divorces in that country may be procured in about five minutes. . . . This was an object lesson for me, I guess, for I have kept away from matrimony and given all my attention to the violin."[97]

Did this ambiguous, partially false statement reflect the inner truth of Ruth's complex personal situation at the time? On the surface, she distances herself from the tendency of "Russian girls" to marry at a tender age and be divorced by twenty, but she might also be drawing a parallel between their lot and hers, *sotto voce* wishing for a quick Russian divorce as a way to concentrate on her violin. Is this the object lesson she was speaking of? After all, like the Russian girls, she, an American girl, had married at the tender age of eighteen, but now that she was (secretly) twenty-three, she had fallen three years behind them in getting a divorce. On the other hand, her fake age of nineteen allowed her a year of grace.

Throughout the previous year, Arthur had been taking an active role in helping to manage Ruth's career so she could concentrate on her violin *in the United States,* and after Russia, it appeared he had had some success in this endeavor. Posselt seemed convinced that her future lay at home. But with whom? A new chapter was about to begin in her life, one that neither she nor her husband could have foreseen at the start of 1935.

The Love of Two R's: 1935–1940

No, I believe that it is best to marry someone who understands the demands and needs of a woman's career.[98]

– Ruth Posselt

The headline in *The Boston Globe* read "Miss Posselt Crowned 'Queen of America on the Violin.'"[99]

A week later, a reporter for the *Journal-Transcript* of Franklin, New Hampshire, wrote about the newly crowned "Queen of the Violin" as "the blond darling" of the concert hall. His impressions of Posselt speak volumes about the treatment of female virtuosos by the American provincial press in the 1930s: "Ruth is the same little girl – quite grown up now, s'il vous plait –who strutted out happily on Concord's Phenix Hall stage thirteen years ago to thrill an enormous audience of New Hampshire music lovers with her startling interpretations of Beethoven. . . . She is rather tall. She has beautiful large brown eyes. And a cluster of gold curls, which fall to a mass on her shoulders. She and I talked for more than an hour. Sometimes, as she reminisced, a wandering look would cross her pretty curved face. Sometimes, too, she would pucker her carmined lips and giggle at something funny we might have said. But for all of me I couldn't quite seem to picture her as the 'Queen of the Violin.' She seems too young and vivacious for the opera or to be recognized as the world's greatest woman violinist. Rather, I thought her the 'Queen of Pulchritude.'"[100]

At the time of this interview, the "Queen of Pulchritude" was wholly and very seriously focused on her violin, as she was preparing the Tchaikovsky Violin Concerto for her upcoming debut with the Boston Symphony Orchestra. This concerto and this performance, on March 25, 1935, would be a major game changer in both Posselt's professional and personal life. The concerto had been in her repertoire since her Boston concert debut seven years earlier with the People's Symphony Orchestra. It had proved a successful vehicle for her with the New York Philharmonic (1928), the Denver Civic Symphony (1931), the Colonne Symphony Orchestra in Paris (1933), the Residentie Orchestra in The Hague (1933), the Concertgebouw in Amsterdam (1933), and at the Kurzaal in Scheveningen (1934). Despite this track record of successful performances, the importance of her debut with the BSO and, even more, the reputation of Serge Koussevitzky for being "a terror," as she later recalled, made her more nervous than usual. She decided, as was her habit before the performance of any major or new work, to try it out for an informed audience before the first rehearsal. This time, she chose for her auditor Richard Burgin, the concertmaster and assistant conductor of the BSO. It would prove a very happy choice.

♩♩♩

Who was Richard Burgin? Born in 1892 in the town of Siedlice outside of Warsaw, Poland (at that time part of the Russian empire), he was the first child of Moisey Burgin, a tradesman and sign painter, and Moisey's first cousin, Rachel Krzyzowska, a factory worker. Burgin began study of the violin at five, after manifesting an ear for music when he was seen trying to conduct from his seat at a concert his music-loving father had brought him to. After studying privately with Jacob Winiecki, a member of the Warsaw Philharmonic, and the famed Polish virtuoso Izydor Lotto (with whom Bronislaw Huberman also studied) in Warsaw, he continued under the guidance of Josef Joachim in Berlin and made his concert debut at the age of eleven, with the Warsaw Philharmonic, in 1903. After the 1905 revolution in Russia, his father took him to America, where he lived and performed as a child prodigy for a couple of years. At that time, he heard the Boston Symphony Orchestra, an event which might have helped determine his professional course. One of his classmates at the St. Petersburg Conservatory, Wolf Graffman, later recalled "young Richard's excitement when he returned from the United States. . . . Everyone clustered around to hear his tales of the New World. 'And now I know exactly what I want to do for the rest of my life!' Richard announced. He then surprised his audience by elucidating, 'I want to be the concertmaster of the Boston Symphony Orchestra.'"[101]

In 1908, Moisey Burgin decided to return to Poland since he could not get used to life in America. On their way back to Warsaw, the Burgins stopped in London, where Richard auditioned a second time for Leopold Auer, the world-famous violin pedagogue at the St. Petersburg Conservatory. Auer had accepted him as a student several years earlier, but Moisey had decided at that time to send him to Berlin rather than St. Petersburg.

The second audition was successful, and Burgin entered the St. Petersburg Conservatory in 1908, graduating four years later with the large silver medal in violin. He then pursued graduate studies in composition with Alexander Glazunov while taking up his first position as concertmaster with the Helsingfors City Orchestra under Georg Schnéevoigt.

Burgin spent eight years in Scandinavia as concertmaster of orchestras in Helsingfors, Stockholm, and Christiania (Oslo); he also led a popular string quartet, served as assistant teacher to Auer in Oslo, and concertized throughout Scandinavia and Russia, popularizing in particular the Sibelius Concerto, which he had studied with its composer. In the summer of 1920, upon Schnéevoigt's recommendation, Burgin auditioned for Pierre Monteux, who had recently assumed directorship of the BSO and was looking for a new concertmaster. Burgin assumed this position in October 1920 and continued in the post after Serge Koussevitzky was named the BSO's conductor in 1924. Burgin began conducting the BSO in the mid-1920s when Koussevitzky was indisposed, or simply did not feel like conducting, and in 1934, the concertmaster was named assistant conductor of the orchestra. He would become associate conductor ten years later.

When Burgin became acquainted with Ruth Posselt, he was a confirmed bachelor. No one knew that he had been married as a very young man in Russia to a fellow student at the conservatory, a pianist, Henrietta Borsch, who served as the young Jascha Heifetz's accompanist in Denmark. Although Richard and Henrietta were in love with each other, their marriage was complicated and unhappy. They were divorced by mutual agreement after less than four years, and the whole experience left Burgin marriage-shy and convinced that marriage was not for him. Therefore, as a very eligible bachelor in Boston, he actively, but diplomatically, avoided romantic relationships with any woman who pursued him, and developed the reputation for being a misogynist.

Posselt would always vividly recall the beginning of her and Burgin's relationship – it was one of her favorite stories, and she told it to anyone and everyone who asked "How did you and your husband meet?" (Mr. Burgin, Richard, or Poppy would replace "husband," depending on who was asking.) And she would reply: "It was my first time with the Boston Symphony and I was still in my twenties. Koussevitzky was Russian, and world famous, and they said at that time he was a terror; I don't know if he was or not, but I was nervous. So, I decided to call Burgin up – I didn't know him at all, but he had the reputation of having a calming influence on Koussevitzky – and ask if he would have a few minutes to listen to some of the Tchaikovsky because, after all . . . He said he would be delighted to. So I went to his house in Jamaica Plain, and I played and I played and he just stood there, smiling. When I finished, he said, 'I think it's wonderful, I don't know what you're so worried about.' I said, 'I don't know if Koussevitzky will like this interpretation,' and he said, 'Anybody will love that interpretation. If you can play it like that, it's marvelous.' And oh, that gave me so much confidence, I'll never forget that."[102]

Boston concertgoers were treated to an unexpected interaction between their beloved concertmaster and the soloist during the performance of the Tchaikovsky. As reported the next day by Warren Storey Smith in *The Boston Post*, it went like this: Miss Posselt's "playing last evening provoked applause that was more than commendation, applause that deserved the overworked characterization, enthusiastic. From Dr. Koussevitzky and his orchestra she received generous and eloquent support, and from at least one member of it a very special service. In the course of the first movement a hair of Miss Posselt's bow became unloosened at one end and hung trailing down until Mr. Burgin arose from the concert master's chair and snapped it off while Miss Posselt in apparent unconcern continued her performance."[103]

The day after the concert, Boaz Piller invited Ruth for tea, and she said, continuing her story: "'Why don't you ask Richard Burgin, too, he was so nice to me.' Piller replied, 'Oh, I could ask him but he probably won't come, he doesn't like women, he thinks they're stupid.' But I said, 'I don't think he thinks I'm stupid, why don't you ask him?' So he did ask him, and Richard said he'd love to come. He already had a little yen for me, I think. Because we used to have tea after that, just he and I, whenever I was in Boston, and we just talked back and forth, back and forth. I don't know, there seemed to be always something interesting to discuss. He could talk about European history, politics, mythology, he spoke four or five languages. I don't know, I was sort of captivated by all that."

Captivated she may have been, but some major obstacles stood in the way of a closer relationship, not the least of which was the fact that Posselt was married. And in 1935 she was still a long way from leaving her husband. However much Burgin may have "daydreamed" about Posselt, and he certainly did, he was not disposed to making any move toward a relationship he genuinely believed could not happen. In fact, the formidable differences between Posselt and Burgin – in age, cultural background, upbringing, interests, politics, just about everything except the violin – while not precluding a relationship, certainly did not facilitate it. There seems little doubt, though, that Posselt did eventually, in the parlance of the day, set her cap for Burgin, but she proceeded very cautiously, and Burgin, true to his gentlemanly nature, and his own insecurities, decided to follow her lead.

In late June, Posselt received a rather ambiguous, worrisome letter from her European manager, De Koos, with the news that he could only book small tours for her in Europe the coming season, and those only on a percentage basis, but he considered such an arrangement unacceptable because she would not earn enough to cover her expenses. He told her that she had played so much in Holland that the music societies wanted to engage other violinists. He would be able to get her engagements in Scheveningen, with the AVRO, and perhaps in France, but it would not be worth her while to come for these engagements alone. He concluded ominously that the general situation in Europe had worsened since last year, and he advised her to stay in America. He copied this letter to Merovitch, hoping the latter could get her engagements the next year. He said business was very, very bad.

Merovitch had succeeded in booking Posselt with the Chicago Symphony and the prominent conductor Frederic Stock in November 1935. Shortly before her concert there, the impressario suffered a nervous breakdown, became violent and ended up being hospitalized in St. Paul, Minnesota.[104] Posselt played the Tchaikovsky concerto in

Chicago on November 28 and 29, and again had a major success. One reviewer in particular drew attention to one of the issues that seemed to be contributing to the difficulty she was having in achieving the kind of career in her home country that her playing deserved:

"For those critics who cherish the unpopular idea that American artists should be allowed a share in the activities of the country's most important artistic institutions, last night's assignment was congenial.

"At the Symphony, a violinist who had the poor judgment to be born here; confirmed this misfortune by studying only in America and followed this unconventional beginning by conquering the capitals of Europe first with her bow before submitting herself to the unfriendly appraisal of her fellow countrymen, was the soloist. . . .

"International sentiment in art operates like the league of nations or The Hague court. There are fifty votes for the European and one for the American. Of necessity, however, the votes cast last night at Orchestra Hall . . . were all pro-American.

"If prejudice was manifested in this limitation, let the doubters be consoled with the reflection that Ruth Posselt returned from Paris bringing assurances from the anti-American press of that city to the effect that she is an artist of whom this country should be proud.

"With this sanction one ventures to lift a timid vote in praise of her performance of the Tchaikovsky concerto with the Chicago Symphony. She is a youngster of 21 [*sic*] but an old artist nevertheless, since she began to play seriously in public fifteen years ago. In that time she has learned the art of addressing and persuading the multitude.

"A charming figure, an artist of abandon, she left her listeners convinced last night of the beauty and variety of her tone, the significance of her phrasing, the amazing resource of her technic, which set off the fireworks of the concerto's last movement with dazzling facility and complete impeccability."[105]

The fact that American-born and -bred concert artists had a harder time making it in America than their European competitors had been the motivation for Olga Samaroff's instituting the Schubert prize six years before. Little had changed by the time of Posselt's appearance in

Chicago, and American artists would remain at a disadvantage for many years more. However, Posselt herself thought there was another reason female violinists had such trouble making a career, and at the beginning of the new year, she brought it up in an interview with a reporter in Richmond, Virginia. He opened his pre-concert article about her with her own words: "'The main reason so few women achieve fame on the concert stage is men. . . . And the men interfere . . . by marrying the artists just when the girls are beginning to play well.' Miss Posselt, who is 21 [*sic*], blonde and starry-eyed, will appear here with the Richmond Symphony tonight as guest artist. She arrived in Richmond yesterday and during the course of a conversation at the Jefferson Hotel (when she was not warning her Pekinese away from the alligators in the lobby pool) Miss Posselt talked of music, matrimony, and her tour of Russia."[106]

Again, Posselt's public comment may have reflected unstated private thoughts about her personal situation at the time. By saying that husbands interfere with a woman's career, she seemed to have in mind the pressure she was feeling from her husband to stay home and damp down her career aspirations. Her habit of speaking about her personal situation in veiled terms to newspaper reporters seems like a revolt against self-censorship, a way of permitting herself to say things that were really on her mind, but which she couldn't speak about because she had to keep them secret.

From the time of the Newcombs' quarrel in Paris, Arthur had tried to convince his wife that she could be happy living with him and having a music career on the side. Posselt wanted more of a career than Arthur wanted for her, however. She was also keenly aware that all her female role models, past and present – artists like Clara Schumann in the nineteenth century and Olga Samaroff, Ernestine Schumann-Heink, Maud Powell, and Erica Morini in the twentieth – had combined big careers in music with marriage. At the same time, Posselt was drawn to the life she had with her non-musician husband precisely because it was private and not part of performing. Despite her early exposure to the public eye, her love for audiences, and her desire to win them over, she was basically a shy and often lonely person, a lot like Ayke

Agus's portrait of Heifetz, really, who had always been her model.[107] Posselt's stage persona was carefully constructed and performed with great skill, both as a way of hiding her "real" self and making it possible for her image to shine and enable her performance. It's possible that her real self did not *wholeheartedly* want to dress up, make up, go out onstage, and "play like a devil or a little angel." That's what her image, or second nature, wanted – and wanted badly. Aware of this conflict, she tried to resolve it by making a necessary compromise between the way she was taught to present herself and her inner "nature," as she had once, in a letter to Arthur, referred to the way she actually felt. So Posselt seemed to be of two minds about her career at a time when it probably was more difficult for a young virtuoso to break into the big time in America, or in Europe, than at any other time till then. "Business was bad, very bad" in Europe, and by 1937 America had slipped into a major recession.

For the entire previous year, Posselt tried assiduously to arrange a second tour of the Soviet Union. Negotiations between her, De Koos, the Soviets, and De Koos's Scandinavian and Finnish management partners went on for months. Posselt initiated them by sending New Year's greetings to Dr. Gabriel Kolischer, the conductor of the Moscow Philharmonic, who replied in March 1936 that he had been following her career and hoped to see her again the following year. He even asked for the time period when she would be free to tour the Soviet Union. That seemed hopeful, so Posselt wrote De Koos of her intention to come to Europe the following season. He wrote by return mail that her news had come too late because in Holland they were already booking for 1937–38, but he promised to try very hard to get her engagements in Holland, Finland, and Scandinavia. He asked for the exact time she had to start in Russia so that he could plan her concerts in Holland.

These plans had to be altered when Koussevitzky engaged Posselt, at her suggestion, to play the Dvořák Violin Concerto with the BSO at the end of October. De Koos informed Kolischer that Posselt had to change her original plans because of a contractual obligation and would like to come to Russia for one week between November 15 and December 20 to play in Leningrad and Moscow. Alternatively, she could come early in 1937 to undertake a more extensive tour.

Fazers Musikhandel in Helsingfors informed De Koos in July that it was too late to arrange engagements for foreign artists in the fall and more important, that the plans Posselt had made in January 1935 with George Fazer, who had since died, were no longer binding on them. They could do nothing to schedule her in the fall season even though they had recently received a most superlative endorsement of her playing from Boaz Piller. De Koos wrote back that Posselt had changed her plans, was coming to Holland in March 1937, and requested bookings in Scandinavia at that time. A few days later, in mid-July, he heard from Moscow that their concert plans regarding Posselt were still unclear. Nothing had changed by the beginning of September. The Soviets were still delaying and little had been settled about appearances in Scandinavia.

In the meantime, Posselt was wholly focused on her second appearance with the BSO, in the prestigious Friday afternoon/Saturday night series. The pre-concert publicity in the Rotogravure section of the September 27 *Boston Herald* put her (and her pet Pekingese) in a photo montage of glittering symphony soloists for the 1936–37 season. Pictured were Myra Hess at the piano; Albert Spalding with his dogs; Jascha Heifetz; Koussevitzky in walking gear; Gregor Piatigorsky, laughing, with cello; the composer Sergei Rachmaninoff; the singer Olga Averino standing in a fur coat; Paul Althouse seated at the piano; Sergei Prokofiev, who would appear as soloist in his own third piano concerto; and Ruth Posselt, "Medford girl who will be a soloist with the Boston Symphony Orchestra, shown at right with her 'Peke.'"

Posselt's rendition of the Dvořák concerto made an unqualified hit with the audience and critics. Moses Smith hailed her as "mistress of a meltingly beautiful lyricism," who "played splendidly, with the entire resources of her instrument and the authority of a virtuoso."[108] "She left not the slightest doubt of her great ability," interpreting the concerto "with much beauty of tone, skill and poise and firmness of bowing," chimed in William Chase, who characterized himself as a "reluctant listener" of the Dvořák, which hadn't been heard in Boston since 1919.[109] Cyrus

Durgin wrote, "She played the long and difficult Dvořák Concerto with admirable clarity and poise, producing a delightfully pure tone." He concluded that "the vital spirit of her performance may have lent a burnish to Dvořák's now rarely heard work that made it appear more interesting than it is. Miss Posselt was given what is commonly termed an 'ovation.' It was most enthusiastic, and every moment of it was richly deserved."[110]

It was Ruth Masters, however, who cast the mantle of artistic legitimacy cum sartorial splendor on Posselt: "It has been gratifying to many to watch Miss Posselt's progress as she emerged from the perilous 'prodigy' stage, to become a legitimate artist. The picture that she presented on Friday afternoon was not the least delightful aspect of her appearance. A dress of red chiffon velvet demurely cut – laced bodice, puffed sleeves and full gathered skirt spreading over side hoops – her hair parted in the middle, bobbed and banged, and of the color which

Titian once made famous for all time – her bland and childlike features – all this resolved into an apparition that was nothing if not a medieval princess turned troubadour."[111]

Posselt's first and second appearances with the Boston Symphony Orchestra confirmed Koussevitzky's judgment that she was "one of the three greatest violinists playing today," the others being Heifetz and Menuhin.[112] As a direct result of Koussevitzky's support, Posselt appeared as soloist with the BSO multiple times, in almost every season from 1934–35 through 1949–50.[113] Of the thirty-nine performances Posselt gave with the BSO during Koussevitzky's tenure, about half were under Koussevitzky himself; the others were with associate conductor Richard Burgin; Koussevitzky's protégé, Leonard Bernstein; and guest conductor George Szell, whom Posselt had met and performed with in Holland. Posselt also came to play a central role in Koussevitzky's commitment to introducing new and American music by giving premieres of several violin concerti, starting with the world premiere of the Hill Violin Concerto in 1938. But we are getting ahead of ourselves.

In mid-December 1936, the news finally came from the Soviets that it was "unfortunately impossible to organize concerts for Miss Posselt in March of 1937 although we hope it will be possible to arrange concerts for her in the 1937–38 season." In order not to cancel the engagements in Europe, which she had hoped to link with a second tour of Russia, Posselt had to find another way of making a European tour worthwhile. She asked Ondříček for advice since he was planning a tour back to his native land that spring. He was happy to suggest that she join him and Gladys for concerts in Czechoslovakia and combine them with the engagements De Koos had booked for her in Holland, Czechoslovakia, and France.

The year 1937 would turn out to be another pivotal one in Posselt's life, especially in her personal affairs, but professionally as well. By January, she and Burgin had become good friends, exchanging pictures with each other and meeting quite frequently for tea and captivating talk. Arthur was working very hard to pay off debts he had incurred in his business ventures, start a new insurance business, and sell a diner,

Marge's Place, that he, Ruth, and his sister-in-law, Marjorie, had operated for several years. Ruth herself was both very worried (about health and financial problems) and quite busy in the months before her European trip; she traveled to Florida for a recital at the University of Florida at Gainesville, and from there she went to New York for a second Town Hall recital. This universally lauded performance received special praise from several critics for its adventuresome "program of unhackneyed material."[114] Such notice seemed to presage many Posselt programs to come, as she began to explore contemporary and little-known music.

Shortly after her Town Hall success, where she premiered several works she had brought back from the Soviet Union by Russian composers, Posselt sailed for Europe for her fourth tour there. Her first appearance was in Stockholm, where she performed a little-known concerto by the Italian Baroque composer GiuseppeTartini that Ondříček had "discovered" and edited. The concert was broadcast throughout Europe. From Stockholm she went to Czechoslovakia for appearances in Ondříček's hometown of Plzen and then Prague, where she played three concertos (Tartini, Dvořák, and Tchaikovsky) with the Czech Philharmonic. Two days later she played the Mozart D Major Concerto in Hilversum, Holland; spent some time in Paris, where she saw Thibaud; and returned to The Hague, where she performed the Bruch Concerto under Paul Paray on the last day of March. Then, it was back to Czechoslovakia for four more recitals with the Ondříčeks in Teplitz, Olmutz, Caslav, and Hradci Kralove. She returned to the States in late April.

After returning from Europe, she underwent major surgery and was hospitalized for two weeks. During her hospital stay, she received anxious telegrams and telephone calls from Burgin; letters from Thibaud that were full of fatherly concern and passionate hope that after her recovery, she would return to Europe for the summer; but no visit from Arthur. Although they were still nominally together, they had begun to go their separate ways, apparently by mutual agreement.

In one of his letters, Thibaud mentioned that he had spoken with his manager in France and Belgium about representing her, and advised her "to give serious consideration to his idea of managing [her] concerts in Europe."[115] When she left the hospital, she wrote to Thibaud that she could not possibly return to Europe during that year due to the post-surgical complications she had suffered (an arterial spasm in her hand) and her need for a complete rest. During her recuperation in Medford, she wrote her first letter to Burgin, who was in Europe visiting his family, in which she reported that she was much better and expected to feel "top-notch" in a week. In closing, she wrote, "Let me know when you'll be back in Boston (a postal-card will do the trick!)"[116]

Although Posselt must have expressed interest in doing business with Thibaud's manager, she did not pursue the plan he urged on her to make an annual tour of Europe and spend time working with him in St. Jean de Luz. Her burgeoning friendship with Burgin had begun to cast him in the role of a professional adviser, one who treated her as an equal and was much nearer to home, and, increasingly, nearer to her heart.

Burgin was very happy to play that role, and he in fact took a proactive part in unofficially "managing" her from the start of their acquaintance. He firmly believed that Posselt's career had suffered mainly from "bad management," and that she needed to establish more personal contacts with notable musicians who would offer her more than all the managers had done for her so far. He understood the music business reality that managers sold their artists in packages and did not compete against themselves. They liked to have one or two "stars" in their "stables," along with other less famous artists. It was the catch-22 of the virtuoso business. One became a star worthy of managerial effort by making money and appealing to large audiences, but the way to make money and get the biggest engagements was to have a manager treating you as a star.

By 1937, Posselt had proven audience appeal and abundant critical acclaim, but she could not compete in ticket sales with the big stars already ensconced in the virtuoso firmament. In his book about the great violinists, Henry Roth gives one, but by far not the only, reason why: "The decade of the 1930s was graced by some of the best violin playing in the history of the art. It was nearly impossible for a new young artist to break into the hierarchy represented by Kreisler, Elman, Heifetz, Menuhin, Milstein, Szigeti, Ricci, and, by 1939, Francescatti."[117]

Yet, Posselt was not really "a new young artist" – she had been playing professionally, though with too many late starts and far too few engagements, since the age of eleven. She was older and more experienced than Roth's exceptional case, Isaac Stern, who did manage "to break into the hierarchy." Moreover, she had been compared favorably, by critics and musicians in Europe and North America, with Heifetz, Menuhin, Milstein, and Francescatti. Finally, we should remember that Francescatti had been hailed in Europe in the same year as Posselt, who was put forward by the Dutch critics as exactly comparable to him. Yet, five years later, Francescatti had made it onto the top rung and Posselt had not. So, the plethora of great violinists in the thirties was not the only reason why some, notably female, virtuosos found an impenetrable ceiling to the heavenly firmament which their male colleagues seemed not to come up against.

The gender bias of Roth's exhaustive study of violin virtuosos has been widely noted, not least because he includes *all* female virtuosos in one chapter and fails to list a single woman in his "hierarchy," not even Erica Morini, who sometimes, along with Maud Powell and two or three women fiddlers of that generation, is mentioned as at least a token among the male greats. Morini, who achieved a bigger career than Posselt and certainly recorded far more, "gave her farewell concert in 1976 after withdrawing from concert life years before. It is thought that she never again touched her violin. She had repeatedly complained of disappointment that due to the narrow-mindedness and prejudice of many managers, women had a much more difficult time achieving success."[118]

In the fall of 1937, Posselt received eloquent confirmation of Morini's plaint in a letter from Haensel & Jones, who had managed her since she was a child: "I regret to inform you," the letter began, "that although we have exerted every effort in your behalf to date we have succeeded in closing just the one contract with the Orchestra in Washington about which you know and there seems to be little prospect of our being able to secure for you the engagements which you rightfully should have. . . . We have gone into this matter very carefully and find that despite the fact that you were offered and pushed in numerous Community Concert cities, the local committees unanimously did not favor a woman violinist and it was impossible to close contracts as anticipated." The letter went on to remind Posselt that they had been hesitant to sign the original agreement without pointing out to her "the general difficulty in the past which we had experienced in endeavoring to book a woman violinist." They had made the agreement with her only "because our faith in your ability and artistic standing was such we would do our very best for you notwithstanding. This we have done but with the unfortunate results that you know. Under these circumstances in all justice to you we feel it best that the existing contract between us be cancelled by mutual consent at the end of the present season, on June 1st, 1938, and we trust with the foregoing frank and candid statements you will agree."[119]

This turn of managerial events did not surprise Burgin. Although he did seem to overlook (or underplay) the gender bias in Haensel & Jones's decision, it confirmed his view that the best route to success for Posselt was via influential musicians, not managers. And he knew very well that the most influential musician at that time in Posselt's modest list of prominent musical backers was Koussevitzky, his boss, and at that time his friend. In fact, plans were already afoot to mount a major performance the following season for Posselt with the BSO.

During the fall Posselt and Burgin's friendship evolved into something more serious and exciting. As Posselt would often recall, "Well, we couldn't stay apart. We'd have dinner, and talk, and we hated to leave each other. Once, I remember, he brought me home about 1:30 a.m., we parked in front of my house, and were doing whatever we were doing, when a police car came down the street, stopped, and the officer flashed the light in the car and said, turning to Richard, 'What's your name?' He said, 'Richard Burgin.' 'Richard Burgin, and I suppose that's Charlie McCarthy over there.'"[120]

A letter from Richard to his "Darling Ruth" suggests that the couple declared their love to each other in early December: "Since you left me last Saturday I am in an exalted state of mind. Those wonderful words you spoke to me that afternoon are still ringing in my ears. They made me feel so sublimely happy that it seems like a dream. You see, sweetheart, for so many years I have been daydreaming about you that it seems hard to believe that this vision has turned into reality. I love you I love you I love you forever Richard."[121]

After writing his declaration of love, Burgin went with the BSO on its annual midwestern tour, and Posselt left for New York en route to Washington, D.C. She and the tenor Richard Tauber had been invited by the White House to perform for President and Mrs. Roosevelt and two hundred guests at the musicale after the annual cabinet dinner. The concert took place on December 14. The next day, Eleanor Roosevelt wrote in her newspaper column: "Last night and this morning we had some really beautiful music in the White House. . . . The young American violinist, Miss Ruth Posselt, was not only a joy to look at but a great pleasure to listen to as well."[122]

RUTH POSSELT BORROWS SUIT IN WHITE HOUSE

Boston Violinist's Accompanist Forgot His Dress
Clothes For Roosevelt Performance

RUTH POSSELT

On the night of the White House concert, back in Boston and after a busy day of orchestra and other rehearsals and lessons, Burgin was daydreaming about his inamorata: "At this moment you are probably getting ready for the concert. Putting on your beautiful dress, rouge, powder, etc. etc. I wish I could be with you and enjoy your playing of all the nice little pieces you are going to perform . . . As it is I'll have to wait for three long days till I shall see you, my angel."[123]

The following day, when he called Ruth in New York, he would learn that the pre-concert preparations at the White House were not quite as he had imagined. As later reported in *The Boston Globe*, Posselt's accompanist, Arpad Sandor, who had flown down to Washington after an afternoon concert in New York without any luggage, realized en route to the White House that he had forgotten his evening dress. "When they arrived at the White House ten minutes before the concert, Posselt asked the staff if they could not find a dress suit for Sandor to borrow." Fortunately, he happened to have a similar build to the president's. The concert began on time, Sandor appeared onstage in appropriate tails, and Posselt herself wore "a turquoise blue lace gown with malines and train. Her program was very well received but she captured the President's heart when she played her last encore, 'Turkey in the Straw.' . . . Cabinet heads and international guests were patting time with their feet, and President Roosevelt, smiling broadly, led the applause."[124]

The same article also reported material from an interview Posselt had given a week prior to the event. Of course, during the interview, she was asked about marriage and whether she thought a female virtuoso had to sacrifice it to a career. The eight-years-married Posselt replied not only with believable disingenuousness, but also with a creditable veiled prediction of the marriage she probably already envisioned for herself in the near future: "What about marriage, she was asked. Must that be sacrificed to a career?" "I don't believe it. Not if one marries the right man. He should be a musician himself, I think, for a happy marriage. I think a woman artist would become weary of constant adulation from a business-man husband, and of course if he didn't sympathize with her career a woman would be wretched. No, I believe that it is best to marry someone who understands the demands and the needs of a woman's career." And who might that be?

Never had Ruth's secret personal and public performing lives been so closely intermeshed as at this time. Immediately after returning to Boston, she went to hear Heifetz play the new Prokofiev concerto, which Burgin, to whom the composer had given the rights to perform the work in America, had given his friend to play. Then, in the home of the composer Edward Burlingame Hill, Posselt played Hill's new violin concerto for Koussevitzky and a select audience. The composer had completed the work the previous summer, with

Burgin's collaboration. Koussevitzky liked what he heard and programmed the world premiere for the 1938–39 season.

Posselt's performance of the Hill Concerto for Violin turned out to be the first of a dozen premieres that she would give from the late 1930s to the mid-1950s, ensuring her rise to prominence in the United States as a champion of contemporary and American music for the violin. Serendipitously, many of Posselt's premieres seem, with biographical hindsight and perhaps in actuality, to express her and Burgin's evolving love relationship as it moved from romance, to intimacy, to secret engagement, to marriage, having a family, and disharmony, and finally, to lasting family happiness. This musical story of firsts in love and performing, which I call "Performing Premieres," will continue through this and the next two chapters. In the remaining pages of this chapter, we will follow how Posselt's first four premier performances were entwined with her and Burgin's lengthy, fraught, and rather original trip to the altar. It all seemed to begin, as noted, at the romantic summit overlooking the Hill.

I. Darling Ruth and Her Dearest Boy
E. B. Hill, *Concerto for Violin*
World Premiere, Boston, November 10, 1938

Edward Burlingham Hill (1872–1960), a graduate of Harvard University and student of John Knowles Paine, completed his musical training in New York, Paris, and, finally, the New England Conservatory. He began teaching at Harvard in 1908, eventually becoming chair of the music department, a position he held until he retired in 1940. His style was considered eclectic, and in his later compositions was influenced by jazz. In the summer of 1933, he wrote a concerto for violin. After revising it during the following winter, he put it aside and returned to it only in the summer of 1937, at which time he added a cadenza with the advice and collaboration of Richard Burgin.[125] Posselt began learning the piece in the fall. By the time of the world premiere, she and Burgin were secretly in love, as evidenced by their respective doodlings on programs Ruth saved of the event:[126]

Scribbled on the Sixth Programme, Friday Afternoon, November 11, at 2:30 o'clock / Saturday Evening, November 12, at 8:15 o'clock, in Richard Burgin's hand:

Richard Burgin

Ruth my darling

I love my darling

Ruth

Scribbled on another copy of the Sixth Programme, Friday Afternoon, November 11, at 2:30 / Saturday Evening, November 12, at 8:15 o'clock, in Ruth Posselt's hand:

Dearest Boy I love

You with all My Heart

With the exception of Alexander Williams in the *The Boston Herald*, who called the Hill concerto a "disappointment" and "dull," the Boston critics greeted the work favorably. Cyrus Durgin, for example, called Professor Hill "among the most resourceful and technically accomplished of American creative musicians," and found the new concerto "polished and very enjoyable."[127] He more lavishly praised Posselt for her "big lustrous tone, accurate pitch, and the poise of her phrasing" and opined that both the public and the composer benefited by the fact that she, "not only a virtuoso fiddler but an excellent musician," was chosen as soloist. Williams concurred, writing that "Miss Posselt, a highly accomplished violinist, played the concerto with great spirit and precision. She was most cordially applauded, as was also Mr. Hill who was in the audience to hear the first performance of his concerto."[128] Williams returned for the Saturday night performance and noted that the concerto was greeted more enthusiastically; he thought that Posselt's performance "seemed actually to have gained in intensity, bravura and emotional depth over the remarkable performance of the matinee. The orchestral playing was on a very high level, and the cheers which were added to the more normal applause were richly deserved."[129]

At the end of the year, Posselt left for her last European tour before the war. The separation from Burgin, by then her secret fiancé, whose diamond she wore openly among her European friends, was wrenching for both of them. Their correspondence from that time, an era without cell phones, emails, text messages, and Skype, speaks to the pangs endured by separated lovers waiting for mail, very snail-like mail: a letter from Boston took a minimum of ten days to reach The Hague. Having arrived late on a cold, rainy New Year's Eve in Paris's North Station and missing her train to Holland, Posselt wrote in despondency, "I feel like weeping violently. I wonder why I ever came to Europe. This career business is hardly worth my suffering heart!"[130] Burgin was already "very, very lonesome, and sad," feeling strange to be in Boston and not see Ruth, confessing "every now and then I find myself listening intently, hoping that my darling sweetheart may open the door and surprise me."[131] Waiting for letters caused Burgin to become so depressed that he forsook writing altogether, leading Posselt to imagine the worst, until he started telegraphing. Despite a whole string of recital and concert successes in Holland and Scandinavia, Posselt could not wait to come home to the man she had decided was her future.

Four months after the Boston performances of the Hill concerto, Posselt premiered it in Washington, D.C., with the National Symphony Orchestra, Hans Kindler conducting. The concerto enjoyed an even more enthusiastic response in the nation's capital, with one critic emphasizing the "all-American" aspects of the performance: "An American girl played a violin concerto by an American composer yesterday afternoon in Constitution Hall, and music lovers of the Nation's Capital recalled her eight times in token of their appreciation. That is news. It should not be, but it is. It is even good news for those who believe that the task of defining the national spirit belongs importantly to the art of music."[132]

Hill himself was particularly impressed by the Washington performance, which he recalled to Posselt many years later in a letter of sympathy written on the occasion of her mother's death: "Curiously enough I had another reason to think of you, before I learned your sad news, last Sunday when Alexander Bloch, a skilled artist in chamber music and conductor of the Florida West Coast Orchestra, played for me the slow movement of my old violin concerto, which recalled the performance in Boston, Brooklyn and especially, Washington."[133]

Despite all the precautions Posselt and Burgin took to hide their love affair from the world, it ultimately became the subject of gossip in BSO circles. According to Posselt's oft-repeated story, the gossip started when "somebody saw me leave Richard's house with him around twelve o' clock, and that started some rumors, and one elderly society matron who had known me for years said to her friend, 'You know, I wouldn't be surprised if Ruth Posselt and Richard Burgin were living in sin!' Somehow, it got to Koussevitzky and Koussevitzky told Richard. The memory still lingered of Monteux having been forced to leave his post with the Boston Symphony because it was revealed he was having an extramarital affair. And so, when Richard told me the gossip about us, he said, 'You know, we have to do something, either we have to get married or we can't see each other, or if we see each other, we have to get home at 9 o'clock.' So we decided to get married."

Before that could happen, however, Posselt had to dissolve her first marriage so quietly that no one would ever hear or speak of it. In May, with Arthur's agreement, she filed for divorce and permission to use her maiden name[134], and she and Burgin went to Europe. They originally intended to stay abroad through July, but increasingly aware of the approaching war, they came home after a month and spent part of the summer together with Ida Posselt in Manomet. The snapshots taken of Ruth that summer show a spontaneous and very happy young woman who is completely carefree, frolicking in the waves, and chatting lovingly with her mother as Richard snaps their picture.

In August, Burgin went to Tanglewood to discuss plans for the so-called Academy at the Berkshire Music Center, of which he was the primary author. He wrote of what transpired to Ruth: "As soon as I arrived (around 5:15 p.m.) we had our first meeting which lasted until 7:30. Nothing was accomplished at this session. Everybody was talking and nobody was listening. I realized that if this is the kind of meetings we are going to have then nothing will be accomplished. After supper, I took Koussy in my hands and made him listen to my plan carefully and asked him to make possible suggestions point by point. I explained every sentence, as if I had to read it to a child. Finally he understood everything and agreed that nothing should be changed in regard to the plan concerning the Academy."[135]

Perhaps fittingly, the Hill was the first concerto Posselt performed with the BSO under Burgin's baton, for the Cambridge series, on November 16, 1939, a year after the world premiere. This performance came a week before Koussevitzky took Posselt and the Hill concerto to New York. The maestro had decided to make some cuts in order to reduce the work's performance time. Posselt had already made some cuts in the first and last movements. She also thought Koussevitzky had taken the slow movement too slowly at the first performances; if the abridged piece were played at the right tempo, the performance time would work out to what Koussevitzky wanted. Koussevitzky agreed that he had taken the second movement too slowly; in addition, he confessed to Burgin that he had completely forgotten the work, and so he asked Posselt to play it for him again at his home. Posselt was happy to oblige.[136]

The New York premiere of the Hill had a solid success. Wrote *The New York Times*: "Miss Posselt in the performance of this work was completely authoritative, musicianly, sincere in her enthusiastic interpretation, and she observed a refinement and distinction of style appropriate to the music. She felt the form of the concert as a whole; her conception was unified. She allowed no nuance or fineness of phrase to escape her. The composer, like the audience, may well have been gratified by the manner in which his latest work was placed before the public."[137] Nevertheless, after its enthusiastic welcome in three cities, Hill's Concerto for Violin passed into oblivion, where it still awaits resurrection.

It had already become apparent that Posselt, who had very catholic, inclusive tastes in music, genuinely liked so-called contemporary music; she played new works not because she had to, but because she wanted to. She was discriminating in which pieces she chose to play or to fight for – to bring to a conductor's attention when she had the power to do so – and she was dedicated to doing everything she could to convince her audiences to like them too. "Ruth's commitment and support of living composers was a powerful example," recalls violinist-composer Ann Casadaban. "She assumed a vital role in the well-being of continuing music creation with this embrace. She did everything in her power to present new works in the very best light possible, and did not let any personal estimation interfere with this end. As a violinist and as a student of composition, this example has assisted me in remaining receptive to new musical works, both in performing and listening to them – even after some unfavorable experiences, including the visceral response of breaking out in hives after one encounter!"[138]

II. A Little Engagement Music
Henriëtte Bosmans, *Concertstuk for Violin*
American Premiere, November 14, 1939

Ten days before the New York and Brooklyn premieres of the Hill Concerto for Violin with the BSO, Posselt gave the first American performance of the Concertstuk for Violin and Orchestra by the Dutch composer and pianist Henriëtte Bosmans, whom she had gotten to know in Holland. The Hartford Symphony was conducted by Leon Barzin (1900–1999).

Bosmans (1895–1952) was a celebrated pianist in Europe who began composing in her teens.[139] Many of her works were inspired by musicians with whom she performed, and the Concertstuk for Violin seemed to have had a romantic provenance as well. In 1934, Bosmans became engaged to a violinist, Francis Koene, who died the following year, and for whom she wrote her concerto. It was given its first performance by Louis Zimmerman in 1935 with the Concertgebouw under Mengelberg, and was played frequently in Holland. While Posselt was still in Europe, at the end of her farewell tour of The Netherlands, she wrote to Bosmans and expressed her interest in the piece. Bosmans sent her the music in March.

The critic for the *Hartford Daily Courant* described the piece and Posselt's performance of it: "The Concertstuk by Henriette Bosmans . . . reflects the tendency to find in the ancient form of the concerto a suitable vehicle for the expression of contemporary ideas. Although it consists of but one extended movement, the Concertstuk seemed to be divided within itself into three chief sections, an allegro at the opening and the close, with an andante cantabile between. The melodic ideas are brief and but little developed, although an ingenious rhythmic construction gives the Concertstuk a comfortable continuity. The orchestration, relying not a little on percussion, is that of a knowing craftsman, but the impression persists that the composition gained its chief distinction last night from the admirable performance of Miss Posselt, who lavished on it not merely a clear, vibrant tone but also a subtlety of phrasing that greatly enhanced its every page."[140] On the same program with the Bosmans, Barzin on the viola joined Posselt for a performance of the Mozart Symphonie Concertante.

Posselt gave six additional performances of Bosmans' Concertstuk. She performed it with the world premiere of the Piston First Violin Concerto in New York with Barzin and his National Orchestral Association (March 18, 1940). Then came two performances with the Cincinnati Orchestra under Eugene Goossens, coupled with the Hindemith Violin Concerto (October 18–19, 1940). She introduced it along with the Piston concerto in Boston with the BSO under Burgin (January 31–February 1, 1941). Her final performance of the Bosmans was with pianist Lukas Foss at Town Hall, New York, in October 1944.

III. From "Living in Sin" to Marital Bliss
Walter Piston, Concerto No. 1 for Violin
World Premiere, March 18, 1940

The world premiere of the Piston Violin Concerto No. 1, in Carnegie Hall, New York, took place five months before Burgin and Posselt were married, and the first Boston performance took place seven months afterwards. American composer Walter Piston (1894–1976) enjoyed a longtime association with Koussevitzky and the BSO from 1926, when he returned from Paris to Harvard University as a member of the music faculty; he remained in that position until his retirement in 1960. In an interview with the composer Peter Westergaard, Piston recalled vividly Koussevitzky's impact on him: "When I returned from France I felt pretty gloomy about the situation of the composer in America. I knew conductors were not interested in what we composers were doing so I was writing only chamber music . . . Koussevitzky asked to see me. He asked, 'Why you no write for orchestra?' I said, 'Because nobody would play it.' And he said 'Write, and I will play.' So I wrote and he played."[141]

Piston took pride in composing music from the point of view of the performers who would play it. "I believe in the contribution of the player to the music as written," he once said, adding that he was "very old-fashioned that way."[142] His first violin concerto was composed in the summer of 1939, and, as Posselt recalled: "Piston was going to enter it into a competition, but after showing it to me and seeing how enthusiastic I was, he said, 'I'd much rather give you the first performance than enter it in this competition.' So, he dedicated the concerto to me and I gave the first performance."[143]

In a mid-September letter to Posselt, Piston reported that he was still working on the score of his concerto, and was eager to have the parts copied as soon as possible. A conversation he had had with

Koussevitzky at Tanglewood, however, convinced him there was little chance of the BSO performing the concerto that season. Therefore, he wrote Posselt, "Please understand that if you get a chance of a performance with some other work you must not consider yourself bound to play mine. I should be very unhappy if you lost an appearance for that reason. The same goes if you do not like it well enough to play it."[144]

Since Koussevitzky was unable to schedule the Piston for the 1939–40 season, Posselt succeeded in getting Leon Barzin to premier it in New York with the National Orchestral Association. At the beginning of March 1940, she hosted a musicale at Burgin's home to play the two concertos, the Bosmans and the Piston, with piano accompaniment, for the Pistons, other musicians, and interested friends. She noted in her disarmingly direct diary that she played the two concertos "splendidly," her accompanist "Mary [Tower] played her best, "Piston beams," "Richard pleased," there were "eats afterwards," and she was "very happy."

This seems an appropriate place to say something about Mary Pumphrey Tower (1892–1947), a gifted pianist who was a close friend and colleague of Posselt's. Mary Pumphrey was a graduate of the well-known Faelton School of Pianoforte in Boston. A coeval of Gladys Posselt and a close friend of Boaz Piller, she had a good reputation as a pianist in the Boston area. Married to a businessman and amateur cellist, Stanley Tower, Mary had two daughters and lived in West Newton. Her professional and personal relationship with Posselt was of many years' duration; most importantly, she served not only as accompanist but as a rehearsal pianist for Posselt in working up several concertos that the violinist either premiered, introduced, or popularized, including those by Hill, Piston, Bosmans, Hindemith, Barber, and Dukelsky. The Towers also socialized with Burgin and Posselt when the latter were courting (in secret) and during the first four years of their marriage. After her husband's death in 1945, Mary Tower moved to California. Tragically, she committed suicide in September 1947.

♩♩♩

On March 1, 1940, Posselt and Tower gave a concert for a large and enthusiastic Medford crowd. The local critic called their playing "the acme of artistry," re-gendering them to praise them: "It was a Kreisler-Lamson duo."[145] A week later, after trying the piece out for Piston, the two women left for New York and preparations with Leon Barzin and his orchestra. Posselt's diaristic jottings throughout the preparations for the premiere provide a telegraphic, matter-of-fact, day-by-day account of what it was like for her to perform a piece no one had heard before. She was under more than the usual pressure since Barzin had designed the whole concert as a showcase for her. She was to play three concertos: the world premiere of the Piston, the New York premiere of the Bosmans, and the Dvořák. As a program note informed the audience, "It is Mr. Barzin's idea to present Miss Posselt in three concertos in order to show the comprehensive repertory demanded of the young artist today."[146]

After hearing the National Orchestral Association play on Saturday night, and judging it "pretty good," Posselt was up early to practice before she and Tower played the three works for Barzin. Things went well, but the conductor was more sanguine about the Piston than the soloist, who characteristically felt responsible for the new work. According to Posselt, Barzin considered the Piston concerto "easy" and only reluctantly agreed to meet with her and Tower before the first orchestra rehearsal, so that she could point out some changes and difficulties in the piece. She insisted that they rehearse with orchestra at least twice before the premiere. Barzin, who thought a run-through on the day of the concert was sufficient, finally agreed to an extra rehearsal when he heard that Piston would be attending the rehearsals, and many musical notables would be present at the concert.

At the first orchestra rehearsal, the Piston, easy as it was, took up the entire three hours due to the orchestra's unfamiliarity with the score. Burgin arrived in New York on Wednesday and heard the rehearsal of the Dvořák before leaving for a concert in New Haven. By the following evening, Posselt had a sore throat and was falling ill with "grippe"; she felt "lousy" for the rehearsal of the Piston the next day, which the composer attended. Fortunately, the concerto was shaping up pretty well. Posselt, however, was not, and went to a doctor recommended by Barzin for injections. By Saturday she was in bed with the flu, feeling miserable, upset, and nervous. "Everyone was worried," she noted.

Despite her illness and bad sinuses, she got up to practice. The day of the premiere, March 18, she had a rehearsal in Carnegie Hall, which Piston attended. After a dry shampoo, a rest, and more practice, she felt "terribly nervous" and "like fainting," so she practiced some more, "until the last minute" – then "Dress. Concert. Play Bosmans & Piston marvelously, no flaws. Dvořák 2nd & 3rd good, flaws in 1st mvt. Back aches awful, hardly can last thru concert. Ache all over. Repeated Piston 3rd mvt, ovations."[147]

The critic for the *New York World-Telegram* explained why the third movement of the Piston was played twice: "After the [Piston], Mr. Barzin came forward to tell the audience he hadn't been satisfied with the orchestra's playing of the last movement and that it would be repeated – indulgence requested and so on. Even an outsider would have known that the repetition went better than the first essay."[148]

Perhaps Posselt regretted not having urged a third rehearsal of the Piston on Barzin *before* the concert. As she had confided to Burgin after she finally got the conductor to take the difficulties in the Piston seriously: "I straightened out Barzin thank heavens. He's just damn lazy, neglectful, & takes life too easy. . . . When I told him Piston was coming Wednesday and Heifetz and the Columbia man to the concert he began to change that wise look on his face."[149]

Also present at the Piston premiere was Benjamin Britten, who commented to Aaron Copland that there "was no composer in England of Piston's age who could turn out anything so expert."[150] Although Piston's first violin concerto was eventually overshadowed by the Barber violin concerto that was its "nearly exact contemporary"[151] – and whose wider fame Posselt did more than anyone to abet – Piston's work had an enthusiastic critical reception. Oscar Thompson in *The New York Sun* (March 19, 1940) noted that "the first and final sections assume the character of a symphonic work plus violin. But it is not unidiomatic; there are clearly defined themes and near the close an orthodox cadenza. . . . This is one of Mr. Piston's best works and Miss Posselt enabled it to present its case convincingly." The critic of the *New York World-Telegram* concurred: "The Piston Concerto is by far one of that composer's best achievements . . . there is much music of a vital, dramatic import in it. . . . Miss Posselt delivered her assignment with rare musicianship and insight. She was in excellent technical fettle and her phrasing deserved praise for its finesse and subtlety. Applause reigned supreme." Francis Perkins in the *New York Herald Tribune* (March 19, 1940) noted that "the violinist ... is faced by an assignment requiring no little dexterity and virtuosity although the orchestra figures as an interpreter of co-ordinate importance rather than as an accompanying ensemble. . . . But much of the solo part was grateful and effective. . . . Miss Posselt . . . accomplished the evening's exacting task admirably."

Posselt's first performance of the Piston with a major symphony orchestra took place when her new husband, Richard Burgin, conducted it, along with the Bosmans Concertstuk, with the BSO on January 31 and February 1, 1941, in Symphony Hall, Boston. Alexander Williams, no fan of contemporary music in general, nevertheless conceded in his review that Piston's concerto was "just good music and a great pleasure to listen to." His most expansive praise, however, was reserved for Posselt: "This is probably as good a place as any to bear witness to Miss Ruth Posselt's extraordinarily fine playing yesterday afternoon. She is a violinist of superb poise. Her phrasing is exquisite, and her tone is singularly pure. Both Mr. Piston, and emphatically Miss Bosmans, benefitted from her handling of the solo parts of their music. You cannot say more of Miss Posselt than to acknowledge that any composer would be flattered to have her undertake to present his work."[152] More than a dozen twentieth-century composers would bear out Williams's opinion in the coming years, including Paul Hindemith, Samuel Barber, Vernon Duke, David Smith, Mabel Daniels, Herbert Fromm, Norman Dello Joio, John Boda, Daniel Pinkham, Efrem Zimbalist, and Alan Sapp.

More friendly to contemporary music, Cyrus Durgin in his review underscored the originality of Burgin's program as a whole: "It has fallen to Richard Burgin to present the most adventurous program of the season thus far at the Boston Symphony concerts. The phrase 'first performance at these concerts' stands beneath the title of all four works on the program." Durgin echoed the New York critics in deeming the Piston concerto one of the composer's "best achievements." About Posselt, Durgin wrote confidentially but glowingly: "By way of stating a fact, let one add that Miss Posselt has been ill and played after only a few rehearsals. No evidence of that was discernible in the poise or technical assurance of her work. She performed as she always does, as a first ranking artist."[153]

It fell to Warren Storey Smith, a longtime follower of Posselt's career, to convey the full romantic and professional significance of her solo appearance with the Boston Symphony under Richard Burgin. Appearing to augur their musical collaboration, he began his review thusly: "A more auspicious occasion than yesterday afternoon's Symphony Concert is not easily imagined. Making their first joint appearance here since their recent marriage, Richard Burgin conducted and Ruth Posselt was the solo violinist. Both outdid themselves in their respective capacities."[154]

IV. How Burgin Lost a Concerto but Gained a Wife
Paul Hindemith, Concerto for Violin
American Premiere (Richard Burgin), April 19, 1940
New York Premiere (Ruth Posselt), January 9, 1941

The fourth part of our musical story-within-a-story, "Performing Premieres," was fortunately told during their lifetimes by both partners in the marriage, which officially began in the summer of 1940, in between the premier performances each gave of the Hindemith Violin Concerto. Therefore, it is fitting to hear both sides of how the Hindemith came to be introduced and popularized in the United States. We begin with one of Burgin's favorite stories.[155]

HOW I CAME TO GIVE THE AMERICAN PREMIERE OF THE HINDEMITH VIOLIN CONCERTO (RICHARD BURGIN)

Hindemith and I were often together in musical endeavors. I played under him, conducted his works, and also played his violin concerto in this country for the first time. I gave the first performance in April 1940, and later Ruth took it over and played it all over the United States.

It came about in a very strange and roundabout way. When Hindemith came to this country, I think it was in 1938 or 1939, and I got to know him, we became very friendly. On the whole, he was not a very easy man to know, but he took a liking to me, and I was very happy about it. And we used to argue about many of his works. I played his quartets, the first and second, and I also liked his Kammermusik No. 4, which I found terribly difficult and still think is a difficult thing.

Anyway, when I got to know Hindemith a little better, I once said to him, "Paul, I have been practicing your Kammermusik No. 4." "Why do you waste your time studying that piece?" he said. "It's not worth the time you are spending." And I said, "I can't understand why you say that. I like it, but why do you write so difficultly for the violin because you're a violist and a violinist." He repeated, "As I said, I don't see why you bother with it." And we got into an argument, but you can't argue with a composer who evaluates his piece not according to *your* ideas. However, I finally found something that stopped him. I said, "You know, Paul, the moment you compose a piece, and the moment it is printed, you lose all jurisdiction because anyone can take it and has the right to express his opinion." He said, "Well, that is true," and there was no more argument. Then he said, "You know, I am going to send you a concerto for violin and orchestra," and added, "Wenige Noten aber schön." ("Fewer notes, but beautiful.")

And that's how we left it.

Finally, he had to go back to Germany – he had come here alone, without his wife – probably to settle his affairs because ultimately, he knew he would come to the United States if he could. He was not very friendly with the Nazis, and they were not very friendly to him. And his wife was Jewish. About two weeks before he was due to leave, I still hadn't heard anything about the new concerto which was supposed to be so beautiful, and with fewer notes – that was very important! For a while I thought that it was one of those nice things that a composer promises you, but forgets about, and there was nothing to be done. But then I thought, "Why does he bother to send it to me? He's published, after all."

And when I went to say good-bye, I said, "Paul, about that concerto you told me you would send me, why do you bother? I can buy it, your publisher is Schott, right?" He said, "Of course, Schott is my publisher. But you can't buy it yet." "Why?" I asked. He replied, "Because it's not yet in print." Then I said, "Listen, could you let me see a manuscript of it, something?" because I was so eager. I had loved his music before I even knew him. "Well," he said, "I'm sorry, I haven't got a manuscript because it isn't written down." I thought he was pulling my leg because he had already told me that he had promised the first performance to a certain violinist, and the premiere was set for September 19 in Holland.[156]

So I said, "How is that possible? It is now May and you tell me it hasn't been printed, it hasn't been composed, there's no manuscript, and yet it's going to be performed on September 19th?!" He said, "I didn't say it's not composed. It is composed, just not written down. I've got it all composed in my head but I haven't written it down yet." Well, such things were new to me. I could not disassociate composing something from writing it down. I still thought that was the same thing. He continued, "Well, you know, I'm taking the boat to Europe and I'll be on the boat six days. There's nothing else to do then, so I'll write it down, and when it's written down my proofreader will check the manuscript, okay it, and then it will be printed and performed."

I finally got the violin concerto, but only in February [1940] and only after writing to the Schott representative in London and pestering them. They at first replied that they had not gotten it yet. At last, they sent me a facsimile of the violin part with a letter asking me to inform them immediately when I would perform it because they had a great demand for the concerto and Mr. Hindemith wouldn't allow anybody to have it until I had performed it. I wrote back that I could tell them nothing until I received the score both for myself and for the conductor.

Well, in February the music arrived and I did perform the Hindemith with the BSO and Koussevitzky, in April. It really is a beautiful work, "beautiful. And with fewer notes."

And now, Posselt's side: [157]

HOW I STOLE THE HINDEMITH CONCERTO FROM MY HUSBAND (RUTH POSSELT)

I remember the day Richard gave the first performance of the Hindemith very well. He didn't want me to come to the concert, and I was so nervous for him. While he was playing, I walked the streets & prayed, sending him courageous thought waves. He had a triumph! Played excellently and received wonderful criticisms. Hindemith was there for the concerts.

On Saturday it rained all day; Richard had had very little sleep since we had gone to the Ballets Russes the previous evening. He was awfully nervous when he left for the concert. The Towers [Mary and Stanley] called for me and we went to the concert. He played the first two movements wonderfully, but the third was not so good – he forgot in one place, and the cadenza wasn't perfect. But he had a big success, and I was happy. He was sad, though, and later told me that my presence in the hall upset him all during the performance. I felt badly, and realized I would probably never go again when he played in public.

About a month later, when Richard was in the hospital recovering from an operation, I admit I sort of stole the Hindemith from him. As a kind of surprise, I learned it in ten days and when he came home, I played it for him. And he was so excited, he said, "You have to play this."

And play it she would, throughout the United States and in Europe; the Hindemith Violin Concerto became one of Posselt's signature pieces, and Hindemith himself one of her closest composer friends and fans. As one critic noted after her performance (under Burgin) at Tanglewood in 1956, "Who but Ruth Posselt plays Paul Hindemith's violin concerto in this country? Stand and be counted. She has championed it virtually since its composition in 1939."[158]

But first, her marriage to Burgin, for as he often quipped when asked about the Hindemith, "I lost a concerto, but gained a wife." They decided to avoid publicity and get married away from Boston and reporters. The Berkshires seemed the perfect spot since Burgin had to be at Tanglewood for the inaugural season of the Berkshire Music Center.

The couple left for the Berkshires early in the morning on June 29, a cool rainy day, and they soon realized that getting wed was hard to do. First, they stopped in the town of Palmer and tried to file marriage intentions but were told they could not do so because they were not residents. When they got to Springfield, the city hall was closed, and further west in Westfield, they were turned down for the same reason as in Palmer. In Lenox, they were told to try Stockbridge since they had rented a cottage there for the summer, which made them residents. The clerk was at home in Stockbridge, so things looked promising, but when he learned that Posselt was divorced, he informed her she had to get a judge's okay to marry again. That received, they finally filed intentions and were told they had to wait five days before they could marry. They went to their cottage, unpacked, shopped for food, had supper at the Red Lion Inn in Stockbridge, and went home to bed, tired but hopeful.

July 3, their wedding day, graced them with lovely weather. Having gotten their license in Stockbridge from town clerk Adam Schilling, they drove to West Stockbridge to find the nearest justice of the peace to marry them. That official, Winthrop Sheerin, turned out to be the owner of a garage in town. He was working on a car when they pulled in, and Burgin asked, "Are you the justice of the peace? We'd like to get married." After washing his hands and grabbing a Bible, still wearing his grease-covered overalls, Sheerin asked Burgin, "Which ceremony do you prefer?" "The shortest," replied Burgin.

Afterwards, Posselt wrote in her diary, "Mr. Sheerin married us in the garage! During the 'ceremony' Richard was a little nervous. I wasn't. Richard phoned Koussie. We drove to Pittsfield to do shopping, had lunch at Hotel Wendell. Both very tired. When we got home, Richard went to Tanglewood, I had a nap. In the evening, we went to see the play *Skylark,* which was very fine. Pouring rain, cold, sandwiches at home, bed late. Phone Ma."

FAMED VIOLINIST A BRIDE

MRS. RICHARD BURGIN

Ruth Posselt Weds Burgin, Symphony Concert Master

Their private elopement made the front page of *The Boston Globe* on July 5: "Famed Violinist a Bride. Ruth Posselt Weds Burgin, Symphony Concert Master." The reporter noted in his article, "The marriage was in line with Miss Posselt's conviction that she could combine matrimony and her musical career only by marrying a musician." Ida wrote to Ruth two days later: "I suppose you have seen the nice picture of you on the front page in the Globe. The Globe reporter phoned me Friday nite & quizzed me. I did not know whether you wanted it broadcast, but he said it came direct from

Pittsfield & that he thought it quite romantic – wanted to know who stood up with you & said you carried out your ideas expressed in an interview two years ago. That you would marry a musician rather than a businessman. I was so afraid that business man would be brought to light as it often happens with the movie stars."[159] But that "business man" remained hidden in the shadows, content with his own new wife, and Posselt's first marriage never came to light.

Her second one got started in the company of Hindemith and other musicians at Tanglewood that summer. On Sunday, July 14, the newlyweds were feted at the summer home of the Speyers (Louis Speyer was the English horn player in the BSO). Perhaps typically,

they were over an hour late to the party trying to find the Speyers' house. But they entered to a raucous chorus, Hindemith blaring the horn, the pianist Jesus Sanroma beating frying pans, and everyone singing the Wedding March. Mrs. Louis Speyer made a wedding cake topped with a bride and groom. Later in the day, the Burgins invited everyone back to their cottage for supper. Their forty-year marriage had begun.

Paul Makanowitsky and Ruth Posselt on the beach at St. Jean de Luz, August 1932.

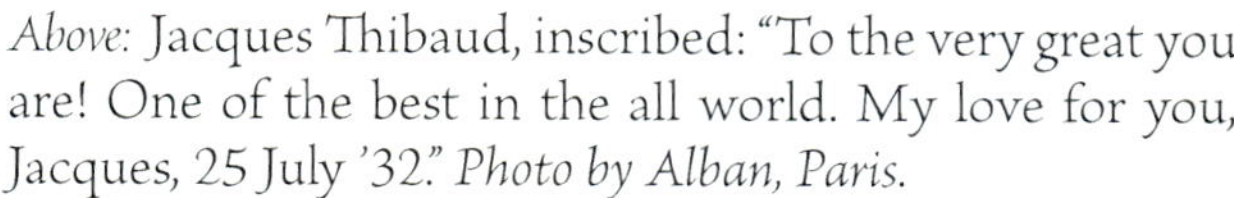

Above: Jacques Thibaud, inscribed: "To the very great you are! One of the best in the all world. My love for you, Jacques, 25 July '32." *Photo by Alban, Paris.*

At right: Mr. Arthur Newcomb and Miss Ruth Posselt aboard ship, January 15, 1932.

Ruth's House, Hermon Pond, Maine, April 1933.

Recital program in Kharkov, USSR, December 19, 1934.

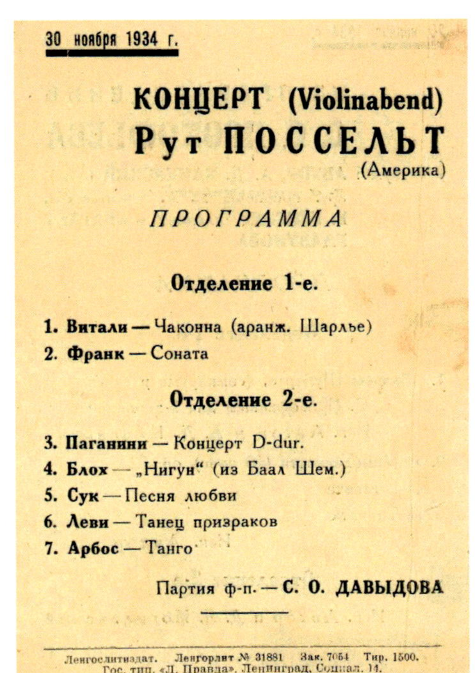

Recital program in Leningrad, USSR, November 30, 1934

Ruth Posselt flyer, 1933, inscribed to her husband, "with my deepest sincerest love, Baby, 1933."

Program of Posselt's concert with the Czech Philharmonic, Prague, March 20, 1937.

Above: Posselt in The Hague, March 1937.

At left: Richard Burgin in 1920. Inscribed to "Ruth Posselt with admiration and love. Jan. 25, 1937, Boston." *Photo by Bachrach, 1920.*

Swedish conductor Georg Schnée-voigt, inscribed "To Miss Ruth Posselt in kind remembrance from Georg Schnéevoigt, 1939 Helsingfors 5th of February."

Henriëtte Bosmans, inscribed "To my genial colleague Ruth Posselt, very thankfully for all musical collaboration and friendly assistance, Henriëtte Bosmans, March, 1940." *Photo by Groot, Amsterdam.*

First page of the manuscript of the Piston Concerto No. 1 for Violin. *Ruth Posselt Archive.*

Ruth and Richard at the 'Towers' camp in New Hampshire, summer 1938.

Paul Hindemith playing the rebec.

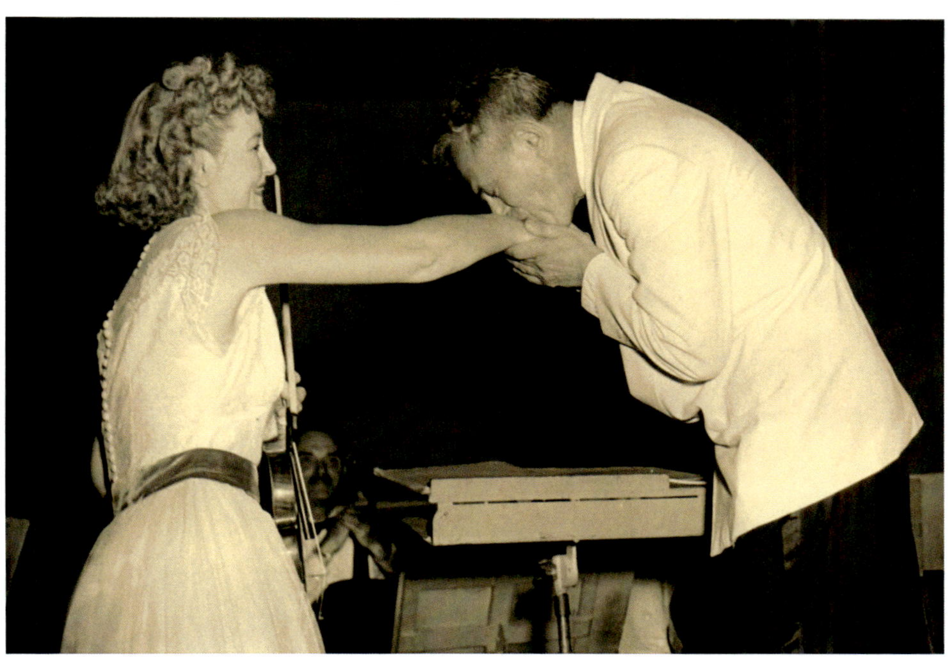

" 'Well Done, my Dear': Richard Burgin, concertmaster of the Boston Symphony Orchestra, who turned conductor last night as his wife, Ruth Posselt, played a violin solo in two compositions, kisses her hand following the performance." February 1, 1941. *Whitestone Photo.*

CHAPTER FIVE

Posselt at Her Peak: 1940–1951

It is increasingly apparent that Miss Posselt is one of the really great violinists of the day.

> – *The Boston Herald,* 1944

Despite her decade-long first marriage, Posselt's second was rather a new experience for her. For the first time in her young life, she appeared in public as part of a pair, even though she retained her maiden name professionally. Not only that, though both were public figures, her husband was more prominent than she. With Burgin, Posselt not only had a very present and onstage husband, she also became a wife outside the privacy of her own home. On one hand, and increasingly with the years, she was proud of that role, but at the beginning of her marriage, she chafed at being seen by people as "only Richard Burgin's wife."

Knowing better than anyone how much his wife deserved the broader recognition her talent warranted, Burgin encouraged Posselt's exposure to musicians in his circle. As had been the case with Edward Hill and Walter Piston the previous summer, Burgin was sure that when Hindemith, who was composer-in-residence at Tanglewood in 1940, heard how well Posselt played his violin concerto, he would need no further convincing that she was the virtuosa for his piece. In August, Posselt played for Hindemith at Tanglewood. First, she and pianist Jesus Sanroma played the Sonata in E two times through; then she and Mary Tower played the Violin Concerto. Ruth judged it "a first class performance" from both of them, and noted that Hindemith was "very enthusiastic."[160] Burgin next wanted to have Koussevitzky hear it, and decided to invite Artur Rodzinski, conductor of the New York Philharmonic, to attend this audition as well. Posselt came down with the flu, however, and it was postponed for two weeks.

September 6, Posselt's twenty-ninth birthday, was the big day – another three-concerto stint for her, albeit with piano, not orchestral accompaniment. At Koussevitzsky's summer home, she played the Bosmans, Piston, and Hindemith concertos for Koussevitzky, Rodzinski, and Hindemith, all of whom praised her to the skies. According to Ruth's diary, Rodzinski said he wished he could have her play the Hindemith in Cleveland, but the concertmaster there was already scheduled to do it. Koussevitzky, however, decided to do the Hindemith with Posselt and the BSO in New Haven, Hartford, and New York the coming season. The Towers, the Burgins, and "Hindy" (Posselt's nickname in her diary for the composer) celebrated with dinner in Pittsfield and then drove back to Boston.

As it turned out, Posselt's *first* public performance of the Hindemith Violin Concerto, together with the Bosmans, took place with the Cincinnati Symphony under Eugene Goossens on October 18–19, 1940. On the day of the concert, she was ill again with influenza – the local doctor painted her throat and gave her inhalation therapy and a vitamin B shot. She confessed in her diary to feeling nervous and suffering from wet hands, but she "talked to herself for courage," and apparently found it. In her opinion – and she was always her own most severe critic – it "was the greatest performance" of her life. The critics concurred that she played brilliantly, "surmounting the work's difficulties with great ease,"[161] and "proving to be the finished artist with superb understanding both of the instrument she has elected to play and of the music."[162]

A month later, she performed the Hindemith concerto with Koussevitzky and the BSO in New Haven. Hindemith, who was teaching at Yale University, attended the concert and was so delighted with Posselt's performance that he baked a cake for her, which, she remembered, he decorated by hand with chocolate frosting and topped with a figure of a blond-haired woman playing the violin. At the small party after the concert, Posselt met Gertrude Hindemith, who wrote her many years later: "Ruth, my dearest, your ears must be ringing today, Paul and I spoke of you with so much affection. . . . Paul is having a concert here [in Stockholm] and a violinist Leo Berlin plays *your* concerto . . . rather well but oh, nothing of your masterful grip & your poetic charm. I can not hear a phrase without thinking how you played it . . . am glad I still have it in my ears & my heart."[163]

At the beginning of the new year, Posselt premiered the Hindemith Violin Concerto in Hartford and New York with Koussevitzky and the BSO. The piece won favor with all the critics except Virgil Thomson, who deemed it "a monotonous and arid three movements."[164] Howard Taubman in the *Times* was most enthusiastic, noting that "Miss Posselt played the difficult score with an easy command of the technical problems," and with "an assured grasp of its creative world. Mr. Hindemith could hardly ask for a more devoted interpreter. Mr. Koussevitzky and his players contributed a resounding performance of their share."[165]

Posselt went on to champion the Hindemith Violin Concerto in the United States. She revived it with the BSO in 1947, playing it in Boston, New Haven, New York and at Tanglewood. She brought it to Los Angeles in 1948 under Alfred Wallenstein and had a success with it despite Wallenstein's doubts that it would win favor. She repeated it at Tanglewood in 1956 under Burgin's baton, a performance they both considered especially fine; hearing from Ruth in a letter that she had recently heard the tape of the concert, Richard imagined her pleasure, saying, "It was good wasn't it?"[166] Posselt chose the Hindemith for what would be her last performance with the BSO, this time with Erich Leinsdorf, in 1964, a rendering hailed by the caption in one Boston review: "Thus Spake Posselt."[167] On the same occasion, Michael Steinberg in *The Boston Globe* called her "an ideal interpreter of Paul Hindemith's Violin Concerto."[168] Her last performance of the Hindemith, very fittingly, took place in October 1971, with Burgin conducting the Faculty Chamber Orchestra he had founded at Florida State University.

♩♩♩

Posselt's initial performances of the Hindemith Violin Concerto heralded the forties, which turned out to be among her happiest times both in her personal life and in her profession. It was during this period that she made her most significant contribution to American music and realized, rather than sacrificing, her personal desire "to live a full life as a woman." At last, Posselt had come into her own, in her home country, as "one of the really great violinists of the day," and she would be at her peak in both the number and the prestige of her concert and recital engagements. As with so many women, in the widest range of professions and jobs, from factory workers to classical artists, the war years in America proved a time, ironically but predictably, of heretofore unexcelled career opportunity. So, in the mid-forties, Posselt became a kind of "Ruth the Riveter" of American classical violinists. Encompassing, and perhaps symbolizing, the fortunate forties in Posselt's story were two first performances she gave of the Barber Violin Concerto, the New York premiere of the original score at the beginning of the decade, and the world premiere of the revised version at its end. And so, the musical story of performing premieres continues.

V. Ten Years of Happiness
Samuel Barber, Concerto for Violin
BSO Premiere, August 16, 1941
New York Premiere, March 14, 1942
World Premiere of the Revised Version, January 7, 1949

A few months after the New York premiere of the Hindemith Violin Concerto, Posselt set to work on preparing the Barber Violin Concerto, the world premiere of which was given by Albert Spalding with the Philadelphia Orchestra in February 1941. The Barber would come to occupy as cherished a place in Posselt's heart and repertoire as the Hindemith. Of all the works for violin she championed, the Barber concerto alone came to win enduring popularity with audiences and violinists alike, and perhaps she is responsible more than anyone for keeping it before the public during the decades when few other violinists were playing it.

Posselt's long relationship with the Barber concerto, and with "Sam" Barber himself, began in 1941, and her first goal was to bring the concerto to Koussevitzky's attention. She had by then become the maestro's favorite violinist; his written lauds appeared on her new circular for her new management firm, Boosey & Hawkes: "Ruth Posselt is one of the greatest violinists of our time, and her inexhaustible repertoire, ranging from the classic to contemporary works, gives her a particularly distinguished place in the world of music art. [Signed:] Serge Koussevitzky."[169] In May, Posselt and Tower played the Barber concerto at Koussevitzky's home for the conductor, Barber, and other guests. The women played the concerto twice through, and Koussevitzky decided to introduce it at the Berkshire Music Festival that summer.

The three-week-long Eighth Annual Berkshire Festival in late July and August of 1941 was a resounding success and drew a record-breaking attendance of 106,000 for its nine concerts. Notables like Eleanor Roosevelt and New York governor Herbert Lehman attended the opening concerts. Enthusiastic supporters of the orchestra filled the chairs in the shed. Thousands more music lovers bought general admission tickets and sat on the spacious lawns of the estate, where they listened without amplifiers, or movie screens.

The program for Saturday, August 16, opened with *A London Symphony* by Vaughan Williams, continued with the first BSO Tanglewood performance of the Barber Violin Concerto, and concluded with two Wagner favorites, "Prelude to Parsifal" and "Overture to Tannhauser." The lyrical Barber concerto allows the solo instrument to sing and also to display virtuosity, especially in the "perpetual motion" last movement. It suited Posselt's lush tone and fleet fingers to a T. Francis Perkins of the *New York Tribune* wrote: "A feature of last night's concert was the unusually intense display of enthusiasm which followed the performance of Samuel Barber's violin concerto. The plaudits lasted for several minutes and the Pennsylvania com-

After the Barber: Burgin applauds; Posselt, Barber, Koussevitzky bow. Tanglewood, August 1941

poser was called to the stage to share several bows with Ruth Posselt and with Dr. Koussevitzky. Both had done very well by Mr. Barber's music." After noting gratuitously, but typically, that Posselt was "the wife of the Boston Symphony's concertmaster, Richard Burgin," Perkins praised her "unerring and impressive technical skill and deftness" and her "tone which preserved its appealing quality, its eveness of texture and fluency throughout its compass."[170]

A few days later, Posselt received a personal note from Barber: "I had been trying to forget your fine performance of my concerto, so I could keep my ears free for some new music, when your letter arrived and recalled to me all over again how beautifully you had played it! I wish there had been two performances, so that I could have sat back and relaxed and enjoyed the second! Perhaps next winter." In closing, he gave his "sincerest thanks for one of the most exciting evenings of my life."[171]

At the beginning of February 1942, Posselt introduced the Barber concerto with the BSO in Providence, Rhode Island, Burgin conducting, and played it the following month with the University of Miami Symphony Orchestra, John Bitter, conductor. The latter per-

formance evoked the usual sexist praise: "She played with utter abandon rarely displayed by women violinists."[172] Three days later came the Boston premiere with the BSO and Koussevitzky, followed by the New York premiere on March 14. The reviews of the New York critics were laudatory and blessedly gender-neutral, drawing particular attention to Posselt's "vibrant" and "luscious" tone. However, the New York performance appeared to have made the most intense, not to say lurid, impression on the well-known literary and social critic Edmund Wilson, who happened to be in the audience, and in whom Posselt's playing seemed to have evoked a musical wet dream: "Blond woman violinist with Portia-like yellow hair – Ruth Posselt – long full black dress and arms bare almost to the shoulders – played Barber concerto, and as I watched the sawing motion of her pretty round arm always held away from her body and saw the bow moving straight across the bridge and eliciting the sweet and tender and rather sentimental strains of the alleged first movement, I realized that violin music was intensely sexual and feminine, even when produced by a man, in the sense that it represents the feeling for a woman of the underpart of the penis lingeringly passing in and out and eliciting exquisite music."[173]

Barber remained friends with the Burgins throughout the forties and followed Posselt's career with interest. He even developed a fondness for their first child, whom he dubbed in one letter to Posselt his "fiancée." At the end of 1948, he made revisions in his violin concerto, prior to Posselt's reviving the piece with Koussevitzky and the BSO. In early December, Ruth wrote to her husband: "I had a letter from Barber saying he has re-written the whole climax to the second movement and also changes in the last movement of his Concerto and is sorry to cause me all this extra work, etc. The fact is, I haven't yet received the music, and if it doesn't come pretty quick he'd better forget all the changes."[174]

Much later in her life, Posselt happened to recall how she came to premier the revised version of the concerto. At first, she told Barber there was "no way" she could play the new version because there wasn't enough time for her to study the new score properly. "But," she continued, "he talked me into it. He sent the music and I had to admit, it was much better. I worked like a beast. And I learned it. We played it in Boston, twice [January 7–8, 1949]. So I knew by the time of New York, I had it."

In Posselt's opinion, if the last movement of the concerto were not played very fast, it would not be effective. She thought Barber's metronome mark "way off – it should be 96, not 76." In Boston, Koussevitzky, who was worried about the piece, took it at a leisurely tempo, and Posselt told him, "Let's do it a little faster in New York." Before the concert in Carnegie Hall, she didn't say anything more, but "in the last movement," she recalled, "he started to go like the speedway in Indianapolis, me chasing after him all the way. He went so fast! But I was happy, and it brought the house down. Anyway, Barber sent me flowers and on the card he wrote, 'To the Peacherino from the Stickerino.' That struck me so funny. I still have the card."[175]

At the end of the year, Posselt took the Barber concerto on the road. She introduced it to Dallas audiences with the Dallas Symphony under Walter Hendl and in Minneapolis with the Minneapolis Symphony under Antal Dorati. She performed it for the last time in Boston, in April 1962, with Burgin conducting, in his valedictory concert as concertmaster of the Boston Symphony Orchestra. Robert Taylor of the *Herald* wrote, "Her intuitive and intellectual understanding of the Concerto brings out interpretive depth and power. She was superb." Cyrus Durgin of the *Globe* echoed, "Miss Posselt performed it superbly . . . In many respects, the Orchestra did its best work of the afternoon accompanying her."[176]

Posselt's own valedictory to her beloved Barber Violin Concerto took place when she played it with the Florida State University Chamber Orchestra under Philip Spurgeon. Ann Taylor Casadaban, who was studying with Posselt at Florida State at the time, recalled:

"I was Ruth's houseguest when she performed the Barber Violin Concerto with the FSU [Florida State University] orchestra. She had informed me of all her pre-concert rituals and I had sense enough to mainly just be around so she wasn't alone, and not be chatty. We drove to the hall in her big American luxury car du jour – I in my orchestra black and she in her colorful, flowing evening gown. The performance was wonderful. After we got back to the house we had a snack and a beer in the sunroom. Somehow Ruth started talking about the electronic organ in the corner and the evening ended with both of us sitting on the bench attempting to play simple tunes from the instruction booklet – her plunking out the right hand and I the left in a *most* elementary fashion. After all the exquisite phrasing and pyrotechniques of the Barber, the irony of this struck me then and made the activity all the more fun and amusing."[177]

Back to the future: the premieres of the early forties, and "Miss Posselt, perhaps the foremost woman violinist of today."[178]

VI. "Ruth Posselt Scores"
David Stanley Smith, Requiem Poem
for Violin and Orchestra
World Premiere, April 6, 1942

After studying composition at Yale University, David Stanley Smith (1877–1949) continued his studies in Paris. Upon returning home, he was appointed instructor in music theory at Yale University in 1903 and remained there until 1946, succeeding his mentor, Horatio Parker, as dean in 1920 and as conductor of the New Haven Symphony Orchestra. Like many American composers, Smith had a long, collegial relationship with Koussevitzky, who, back in November 1938, had raved about Posselt's playing backstage after a BSO concert in New Haven. Koussevitzky even suggested at that time that Smith hire her to play with his orchestra. Perhaps the two met in Boston the following spring when Burgin included Smith's Fourth Symphony, with the composer conducting, on his program with the BSO. It is most probable that Smith heard Posselt's performance of the Hindemith with the BSO in the fall of 1940, and that decided him on following Koussevitzsky's advice and hiring her to give the first performance of his Requiem Poem. Whatever the exact circumstances, Posselt premiered Smith's work with the New Haven Symphony Orchestra, Smith conducting, in Woolsey Hall, New Haven, on April 6, 1942. At the same concert she played Lalo's Symphonie Espagnole.

According to the program note, the only portion of the Requiem Mass that inspired Smith in writing his Requiem Poem "is the short prayer which opens the Mass and which is repeated many times as the main text of the liturgy – *requiem aeternam dona eis Domine; lux perpetua luceat eis.* ('Lord, grant them eternal rest, and may perpetual light shine upon them.'). There is pathos in the first melody, but the terror and despair of the *Dies Irae* are absent. The score contains passages of hope and even of triumph. Towards the end, Gregorian harmonies serve as an introduction to a wandering melody for muted violin over a sustained B flat major chord. This concluding section may be taken as a musical symbol of the soul's ascent. The 'Requiem' is neither a concerto nor a show piece for a solo instrument. There is no scholastic development of themes. The violin, with its great power of emotion, is here an expressive vehicle for conveying the feelings and reflections inspired by the text."[179]

"Miss Posselt Scores" read the headline in the *New Haven Register* the next day, and the review went on to cite the violinist's mastery of contemporary compositions: "The collaboration of Ruth Posselt in Professor Smith's Requiem was a fortunate one. Hers is a talent as fresh and confident as the concertgoer may find in many a season. A tone naturally opulent, and never forced in those sweeping passages which soar over a mass movement of orchestral proportions, is joined to a musicianship which is sensed by the listener even if he does not know of her mastery of half a dozen Concertos by contemporary composers. Charm of personality and intensity of expression in performance augment a fine technique and reassuring authority.

The audience accepted her last evening at face value (which is considerable!) and let her go only after a prolonged demonstration on the basis of very real accomplishment, which, without precise count, seemed to set the season's record for calls."[180]

VII. *"All through it I could feel the baby kicking around"* Vladimir Dukelsky, Violin Concerto in G Minor World Premiere, Boston, March 18/19/20, 1943 New York Premiere, January 5/7, 1944

When the New Haven critic noted Posselt's "mastery of half a dozen Concertos by contemporary composers," the indefatigable virtuosa was beginning the process of mastering a seventh, the Violin Concerto in G Minor by Vladimir Dukelsky, better known as Vernon Duke (1903–1969). At the time of his collaboration with Posselt, Duke was still using his birth name exclusively for his classical compositions, to distinguish them from the popular hits which had earned him both fame and fortune, allowing him to quip, "Vernon Duke supports Dukelsky."

Dukelsky and Posselt became acquainted in late 1939 at a time when the composer was considering writing a violin concerto. He wrote in his memoir, *Passport to Paris*, that the idea originated with Heifetz at a party where the great violinist and he were jamming, and Heifetz said, "Why don't you write a violin concerto? I'll play it if it turns out well."[181] By February of the new year, Dukelsky had already apparently consulted with Posselt, inscribing a picture to her: "To Ruth Posselt, with whom it has been a joy to collaborate, with my true admiration and my friendship, Vladimir Dukelsky." A little more than a month later, the composer attended Posselt's world premiere performance of the Piston Violin Concerto in Carnegie Hall.

While composing his concerto, Dukelsky "spent a lot of time studying the violin's literature," and "long hours taming the violin, an instrument that doesn't lend itself to imaginative experiments."[182] At some point in the composition process, which began in 1940 and more or less concluded the next year,[183] he asked Posselt to look at the piece as he had sketched it out for violin and piano. Dukelsky is not precise about when he finished the concerto, but suggests it was in the months after the October 1940 opening of his Broadway show *Cabin in the Sky*. He sent it to Heifetz, hoping the concerto would also be a hit. Eight months later, however, Heifetz wrote him that the work did "not appeal to me to my *entire satisfaction*."[184]

Irked at Heifetz's response, but still confident that he had written "a damn good concerto,"[185] Dukelsky turned to Posselt, who had been with the work at the start and whom he considered "one of the few really good violinists of her sex."[186] At the end of January 1942, shortly after the death of Koussevitzky's wife, Natalie, Dukelsky (now officially renamed Vernon Duke) sent Posselt the violin part of the concerto in manuscript, with the dedication "To Ruth Posselt."

In the spring, after her triumph with the Barber concerto in New York (which Dukelsky attended) and Smith's Requiem in New Haven, Posselt got to work on the concerto in earnest. The first step was an audition (with Mary Tower at the piano) for Koussevitzky in the Berkshires, on July 3, which happened to be her second wedding anniversary. Tower arrived at the Burgins' mosquito-infested cottage on June 29, spending the next day in bed with a cold. Burgin also had a bad cold, and Posselt was suffering her usual pre-performance aches, pains, and nerves. Posselt often said that most performers suffer them, some, like her, before they go on stage, and a few after they play, but the worst-case scenario was being nervous *while* one is performing. The first piano rehearsal of the Dukelsky did not go well, and during the whole pre-audition ordeal, Posselt felt miserable. After a run-through at Tanglewood, Posselt and Tower went to Koussevitzsky's, where they played the concerto two times through, the "first time pretty good, the second – marvellous. Everyone enthusiastic. Dukelsky there. Calls me 'angel.' K kisses me. Glad."[187]

Posselt completed the Tanglewood summer season in fine fettle. Appearing with the Berkshire Music Center Orchestra led by Koussevitzky on a damp, muggy Sunday afternoon in early August, she played the Tchaikovsky Violin Concerto to a shouting and cheering crowd of 3,300 fans. She noted in her diary that Boris Goldovsky, then the director of the opera department at Tanglewood, said it was "the finest Tchaikovsky Concerto he had ever heard." The Burgins celebrated with the Piatigorskys at a post-concert supper at the Curtis Hotel in Lenox.

Koussevitzky programmed the world premiere of the Dukelsky Violin Concerto for the spring of the 1942–43 season, but he decided to have Burgin, then still assistant conductor, perform it. The Dukelsky would prove to be the only world premiere the Burgins did together as musical collaborators, and it is rather a romantic coincidence that this professional premiere had a secret, personal "premiere" accompanying its preparation and performance.[188] "After we were married a couple of years," Posselt never tired of recollecting, "I realized that I wasn't getting any younger and wanted to experience a full life as a woman. So, one evening I asked Richard what he would think if we had a baby. He beamed and said, 'I think it would be wonderful!' Then, he added, 'But I think it would be terrible if it made you give up your career.' I replied that I didn't see why I couldn't do both."

Whether things happened this way or not, the fact remains that Posselt was unusual among female virtuosos of her generation and earlier in that she not only did not give up her career for marriage, she managed to combine a career with marriage and full-time motherhood. In the fifties, when traditional gender roles had become the norm again, in an interview for the *Miami Herald*, Posselt noted proudly, if perhaps a trifle defensively, that she has "accomplished three things that are considered 'practically impossible' by most viewers of the musical scene. She has successfully hurdled the gap between prodigy and mature artist. She has been happily married for 13 years to a 'working musician' and . . . she is also happily mothering two children ('most female concert artists,' she has noticed, 'don't have children') and succeeds in spending as much time as most mothers with her offspring."[189] All very true, but "having it all" proved not so "easy and natural" as she averred in the same interview.

Posselt's first challenge in becoming a mother while concertizing was intense morning sickness. Almost no one besides her husband knew she was pregnant, not even her mother, who put her symptoms down to her daughter's usual pre-concert "disturbances," or "weak nerves." Burgin knew better, and he worried, not so much about her pregnancy as about *her* worrying and pessimistic moods, especially when he had to be away with the orchestra on its annual western tour in December. While encouraging his wife to play, Burgin wished she would not take "small" concerts so seriously, writing her three days before an appearance in Greenfield, Massachusetts: "Please do not take any chances with your health should you feel that you are too weak to play the concert in Greenfield. . . . In any case should you decide to play, then take it easy. It is the type of an engagement an artist has to take in order to earn something and it adds very little to his glory or satisfaction. Reserve your strength for more important appearances."[190]

The upcoming Dukelsky premiere was such an important appearance. Although Mary Tower had worked with Posselt in preparing the Dukelsky the previous summer, she was unable, for personal reasons, to act as rehearsal pianist during the winter. Her place was taken by the brilliant young pianist Luise Vosgerchian (1924–2000), a former student of Gladys Ondříček and, later, professor of music at Harvard University. This was the beginning of a long and fruitful professional collaboration (and friendship) between Posselt and Vosgerchian which lasted until the mid-sixties. The two toured together in the mid-forties, and from 1948 to 1961 gave several critically acclaimed recitals in New York, Boston, and elsewhere in New England.

By January, Posselt had reservations about the Dukelsky cadenza: "The only thing I like are the opening five chords and the melody at the end plus the few measures (four to be exact) just before this melody begins. Everything else I want changed. Anyway I think it's too long," she wrote to Burgin, who was in New York playing his own premiere, of the Lopatnikoff Violin Concerto, with the BSO, and who planned to see Dukelsky while he was there.[191] Dukelsky dedicated his concerto to Ruth Posselt and in the program for the New York premiere generously acknowledged her input: "I had some trouble with the long cadenza in the opening *Allegro* and owe a word of thanks to Miss Posselt for her helpful suggestions."[192]

The full score of the Violin Concerto was still in manuscript when the rehearsals for the premier performances took place. Winthrop Tryon, in a *Christian Science Monitor* article previewing Dukelsky's work, described the score impressionistically as an "interesting document, and original, indeed, the notes for the various instruments being set down, as if provisionally, in lead pencil, and the solo part emerging from the middle of the page in red ink, as though predetermined and there to stay. Here, sure enough, was music in the process of the making." For her part, Posselt expressed her liking for the piece: "The composer has had regard for his proportions. . . . It has been scored with such care, too, that the solo part has a fair chance, right through, of reaching the audience. I would say [the orchestration] is transparent. The composer tells all he wants to with a minimum of accompanying sonority. His concerto . . . has a good deal of the character of chamber music."[193]

"The concerto was splendidly received both at Sanders Theater, Cambridge, and Symphony Hall, Boston – Ruth Posselt's virtuoso performance helped a lot," wrote Dukelsky in his memoirs.[194] Indeed, Posselt's performance was roundly praised. The work, particularly the first movement, is extremely difficult, presenting formidable challenges to the soloist in the harmonic language, unexpected intervals, numerous double stops including octaves, many high notes, and the quick tempo and short note values.[195] As the *Boston Globe* critic noted, "The composer has produced a striking vehicle for virtuoso fiddlers." Rudolph Elie of *The Boston Herald* wrote that Posselt "is, without exaggeration, one of the more exciting performers of the day in either sex." There was some carping about the "meagreness" of the accompaniment, but this was stated indirectly, as an expected consequence of Dukelsky's desire "to write an effective solo part that would not be obscured or dominated by the orchestra."[196]

The premiere of the Dukelsky was celebrated by Posselt's mother and sister Marjorie in Fort Lauderdale, Florida. Marjorie publicized the radio broadcast of the premiere, sending Ruth's picture to the *Miami Herald* and also putting ads in the Miami and Fort Lauderdale papers. It turned out the owners of a local dancing school knew Dukelsky well – the founder of the school, Betty Barrett, had danced in one of his Broadway shows. They suggested inviting the public to the dance studio to hear Posselt's broadcast. Ida wrote to Ruth that they "assembled the biggest radio [they] could find and had [her] picture in front of the studio, inviting the public. Marge made a lot of it, she is so proud of you – bought me a mammoth bunch of sweet peas which are blooming now – pink ones – and of course made me stand up as she introduced me as the mother of Ruth Posselt. That is the third time I have had to make a bow. They all said, 'I knew it, you both look alike' – the contour and expression, I suppose."[197]

As for the "the brilliant soloist" herself, she remembered the first performance of the Dukelsky concerto for another reason: "All through it, I could feel the baby kicking around. Someone who sent me flowers and knew I was going to have a baby, wrote on the enclosed card, 'No wonder it was good. There were three people involved, Richard was conducting, you were playing and so was the baby.'"

The story of how Posselt came to give the first performance of the Dukelsky Violin Concerto in New York with Artur Rodzinski and the New York Philharmonic is complicated and interesting for the light it sheds on how such premieres were arranged at the time. To begin with, the New York premiere of the Dukelsky concerto somehow became inextricably wound up with the premieres of two different violin concertos by Bohuslav Martinů, whom Posselt had become colleagues with at Tanglewood in 1941 and 1942, and whose Concerto da Camera she had agreed to premier with the New York Philharmonic in the 1943–44 season, before Dukelsky entered the picture. Then, in June 1943, Mischa Elman suddenly announced in *The New York Times* that he would give the world premiere of a Martinů concerto with Koussevitzky and the BSO in the coming season.

Elman's announcement caught everyone by surprise. Hans Heinsheimer, Posselt's manager at Boosey & Hawkes, in reply to a query by Bruno Zirato, business manager of the New York Philharmonic, wrote that he, Heinsheimer, knew nothing about the Martinů world premiere Elman had announced, that the concerto for which Posselt had been engaged (by the Philharmonic) was a world premiere, and he would respect the contract he had with the New York Philharmonic, adding "but on the other hand, if Martinů is going to write another violin concerto for Elman, there is nothing we can do about it."[198] Heinsheimer promised to contact Martinů and find out what was what.

Rodzinski, the conductor of the Philharmonic, apparently had no idea which Martinů concerto his orchestra had contracted with Posselt to premier, only that it was a world premiere. When asked, he replied to Zirato: "In case Martinů did not write a second violin concerto for Elman, and in order to save Miss Posselt any embarrassing situation with Koussevitzky on whom she and her husband depend, *and in order to still have a premiere with our orchestra*, I would suggest switching Posselt from her January date to any other date before December which you might find suitable."[199]

By late July, Martinů was hurrying to get the piano score of the Concerto da Camera to Posselt, so she could begin studying it and correct mistakes in the violin part. In the meanwhile, Dukelsky, who had learned that Koussevitzky had decided *not* to do his concerto in New York with Posselt, as he had expected, had taken the initiative with Rodzinski and was trying to get him to schedule Posselt in his concerto. He wrote Posselt that Rodzinski said there was certainly a good chance of her playing his concerto with the Philharmonic – though she had already been contracted to play the Martinů. Rodzinski decided to settle the whole business in the fall after consulting with Arthur Judson, the manager of the New York Philharmonic.

Dukelsky tried to persuade Posselt to intercede with Rodzinski on his behalf: "Now listen, my wonderful girl. Really and truly – if *you* prefer my concerto to Martinu's – and are willing to *say so* to Rodzinski, I know that he will make up his mind accordingly! I feel certain that the matter is now up to you – and *you only*. . . . If you see greater possibilities in the Martinu – good luck and bless you; far be it from me to even attempt to dissuade you from doing it. But I know I wrote a damned good concerto and we both know had a great success with it and *what's more important* that you'll repeat that success in New York. The time to act is now. It is inconceivable in retrospect that Koussy didn't see fit to bring you and my concerto to New York after the fine Boston results."[200] Before Dukelsky mailed this letter, Burgin had a talk with him and explained that the decision on whether Rodzinski did his concerto now rested mainly with Judson, and that Posselt would have little influence on the outcome.

As it happened, very shortly after receiving Dukelsky's pleas, Posselt went into labor. On August 4, she gave birth to her first child, a daughter, Diana. At the end of the month, Bruno Zirato, after a call from Heinsheimer, informed Rodzinski that Posselt would be playing the Dukelsky instead of the Martinů with the Philharmonic. He added: "Elman is appearing with the Boston Symphony on December 31st and January 1st in Boston, and January 7th in New York. Heinsheimer expects Martinu in his office tomorrow and will 'phone me the information about the Second Symphony."[201] On the same day, Heinsheimer wrote to Posselt, congratulating her on the birth of her baby and telling her he had notified Rodzinski and Zirato that it was all right for her to play the Dukelsky in New York.[202]

A few days later, Martinů wrote Posselt, sending congratulations from him and his wife on the birth of her little girl and expressing regret at the "less good news" that she would not be playing his Concerto da Camera. He realized that her playing it "might have caused some confusion with the concerto Mischa is doing, even though the two pieces represent different genres."[203] He asked her to return the piano score and violin part in the hope that he might still be able to set up a performance for the coming season.

In the end, Mischa Elman did the world premiere of the Martinů Second Violin Concerto with the BSO and Koussevitzky on December 31 and January 1 in Boston and on January 7, 1944, in New York. On January 5 and 7, in the afternoon, Posselt gave the New York premiere of the Dukelsky Violin Concerto with Artur Rodzinski and the New York Philharmonic.

In *Passport to Paris*, Vernon Duke recalled that "January 5, 1944, was a bad day for me, because that same evening my Violin Concerto, picked up by Artur Rodzinski, failed to repeat its Boston success at a New York Philharmonic concert in Carnegie Hall, despite the efforts of Ruth Posselt, its creator, and the thorough and incisive preparation given my piece by Lennie Bernstein, then the Philharmonic's assistant conductor." Duke laid the "failure" of the performance squarely at the door of Rodzinski, whose earlier illness had led to Bernstein's preparing the work in his stead but who "not two hours before the concert, suddenly recovered and conducted the work with which he was not overly familiar; . . . the orchestral accompaniment was understandably insecure, the tempi erratic, the public reception on the cool side."[204]

Duke's assessment of the New York performance is somewhat at odds with the critics'. The orchestra's accompaniment may have sounded "ragged" to him, and Rodzinski may have been unfamiliar with the work, but such flaws went unnoticed – indeed, one critic wrote that "Mr. Rodzinski provided a well proportioned, carefully adjusted accompaniment." The most damning criticism came from Olin Downes and focused squarely on the concerto itself: "New works placed by Dr. Rodzinski on the program of the New York Philharmonic-Symphony Orchestra's concert last night in Carnegie Hall [included] the concerto of Vladimir Dukelsky for violin and orchestra, which Ruth Posselt played superbly. . . . Unfortunately, she triumphed . . . in spite of the marked inferiority of tedious and labored music. Her tone is richer and has more color and individuality than ever before. Her technic is astonishing, and her intonation in octaves, or double stops, as in simple cantilena, one of its finest attributes. She was called back repeatedly to the stage and at last she brought Mr. Dukelsky with her."[205]

Dukelsky seemed to have done himself a disservice by stressing the failure of the New York performance. The critic for *The New Yorker* deemed "Mr. Dukelsky's concerto . . . a fresh and interesting essay, marked by certain perkiness and the melodic ease one expects from a man who turns out fetching popular airs when he signs himself Vernon Duke."[206] Rodzinski told Posselt he liked the piece; Bernstein, who admitted to Duke that at first he didn't "get" his piece, came to like it very much once he knew it; Posselt obviously thought well of it, and Burgin, who probably knew the score as well as the composer, wrote his wife after hearing Elman play the second Martinů concerto: "It is more grateful than the other Martinu concerto but I am very glad that you did not decide to play it. Dukelsky is definitely more interesting and original (also more brilliant) than either of the Martinu concerti."[207]

Having a baby not only did not put the brakes on Posselt's career, it spurred her on to a greater number of performances, more widespread recognition in her home country, and greater personal satisfaction than had been the case since her successes in Europe and the Soviet Union a decade before. Perhaps her postpartum flourishing as a violinist represented the chance confluence of external factors, but it does back up her later comment to an interviewer that after having her children, she felt she played better than ever before. Whatever the case, in the months prior to the New York premiere of the Dukelsky, she gave several recitals at venues close to home, and then left her baby in the care of her husband and a live-in nurse to play with the Cincinnati Symphony and make her debut with the Pittsburgh Symphony.

VIII. Postpartum Highs
Aaron Copland, Sonata for Violin and Piano
World Premiere, New York, January 17, 1944

Following hard upon the Dukelsky in New York, Posselt gave her eighth premiere in six years, and her last until the early fifties, "the first performance anywhere" (as noted on the program) of Aaron Copland's Sonata for Violin and Piano, with the composer at the piano, in New York Times Hall. At this premiere, Virgil Thomson, who had bashed Hindemith's concerto, was almost wholly content, "suspecting" that Aaron Copland's Sonata for Violin and Piano "is one of its author's most satisfying pieces," and concluding, "Ruth Posselt played the violin part with perfect tone and perfect rhythm. A beautiful piece cleanly and clearly read."[208] The first performance was broadcast a month later on WNYC as part of the Fifth Annual American Music Festival.[209] Posselt, now represented by Aaron Richmond Concert Management, had already introduced the Copland sonata to Boston audiences, including it in her Jordan Hall Celebrity Series recital program at the end of January.

This proved to be a landmark performance in Posselt's professional journey, which had, in a sense, begun in the same Jordan Hall, back in 1920, when Ondříček sneaked his eight-year-old prodigy onto the program of Czechoslovak music performed by the students in his school. At that time, she was hailed as "the real American prodigy of whom Boston could be proud." Almost a quarter century later, Boston demonstrated its pride in Posselt in no uncertain terms. According to *The Boston Herald*:

"It is increasingly evident that Miss Posselt is one of the really great violinists of the day. She is that rarest of all beasts of the musical field: a musician's musician and an audience's musician at one and the same time. That is to say, the most demanding musician can have nothing but admiration for her technical attainments, her musical conceptions and her means of conveying her conceptions to the audience. There is no pretence, musical or otherwise. There is no playing to the gallery to make easy things look hard and hard things look easy. There is no distortion of musical values, no capriciousness, no condescension, no false temperament. There is nothing in the way of trickery, in short, which any honest musician would not himself employ under similar circumstances.

"From the box-office standpoint Miss Posselt is the ideal performer. She has great personal attractiveness but does not throw it about. She has a wonderful sensitive bow, and with it achieves a glorious tone. She can whip up a fine, exciting climax, but never does so pointlessly. She plays just enough marshmallow on her program to endear herself to all. And she is gracious with her accompanists, elevates them to the position of partners and gives them credit for their work not because she has to but because she wants to. She conveys, in sum, the idea that she likes to do what she does and that she hopes everyone is having as much fun as she is. (They are.)

"A detailed report on her performance yesterday is hardly possible now, but it must be stated, though, that hers was the most beautiful traversal of the Bach A major Sonata anyone is ever likely to hear. Moreover, it must be said that Lukas Foss' accompaniments throughout were incredibly good and were a notable contribution to the distinction of the recital."[210]

AT SPRINGFIELD SYMPHONY Orchestra concert last night in Municipal Auditorium. Left to right: Mayor Anderson, Miss Ruth Posselt, Richard Burgin, conductor, and Governor's Councilor James S. Bulkley, president of the Friends of the Symphony.

Springfield Symphony Concert Wins Applause of Thousands

In the spring, Posselt and Burgin gave their first concert as new parents, "to the applause of thousands," when she performed the Tchaikovsky, and he guest-conducted the recently founded Springfield (Massachusetts) Symphony. This was the music that had initiated their relationship back in 1935 when Burgin had unobtrusively plucked the trailing hairs from Posselt's bow. After the concert, the Springfield orchestra made the Burgins a gift of the performance on 78 rpm records in a hand-painted boxed set, which turned out to be the sole recording of the Tchaikovsky she ever made. Fortunately, and thanks to the magnificent digitally remastering of the old records, this performance is now available on CD.

The Burgins spent the summer of 1944 in Cotuit, Massachusetts, enjoying parenthood and the beach, but at the beginning of August, they both had to be at Tanglewood, where the new mother performed the Mozart D Major Violin Concerto with the BSO. The concert was broadcast, and the announcer commented, "Posselt makes a charming appearance in her emerald green dress against the background of the men in the orchestra." A sketch by Carl Meier appeared in *The Berkshire Eagle,* accompanying a vivid, *staccato* commentary on the concert: "A symphony in G minor, composed by Mozart in his youth, is followed by the concerto in D major, No. 4, K. 218, for violin. Ruth Posselt is soloist. She is blonde, young, in a blue, gauzy dress with a few spangles. She keeps a small handkerchief under Dr. Koussevitzky's music stand to dry the perspiration from fingers and fingerboard. Her performance is exquisite. The audience claps ecstatically. She shakes hands with Dr. Koussevitzky, who is smiling, nodding, trying to leave the stage to her. She shakes hands with particular warmth and affection, with the concertmaster, Richard Burgin. He is her husband."[211]

Of this performance, which took place on the day after her daughter's first birthday, Ruth later wrote to her sister Marjorie, who was also born on August 4, that she had been thinking of her baby daughter all during the slow movement and put her whole heart and soul into it. Some sort of familial-musical telepathy seemed to have been on the airwaves, for down in Fort Lauderdale, Florida, Marjorie was listening to the radio broadcast of the concert and was having thoughts similar to Ruth's as she was playing: "I was almost unconscious at the time," she wrote Ruth weeks later, "– but a most delightful ethereal sensation, intermingled with wondrous thoughts of Diana – & *you* being a mother – the most divine part of it all – & I wrote of it to Ma before your letter came as it was in the Andante that Diana was before me; so you see, I felt the same way & it was so beautiful. My letter to Ma – concerning your playing – and your letter to me just crossed each other."[212]

♪♪♪

The 1945–46 season ushered in a new opportunity in Posselt's performing life. Marks Levine, the managing director of the National Concert and Artists Corporation (NCAC), whom Isaac Stern described as "a hard-boiled, hard-bitten New Yorker . . . with the warmth of a slightly gelatinous iceberg,"[213] took Posselt under his management. She became part of the Civic Association circuit, which enabled her to go on annual concert and recital tours that exposed her to audiences in small and medium-sized cities, mainly in the Midwest (Ohio, Kansas, Missouri, Wisconsin, Iowa) and Northeast (New York state, Maryland, Virginia, and, of course, Massachusetts). Such tours were a major focus of her musical endeavors from 1945 through 1947.

Posselt was ambivalent about the stresses of going on tour, especially for a woman with a baby at home. She tired of the steady grind of playing in scores of cities where all she really saw was the railroad station, the concert hall, and the hotel; of playing the same pieces over and over again no matter how the audiences applauded; of living out of a suitcase; and, most of all, being alone and far from home. On the other hand, it was always important for her to be working, and she liked earning even the modest fees NCAC paid – from $450 to $550 per recital and around $600 for concert performances – and she liked the fact that her contract with NCAC made her competitive with her male peers, old and young alike, violinists like Mischa Elman and the up-and-coming Isaac Stern.

Everything changed after the war, when society's ideas of what women should be doing with their lives rolled backward to pre-war norms. Men were flowing back into the economy and needed jobs or to train for jobs in order to support their families; male violinists from abroad were flocking to America, and Posselt's male competition re-acquired its edge. Civic Association organizations across the country, in almost all cases run by women, fell back into their old habit of preferring male artists over female. It was the same old story that in fact had never stopped humming in the background, to wit, Marks Levine's advice in a letter to Posselt that she should use a male accompanist for her civic recitals because of "the solidity a male lends to a woman artist."[214] By spring 1946, Levine was already sensing the writing on the wall, telling

Posselt he was not hopeful about orchestra engagements for the upcoming season because she had already appeared with a good many of the orchestras, and they did not repeat so soon. Hadn't she heard exactly the same explanation for her dwindling engagements (though for a different reason) a decade ago from her European manager, De Koos? Fortunately, the Boston Symphony Orchestra did not fall into the group of orchestras Levine was speaking about; they soon inquired about Posselt's availability for a pair of concerts early the following year.

In February 1947, Posselt appeared with the BSO after a two-year hiatus, reviving the Hindemith Concerto, with Leonard Bernstein conducting, for a total of five performances, two in Boston (February 7–8), one in New Haven (February 11), one in New York (February 15), and one at Tanglewood the following summer. The first four performances of the Hindemith revival coincided with the start of Posselt's second pregnancy (she again was suffering "acute nausea"), and the last came about a month after the birth of her son, Richard, on June 30, 1947, after a long, hard labor. "Warmest congratulations Heartiest wishes to mother and son," telegraphed Koussevitzky on July 1. On July 19, Posselt took the train to Pittsfield with her two children and their nurse.

The end of 1947 brought the inevitable news that Posselt would be dropped from the NCAC roster at the conclusion of the current season. As was his wont, Burgin tried to help his wife accept this reverse, philosophically: "The letter you received from Levine was no surprise to me. Actually it has not changed your status at all. The few engagements NCAC procured for you were neither very remunerative, nor did they add much glory to you as an artist. We should not feel very bad about it. Maybe it is all for the better. One thing, I feel, is certain: We must find an outlet for your musical activity; some sort of activity which may seem less 'glamorous' but is certainly more worthwhile. It would be shameful if your great talent should go to waste, and also, it would make you unhappy if you could not work professionally. I know that it will be difficult to find the right type of work for you, but we will succeed, I am sure of it."[215]

Burgin's reaction was certainly sincere and well-meaning, but it offered the kind of encouragement that is far easier to give than receive. Yet, Posselt appeared to adopt her husband's viewpoint, noting to more than one interviewer that after she married and had children, she felt her life had become richer and as a result, she played even better than she had before. As regards her playing, which gained depth and maturity with the years, she was no doubt right, but that did not mean that making the transition from "virtuoso, wife, and mother" to "concertmaster's wife, mother, and a fine violinist in her own right" was so easily accomplished as Burgin and she herself hoped it would be. The new fifties priorities in Posselt's life, in which, despite her professional accomplishments, she claimed that her paramount interest was her marriage, home, and family, took awhile to get used to and accept with equanimity. She was successful in projecting her new persona, or in confirming the projections of her listeners, however. In March 1948, she and Luise Vosgerchian gave a Jordan Hall recital that was hailed as "truly one of the high points of the season, partly for the program they offered, but mostly because of the high technical skill and the artistic integrity of their playing."[216] After the concert, Posselt received a letter from a longtime female admirer and supporter who was also a violinist, who wrote: "Ruth, I never heard you play so beautifully as yesterday – it was truly an outstanding concert and I stayed up in the clouds for hours afterward! *I told Richard I think it must be living with him and having babies* – anyway it was gorgeous and thrilling playing that you did and I will never forget it."[217]

Posselt ended the forties with a new manager, David Libidins, who, Levine's opinion notwithstanding, was successful in securing some important orchestra appearances for her under prominent conductors, such as Wallenstein, Monteux, and Dorati, with the Los Angeles, Chicago, and Minneapolis orchestras. Libidins wrote to his partner, Aaron Richmond, that he was "simply thrilled with [Posselt's] success. She was great in Chicago and got marvelous notices and now she came from Los Angeles where she played with the Philharmonic and made a definite hit. I am not judging this only by the newspapers but all [the L.A.] office was at the concert and they wrote me that she got ovation after ovation and was called and recalled back on the stage many, many times."[218] The ovation was for the Hindemith Violin Concerto, which Wallenstein at first was chary of doing, thinking his musically unsophisticated audience would not like it.

The last year of Posselt's most successful decade got off to a flying start with the world premiere of the revised version of the Barber Violin Concerto. In late spring, the Burgins mounted a tour of Finland, Norway, Poland, and France, the only professional tour they made together, with Burgin conducting and Posselt appearing as soloist. These turned out to be Posselt's last appearances in Europe.

Despite the enormous success she had in Helsinki (where she played the Hindemith and Tchaikovsky concertos, and Sibelius himself told her she was "wonderful") and Warsaw (where, she reported, the audience "clapped, cheered and shouted for 20 minutes after my performance"), this last tour was a mixed blessing. Constant worry over the children at home, exposure to the devastation caused by the war in Poland, hearing the survival tales of members of Richard's family, whom he had not seen for over ten years and she had never met – all of these things, plus the stresses of travel in post-war eastern Europe, left Posselt exhausted and extremely anxious when she returned home.

The night before she left for Tanglewood, where she would play the Bach Double Concerto with her husband in July, Posselt visited with her mother who thought Ruth looked tired and ill. On Diana's sixth birthday, Ruth noted in her diary that they had celebrated with a cake and ice cream, but it was not much of a celebration since she was not very well. A couple weeks later Ruth received a letter from her mother, who offered her diagnosis: "I think the whole trouble with you is too much *work*, excitement, worry over children & all accomplished in so short a time, 6 weeks, playing, travelling, recording & the excitement of a foreign country & meeting so distinguished a living composer! Sibelius! . . . I think you are a brick to do what you have done this summer & feeling so wretched! – you should have been in some quiet place, trying to get caught up with your sleep – sweet sleep – that will do wonders for you, more than anything else – now listen to your mother who has been thru it all & knows & who went a whole week once without a wink of sleep – so don't go or sacrifice your rest."[219]

A week after this letter was written, Posselt's wretchedness and sleeplessness had worsened into an emotional crisis which ultimately brought her to a prominent Boston psychiatrist who treated her off and on for several years.

The fortunate forties had ended and the fraught fifties would shortly begin.

The Towers (Stanley, Mary, and Barbara) and the Burgins (Ruth and Richard), Tanglewood, 1940.

"It was good wasn't it?" Posselt and Burgin take their bows after the Hindemith at Tanglewood, July 29, 1956.

Vladimir Dukelsky, inscribed "To Ruth Posselt, with whom it has been a joy to collaborate, with my true admiration and my friendship, Vladimir Dukelsky, February 10, 1940." *Photo by Laskin, St. Louis.*

Posselt Playing the Mozart D Major Violin Concerto at Tanglewood. *Sketch by Carl Meier.*

Gregor Piatigorsky (?), Ruth Posselt, and Bohuslav Martinů, Tanglewood, 1942.

Ruth and baby Diana, early fall, 1943.

At right: Flyer, "Ruth Posselt, One of the Greatest Violinists of Our Time," October 1944.

Below: Posselt and Burgin rehearsing the Bach Double Concerto in Symphony Hall, 1949.

Igor Stravinsky, inscribed "To Ruth Posselt, the beautiful virtuoso, Warmest wishes, I. Stravinsky, 1946."

Ruth Posselt receiving flowers after her performance of the Lalo Symphonie Espagnole with the Springfield Symphony, October 22, 1947.

At left: The Burgins, early July 1947. Ruth is holding her son. *Photo by Mitchell Studio, Pittsfield, Mass.*

Opposite page: Arms akimbo redux: Ruth Posselt chats with Leonard Bernstein backstage after the Hindemith, July, 1947. *Photo by Mitchell.*

After the Hindemith at Tanglewood. Left to right: Richard Burgin, Ruth Posselt, and Leonard Bernstein, July 1947.

Posselt and Burgin arrive in Warsaw and are greeted by Burgin's brother, Juliusz (far right), June 1949.

Posselt smiles at concertmaster Burgin after playing the Bach E Major Concerto, Tanglewood, 1950.

CHAPTER SIX

Nerves, Nostrums, and New Musical Outlets: 1951–1964

I struck out the sentence in which [the interviewer] mentions that at the age of three you decided to study violin. I did not think that at this age anybody would be apt to make such a "foolish" decision.

— Richard Burgin, Letter to Ruth Posselt

The profession of virtuoso violinist has always been a high-stress, high-risk, brutally competitive line of work, where being among the best is absolutely no guarantee of reaching the top. With possibly one or two exceptions, the top ten violinists of the twentieth century (in terms of earning power, reputation, audience appeal, and even ability) were probably no better at what they did overall than many of their colleagues who never made it into the circle of the elect. In the virtuoso business (my coinage) one can justify why Heifetz, for example, deserved to be called "God's fiddler," but one could never tell a worthy aspirant to that lofty position how to win the title.

As Itzhak Perlman notes in *The Art of the Violin,* any violinist who can continue to play well and be successful after forty is really remarkable – "so many things can go wrong." And, I would add, judgments are solidly subjective. The case of Yehudi Menuhin proves, at least to some connoisseurs of the art, that things can go very wrong, but audiences will still spend money to hear you, and you can command high fees for playing badly, even very badly. [220] Mental problems and breakdowns, extreme nerves and self-destructive behavior, neuroses and even psychoses, are certainly not unknown to virtuosi. Indeed, some of them have even become as famous, or more famous, for *not* succeeding as for succeeding. Izydor Lotto, Michael Rabin, Boris Goldstein, Joseph Hassid, and Ervin Nyiregyhazi are names remembered today mainly because of their tragic disappearances from the concert stage due to emotional and mental problems.

Some have argued that child prodigies are bound to grow up with more than their share of nervous ailments, but it's unlikely that is true for them any more than for high-powered performers in any field who from a very young age have had to work very hard and concentratedly at attaining excellence. Part of the unfairness of the virtuoso's fate stems from the obvious facts that few if any virtuosi choose their profession, the vast majority of their audience has little or no idea about quality violin playing, and even the most informed music critics – and they are few – often make their judgments on more or less subjective, extrinsic criteria (as many of the reviews cited in this book illustrate).

The "happiest" virtuosi, the ones most content with their lives, appear to be those who are judges of themselves, who set the standard of performance they want to meet and know they can achieve, at least most of the time. They also seem to know, or realize at some point, that life is much more than playing the violin perfectly, and they manage to find someone or, preferably, something that transcends their single-voiced instrument.

My own studies of the lives of virtuosi, and my life with my mother, have made me realize one thing: these exceptionally talented people run the narcissistic risk of becoming prisoners of performance, or perhaps, more narrowly, of their self-image as performers. However, I think they may *have to* cultivate this focus on image, in order to become what they are driven, for one reason or another, to be.

When I quixotically decided to take some violin lessons at the "hopeless" age of sixty – I had studied for two years as a schoolgirl, but gave up in frustration – my teacher recommended I practice in front of the mirror in order to try to self-correct how I was holding the violin, how I was drawing the bow, how my posture was, etc. I found this impossible to do. What I saw in the real mirror was too different from what I saw in my mind. My inner mirror was way out of sync with what was reflected back at me, and I realized there was no way I could ever bring them together. To paraphrase Shakespeare's Macbeth, the real violinist I saw in the mirror contradicted the fantasy one in my wishful imagination.

SYMPHONY SOLOIST— R u t h Posselt, American violinist, pictured on arrival here to play with the Pittsburgh Symphony Orchestra. As guest soloist, she will play the Dvorak Concerto at concerts in Syria Mosque tonight and Sunday afternoon.

I imagine that for violin prodigies growing up, the image in the mirror eventually becomes the one in their minds, and there is the rub, for inevitably their mental image takes on a life of its own – they no longer need to look in the mirror, their mirror-memory is inside them, permanently, just like their finger-memory is in their left hands. Somehow, the photographer of the *Pittsburgh Sun-Telegraph* caught this idea of performing as mirroring self in his 1943 shot of Posselt playing in front of a mirror.[221] In this photo, the reflected Ruth Posselt bears a striking resemblance to the real Posselt's typically posed, distant look in many putatively candid photos. People occasionally noticed the same look while conversing with her in real life.

Most of the *Wunderkinder* of Posselt's vintage were not beaten into virtuosity as Paganini allegedly was, but they were often "killed" into it with kindness, or doting attention, offered as a reward for focusing unilaterally on their violins and inner images as violinists. Menuhin's mother was said to be notorious for her domineering nature and her overprotectiveness of her son. Heifetz came to resent his controlling father mightily, but he worshipped the teacher who replaced him and never seemed to realize how little Professor Auer really had to teach him. And Heifetz is the case in point. He has been called "God's fiddler," and, to develop the implied metaphor, like God he was AL-ONE. "It's lonely at the top," he confesses towards the end of the moving documentary film about him, citing the cliché about the wages of success.[222]

But, it's lonely at the near-top, too, and at the not-quite-near-the-top; it may be lonelier still in the middle, or at the bottom. Practicing is lonely, touring is lonely, hotel rooms are suicidally lonely – no one but you, your violin, and your reflection in the inevitable mirror, internal or external. Posselt used to tell her students (and I have heard this from other violinists) that in order truly to master a difficult passage you have to play it thirty times while staring out the window. That's finger-memory and mirror-memory working in concert while the violinist remains a detached onlooker on life out there. That's aloneness, apartness. At the height of her career, in the forties, Posselt was often aware of four lonesome souls – her, her husband, and her children – especially when she went on tour. This is touchingly clear from the letters the Burgins wrote to each other on the same day in January 1945 when Posselt had just played in Indianapolis and Burgin was home in Brookline: "How's the baby? I played like a god! The criticisms were surprisingly good. I have a sore throat and feel miserable, but I left Indianapolis instead of staying in bed as hotel was so filthy. Killed three cockroaches. Today was 1st time I cried, but I controlled myself until now. I'm terribly lonesome, not cut out for a career. Haven't slept."[223]

Her husband felt equally alone: "Yesterday I did not write you, but you know sweetheart, I am thinking of you every minute of the day and at times I feel *terribly* lonesome without you, so lonesome that I don't dare to look at the baby at those moments because I could almost cry for not having you around the home, that is around me and the baby."[224]

Heifetz was lonely at the top; Posselt was lonely wherever she was, and sometimes, I think, *whomever* she was with. Burgin understood, and seemed to have validated the loneliness necessitated by his wife's career: "After your telephone call I suddenly felt a sadness coming over me, thinking of your being so far away from us, all alone, cooped up in a hotel room with violin practicing to look forward to – trains, hotels, sleepless nights, practicing the same pieces over and over again – it seems like a steady dull grind. But that's the way a career turns out to be. All you can do, my sweetheart, is to make the best of it. And by that I mean – to take it easy and not to waste energy. Don't waste your precious nerves. It does not pay to get upset about trifles. Just laugh it off. Darling, I love you so much, it makes me mad when you get nervous playing in those one-horse towns. Besides I am convinced that all the others have a much more matter of fact attitude to this type of concert. Please think of your health more than of your harmonics. You mean much more to me than all your beautiful fiddle playing put together."[225]

When an interviewer asked little Ruth Posselt back in her childhood, "Don't you get frightened when you come out on stage and see all the people?" she had a good (and unrehearsed) answer:"Why, I don't think about the people, I just think about my music and I play and I play and that's all." Little Ruth had no stage fright because she wasn't yet conscious of being in a sound-mirror that reflected only her own sound.

The way out of such loneliness is for the virtuoso to find a productive and satisfying life outside his or her inner image. To find someone or, better, some*thing* that doesn't reflect him or her to perfection. But the longer a person is obsessed with the perfection of her image, the harder it is to live unaware of it, or in spite of it. It must be very scary and lonely to lack her image – who's going to keep her company? It must be terrifying to have things "happen" to one – even pleasant things – without one's preparing for them. Life can be panicky and very fraught when one approaches it without rehearsing and practicing, when one's fingers aren't able to move independently, when one can't just walk out there and "play and play and that's all."

When Posselt reached the age of conscious awareness of what she had to do to perform for people, she started to suffer normal nervousness, but she learned how to master her nerves, as every successful performer must. Yet, every successful performance provides incentive for the performer to stay focused on the image of perfection, that image she sees or hears even when interacting with other people. It's as if when an interlocutor says something that recalls something you said or felt, instead of responding to the person you're talking to, you look into an inner mirror and respond to yourself while projecting that response to the person you're interacting with.

What Posselt saw in Warsaw in 1949, and what she heard Burgin's family remembering, seemed to have had a shattering, reality-correcting impact on her. Though the performances she gave there were comforting mirror reflections – the familiar "triumphs," "greatest performance of my life," "greatest ovation I ever had," etc. – the reality she actually saw in devastated Warsaw was way outside her mirror. Something about that whole trip gave her a terrible scare, or just a massive dose of real life.

Characteristically, my mother never went into any detail about the *real* fears she suffered from. The closest she came was on the day of my father's funeral when she said to me that *personally*, not professionally, she had been afraid and insecure her whole life. I believe that was true although it took me a long time to recognize the insecurity part. Even when she was affected by dementia in the last three or four years of her life and claimed to be seeing the ghost of my father, she resisted any suggestion that she was "just seeing things," saying that she always thought she had a strong mind. As one of my friends said, "Your mother was a formidable woman."

After the most severe indications of her emotional crisis occurred, in August 1949, she was under a psychiatrist's care throughout the fall and maybe into the new year. She insisted, however, on carrying out her engagements with the Oklahoma City, Dallas, and Minneapolis orchestras in December, and they all went off splendidly. In each city, and before each concert, she saw a local psychiatrist – her doctor in Boston provided her with referrals.

Before she left home in November, she wrote her husband a brief but very touching note that may provide some insight into her troubles at this time: "If I should be tearful when you leave me on the train, please know that I tried awfully hard *not to be,* because I don't want you to worry & be sad. I want to make you happy – that's why I'm going on this trip. To make me strong & more *self-reliant,* because I love you more than anyone else in the world. Your happiness is my existence and I shall fight with all my strength these two weeks away from you. If I should weaken at times, be strong & encourage me, but *please don't worry.* I love you my wonderful darling. Take care of yourself, & our two little angels."

My mother often said that her psychiatrist helped her a great deal. She claimed he told her she was neurotic, but had such good defenses that psychoanalysis would do her no good. He apparently encouraged her to learn to live with her neuroses, and that's what she ultimately did.

But her life changed. Her career, too. Professionally, most of the changes were due to factors beyond her control. She gave up touring, in part perhaps for personal reasons, but mainly because she could not get engagements with a sufficient number of top-flight orchestras to make it worth her while. Major orchestras simply were not hiring middle-aged ("mature") female violinists, either in the United States or in the rest of the world. If Perlman's statement is true that having a successful career after age forty is an achievement for any virtuoso, it was triply true for a female virtuoso of Posselt's generation. Indeed, one feminist scholar has theorized that a mature woman playing what is considered that most "feminine" of all instruments, the violin, actually discomforts members of the audience – at least, subconsciously – because it constitutes "an interruption rather than affirmation of femininity."[226]

From 1950 to 1964, Posselt's concert career was centered on appearances with the Boston Symphony Orchestra. More than one Boston critic noted her "in-law" status with the orchestra. Who benefitted the most from this "family" relationship depends on one's point of view. The Boston Symphony certainly got a real bargain since Posselt, being female in a male-dominated profession, played the highest quality performances for less money than any of her male peers would have received, never mind the two superstars to whom Koussevitzky, her first and most ardent patron, compared her. Yet, for Posselt herself, her "special relationship" with one of the world's greatest orchestras, as the Boston Symphony was during her heyday, was something to be proud of. During the last fourteen years of her association with the orchestra, she appeared twenty-seven times (with Charles Munch, who replaced Koussevitzky as music director in 1950–51, Richard Burgin, and Erich Leinsdorf, who became music director in 1962). She appeared with the BSO in Boston, Tanglewood, Providence, New York, and Brooklyn, performing concertos of Bach, Lalo, Hindemith, Bruch, Mozart, Dvořák, and Barber. During the fifties, Posselt introduced three more new works to American and BSO audiences: the violin concerti by Jean Rivier and Aram Khachaturian, and the Tartiniana of Luigi Dallapiccola. These premieres, especially the Khachaturian, which was done with Burgin, recapitulate and bring to a close our musical story within a story, "Performing Premieres," the first themes of which sounded in chapter 4.

IX. *"Ruth Posselt Day at the Symphony"*[227]
Jean Rivier, Violin Concerto
Boston Premiere, February 2/3, 1951
New York Premiere, February 16/17, 1951

After receiving a bachelor's degree in philosophy and serving in World War I, where his health was ruined by mustard gas, the French composer Jean Rivier (1896–1987) studied at the Paris Conservatory, won first prize in counterpoint and fugue, and "became a prominent interwar composer, taking a leading role in the Groupe du Triton."[228] After the war he was professor of composition at the conservatory for eighteen years. Few of Rivier's compositions (several symphonies, suites, choral and chamber music) have stood the test of time, and despite its initial success, his short violin concerto, composed in 1948, is particularly elusive – it does not even appear on several lists of his works.

The American composer Irving Fine, whose chamber music Posselt performed now and again, showed her the score of the Rivier Violin Concerto at Tanglewood in 1950. He had heard it in Paris the previous season where it had a terrific success. Sixteen minutes in length, the concerto has three movements, marked *Allegro non troppo e leggiero* (in sonata form with a very brief development section); *Lento molto*; and *Allegro violento,* which ends in a long cadenza for the solo instrument. Charles Munch, in his second season as music director of the BSO, decided to perform it with Posselt as soloist. On the same program, Posselt played Ernest Bloch's *Baal Shem: Three Pictures of Chassidic Life*, a first for the BSO concerts, as well as her first concert performance of these pieces, which she had programmed in recitals, especially the Nigun, since the early 1930s.

In a Boston newspaper interview that appeared before the Rivier premiere, she commented: "Much of the time this is just like chamber music – combinations of small groups of contrasting instruments. The piece has a very clean, clear, and transparent orchestration, but at times it is really spectacular and colorful! You might classify Rivier as a neo-classicist: his style seems like an outgrowth of Albert Roussel's – very precise, contrapuntal, and often beautifully lyrical: in short – very French!"[229]

Although Posselt's performances of the piece were uniformly lauded in New York and Boston, none of the critics could find anything positive to say about the concerto itself: *The New York Times* critic described it as an "amorphous, empty composition, most articulate in its central slow section, but fragmentary, episodic and restless, with constantly changing orchestral combinations that had no relation to one another or to the tricky solo part, and a long conventional cadenza, that had nothing to do with the modernistic nature of the work as an entity, curiously lacking in personality."[230] Jerome Bohm in the *Herald Tribune* predicted, rightly, that "Rivier's Violin Concerto is hardly likely to become a permanent addition to the slender literature of worthwhile concertos for this instrument." He also liked the modal slow movement best, but blamed the aridity of the other movements on "the devil-may-care mood inherent in so much contemporary French music," concluding that Rivier's concerto "is hardly music worthy of the attentions of so gifted a violinist or of a conductor of Mr. Munch's caliber."[231]

The Boston critics expressed a bit more enthusiasm, but mainly for Posselt's sartorial and violinistic splendor. "Strikingly gowned in royal blue, playing with a mastery few violinists possess," began Harold Rogers in *The Christian Science Monitor;* he then went on to praise Posselt "for meeting the challenges of the concerto's unconventional ranging melodies, doublestops of fourths and fifths and intricate cadenza, in which the composer throws the book at the fiddler." Rudolph Elie in *The Boston Herald* found Jean Rivier's Concerto for Violin to be a work "of rather slim merit," but wrote that Posselt "was in the top of her form," and revealed herself "clearly one of our foremost women violin virtuosi." In *The Boston Daily Globe*, Cyrus Durgin began by admiring "Miss Posselt's courage and enterprise in working up this Concerto by Rivier, a composer little known here. As someone in the audience dubiously asked: 'How often can she hope to play it?'"[232]

The performances of the Rivier Violin Concerto and Bloch's *Baal Shem* heralded the beginning of a fraught period in Posselt's personal and professional life. The next three or four years were marked by personal loss, marital difficulties, new musical initiatives, and a slow, rueful acceptance of a new attitude to her profession. In mid-January 1950, Posselt's older sister Molly had succombed to metastatic breast cancer. Then, at the beginning of March 1951, her sister Marjorie suffered a psychotic break in Florida, which led to a brief institutionalization, after which Ruth brought her up to Boston for medical attention. Worst of all, a month later, Ida Posselt had a cerebral hemorrhage and died after ten days in a coma.

In her last letter to Ruth, written the day before her stroke, Ida had in a sense summed up her "baby's" whole career. She recalled its start when she took Ruth to play for Walter Damrosch in 1928, and then commented on the review Ruth had recently received for her performance of the Hindemith Violin Concerto with the Harvard-Radcliffe Orchestra, the last concert of Ruth's that she would attend – "I thought they spoke very finely of you *honoring* them in playing for them." There is little doubt that Ida had seen all her hopes for her youngest daughter realized. Whether Posselt gave any thought to the strange farewell quality of her mother's last letter, Ida's death affected her profoundly. During the ten days her mother lay unconscious in the hospital, Ruth apparently never lost hope that she would recover. Her death, on April 15, caused Ruth to be openly distraught at home, even in front of her young children, from whom she normally hid her emotional distress. The day her mother died was the only time I remember as a child seeing my mother so uncontrollably upset. The loss of her mother ushered in several months of quiet despair, and it proved irreplaceable, resonating within her to her dying day. She later specifically remembered the year of her mother's death as a time when she suffered "from a serious phobia," which she once described to me as a fear of going insane. She may, however, have used the phrase "serious phobia" in a general sense to describe the emotional turmoil and intense feelings of fear and abandonment she must have suffered in the aftermath of her mother's death.

To help relieve those feelings, she turned to work, specifically some new professional initiatives, in which she hoped to find a rewarding musical outlet for her talents. As it turned out, this new musical outlet, chamber music, involved two members of the Boston Symphony, Joseph de Pasquale and Samuel Mayes, hired by Koussevitzky as principal viola and principal cello in 1947 and 1948, respectively.

By choice, or necessity, or a combination of both, Posselt had decided to pursue her career in directions that would allow her to base her life in Boston. This was not an easy transition to make even though she had never wholeheartedly embraced the peripatetic lifestyle of touring virtuoso. Her main desire as she approached midlife was to remain at the top of her game as a violinist, and to be active in her profession while devoting herself to her husband and children. At the same time, it was very important to Posselt to believe in her own independence and earn her own money.

During her whole life, she looked on playing the violin as paid work. She rarely spoke about music making in abstract, poetic, or spiritual terms. Whatever she *felt* about the music she played, she put into her playing and left it for her listeners to describe in words. Although she once noted in an interview that she considered chamber music the "epitome" of music making, that was the extent of her eloquence on the subject.

In the winter of 1951, Posselt formed a duo with Samuel Mayes and a piano trio with Mayes and a young pianist, Joseph Rezits. When Joseph de Pasquale teamed up with Posselt and Mayes the following winter, the Bel Arte Trio was born. It existed for ten years, played regularly in the Boston area and at Tanglewood, and made several recordings. Mayes left the group and was replaced by Martin Hoherman, cellist in the BSO, from 1954 to 1959, but he rejoined it for the last two years of the trio's existence.

Posselt's work in chamber music gave her the possibility of recording, something she had long wanted to do but had been denied the opportunity, in part, perhaps, because of the contemporary nature of her repertory. How many times she was asked why she didn't record the Hindemith, Barber, and Piston concertos! And how much she wanted to! But, in the forties, no one at the major recording companies, especially at RCA for whom the BSO recorded, wanted to risk recording her signature performances of these or other contemporary works. By the fifties, attitudes toward new music, especially chamber music, were changing, and a number of small, local record companies were springing up, willing to take a chance.

The first of the recordings Posselt made was *Album of 20th Century Violin Music*, with pianist Allan Sly, which was released in April 1951 by Academy Records. The following October, Festival Recordings issued an LP of Posselt and Mayes playing the Haydn Duet and the Martinů Duo, both for violin and cello. The disk also included the Fauré Sonata for Violin and Piano, op. 108 (with the pianist Joseph Rezits). In addition, The Bel Arte Trio made several recordings for Allegro-Elite and Decca records. (A list of Posselt's commercial and noncommercial recordings can be found in the Discography.)

The Bel Arte Trio began giving concerts in the winter of 1952. It proved enormously successful at its Boston debut in Jordan Hall, which, in the words of one critic, came "alive again, swarming to the last crevice with eager listeners." This was surprising because at the time, string trios, as opposed to quartets, were considered a kind of stepchild of ensemble music because of a severely limited repertory. Yet, as one critic noted, "the Bel Arte Trio was able to assemble a program both refreshing and original for it offered works very seldom performed."[233] After this concert, the BSO made its historic first tour to Europe, Posselt lost her trio partners, and she and her husband were separated for six weeks, the first time they had been apart so long since their secret engagement back in 1939.

However, both her duo and her trio were back to playing again at the beginning of the Tanglewood season. On July 5, in the Theater Concert Hall at Tanglewood, the Burgins played the Bach Concerto for Two Violins with the BSO under Munch's direction. A few days later the Bel Arte Trio appeared in the same hall in the first of four weekly concerts sponsored by the Elizabeth Sprague Coolidge Foundation at the Library of Congress.

At the time of these two duo and trio appearances, the Burgins' marriage was in a period of stress that simmered in the background for a few years, but never really came to a visible boil. Whatever the problems were, they eventually worked them out between themselves, as their relationship evolved from a passionate romance into the kind of "family happiness" that is described by Leo Tolstoy in his 1858 eponymous novella.

Posselt had in fact already begun incorporating a family narrative into her public story at the end of the forties, to wit, "Burgin Tots Budding Pianists," an article that appeared in mid-June 1949, in *The Christian Science Monitor,* when the tots' parents were touring in Sweden and Poland. She gave an updated redaction of her "family happiness" in a

press interview with the whole family during her "working vacation" in Miami Beach in June 1953. Here's the gist of what she and the rest of the family said, as quoted by Milt Sosin in *The Miami Daily News*:

HUSBAND AND TWO CHILDREN

Her Severest Critics to Attend Violinist's Concert at Beach[234]

"'It will be long past Dickie's bedtime,' Posselt began, ' but he's only five, and he may fall asleep [at the concert].'"

"Diana," explained the journalist, "who plays both the violin and piano, is just the age her mother was when she made her debut in Carnegie Hall. 'I play duets sometimes at home with mommy,' Diana related proudly. 'Sometimes I play accompaniment for her on the piano.'

"'The selection the children probably like best,' Posselt continued, 'is the Bach Double Concerto for violin, and they like it most when my husband and I practice it at home. One day when we had been playing the Bach Double, Dickie had come in and sat silently listening. When we got all through, he looked up and said, "You know, mommy, I like that; play it again."'

"What happens, when you're in an audience and your wife hits a 'clinker,' Burgin was asked. Burgin darted a quick glance at his wife, smiled, and responded loyally, 'She doesn't hit 'clinkers.'"

People sometimes marveled at the longevity of the Burgins' marriage, and their manifest love and affection for each other – how was it possible for two world-class violinists with healthy egos and their own strong ideas and opinions to stay together for so long and still actually love each other? Despite the tensions inevitably caused by manifold differences in their ages, backgrounds, interests, personalities, tastes, and even outlooks on life, the answer is probably simple: they did love each other, and they needed each other more than they needed to part. They also respected each other's areas of superiority and expertise in musical and other matters. Burgin considered his wife far superior to himself *as a soloist*, and Posselt looked up to Burgin's knowledge and experience in almost all other matters, musical and nonmusical. While sharing important things (music, their children, their home), they also spent time apart. And it is clear from the letters they wrote each other throughout their relationship, and particularly during the rough patches, that absence made their hearts grow fonder. They acknowledged this to each other. During the turmoil of the early fifties, they did not shy away from confronting their problems and trying to resolve them.

And, as my brother once so truly remarked, they had their music. Professionally, Burgin and Posselt were a partnership in addition to being individual artists, and they were seen as such, by their friends, their colleagues, the critics, and the concert-going public at large. Their musical collaboration began before they married, and continued to grow and expand, even as Posselt's career blossomed. "Every time I hear Ruth Posselt play the violin," wrote a *Boston Globe* critic in 1953, "I wonder how she does it. Being wife, mother, housekeeper and so on is enough for most young women. But each time she plays in public – which is all too infrequently – she does better than the last. The tone is deeper; the technique more secure; the musicianship more rounded. Which is a roundabout way of saying that she was the star of the show last night."[235]

This comment was made in a review of a concert by the Cambridge Society for Early Music (CSEM), which became a second important chamber music venue for Posselt in the 1950s. The CSEM was under the direction of Erwin Bodky (1896–1958), a refugee from Nazi Germany, who had come to the United States with his family in 1940. A former professor at the Berlin Academy of Music, Bodky founded the Early Music Society in 1942; the first series of concerts by the society, originally called the Cambridge Collegium Musicum, was given in Houghton Library at Harvard University. In its sixth season, 1949–1950, the CSEM moved to Sanders Theater in Cambridge. Most of the musicians who played in the ensemble were members of the BSO – James Pappoutsakis (flute), Eugene Lehner (viola), Samuel Mayes (cello), Louis Speyer (English horn), James Stagliano (French horn), Pasquale Cardillo (clarinet), Georges Moleux (bass), Phillip Kaplan (flute), Ralph Gomberg (oboe), George Zazofsky (violin), Harry Dickson (violin), Joseph de Pasquale (viola), and Richard Burgin (violin), among others. Posselt was a frequent soloist with the group for four seasons, 1952–1956.[236]

Posselt and Burgin appeared with the CSEM in several programs over the years, but only rarely together as soloists in the same work. On December 1, 1952, they gave a performance of Handel's Sonata in E Major for Two Violins and Continuo which was praised for its "fleet interplay," "rhythmic animation," and "intonation and phrasing that brought delight to the most exacting ear."[237] Four years later, they were featured in a program called "Italian Masters of the Baroque Era," playing Vivaldi's Sonata in E Minor for Two Violins and Albinoni's Sonata in A Major for Two Violins. The only recording of Burgin and Posselt playing violin together is *Italian Music for Strings of the Baroque Period,* issued by Kapp in the late fifties.

After Koussevitzky's death in June 1951, his lifelong commitment to commissioning new works was carried on by the Koussevitzky Music Foundation at the Library of Congress, overseen by his widow, Olga Koussevitzky. At the end of March 1953, the foundation sponsored an orchestral program of works it had commissioned in New York, under the direction of Leonard Bernstein, Koussevitzky's protégé, who had been his personal choice to replace him as music director of the BSO but was rejected by the Board of Trustees. All the works on the program were heard in New York for the first time. Bernstein had known and worked with Posselt for several years; in 1947, he had directed her in highly successful performances of the Hindemith Violin Concerto, and he was well aware of her abiding interest in new music. She was a natural choice to play Tartiniana, a piece for violin and orchestra by the Italian composer and pianist Luigi Dallapiccola (1904–1975).

X. A Host with Her Single Fiddle
Luigi Dallapiccola, Tartiniana
American Premiere, New York, March 29, 1953

As a composer, Dallapiccola combined an interest in early music, the madrigalists, and Italian Baroque polyphonists with twentieth-century serialist music. He was the principal Italian composer to employ the twelve-tone method, which he adopted in 1942, yet he never strayed from his roots in Italian polyphonic traditions.

Posselt's performance of the Tartiniana, written in 1951, was an American premiere of "music written with vigor and humor, and in the slow movement, with an atmosphere and fantasy that may not strictly be Tartinian," according to Olin Downes, who added, "We found the last movement rather repetitious in quality, in spite of some novel effects inserted in it. In this music, Miss Posselt was a host with her single fiddle and her musicianly treatment of its figurations and melodic strains woven into the orchestral fabric."[238] The concert enjoyed an enthusiastic response from a packed Town Hall audience that included many colleagues and followers of Koussevitzky. Posselt's performance of the Tartiniana, which was recorded by Columbia Records, was duly acknowledged by Olga Koussevitzky and, three years later, by Dallapiccola himself, who wrote that he "could not have desired a better performance of [his] little Tartiniana."[239]

Burgin and Posselt had already introduced several works for violin to Boston audiences – concertos by Hill, Bosmans, Piston, and Dukelsky. In the summer of 1954, they performed the Khachaturian Violin Concerto, a first for the BSO.

XI/XII. *Storm, Stress, and a New Dawn*
Aram Khachaturian, Violin Concerto
BSO/Tanglewood premiere, August 1, 1954
BSO/Boston premiere, October 28/29, 1955

Aram Khachaturian's Violin Concerto in D Minor, dedicated to the Russian violinist David Oistrakh and premiered by him in Moscow on September 16, 1940, made its way to Boston audiences slowly. After Arthur Fiedler conducted it at the Pops in 1945, the Boston Symphony played the concerto for the first time at Tanglewood in August 1954 with Burgin as conductor and Posselt as soloist.[240] The following year, they performed it in Symphony Hall.

The Tanglewood and Boston Posselt-Burgin performances of the Khachaturian were two of the high points of the violinist's career. Olin Downes enthused:

Richard Burgin, concertmaster of the Boston Symphony, will conduct the orchestra tomorrow afternoon when his wife, Ruth Posselt, will be the violin soloist. Here they discuss plans for the program.

"Miss Posselt played it with fiery virtuosity, with bravura and exceptional accuracy, a vibrant and sensuous tone and a style that went well with the nature of the music. The concerto could well be performed more often than has yet been the case. It is at the least a welcome addition to the rather restricted literature of the violin in this field."[241]

The 1732 Guarnerius del Gesu which Posselt used for this performance became her prized possession, her "baby," four years later. Before finding the Guarnerius, she played a Guadagnini, which she also liked very much but always considered a bit large for her very small hands. The Guarnerius, an unusually small full-size violin, suited her to a T. It was sold after her death and is now known as the Posselt-Philipp Guarnerius.

The Tanglewood premiere of the Khachaturian was not without its dramatic moments. In *The Berkshire Eagle,* under the headline "Festival Artists Win Over Storm, Broken Violin String," critic Jay C. Rosenfeld wrote:

"Burgin's accompaniment to the Khachaturian concerto in which his wife, violinist Ruth Posselt, was the soloist was a remarkable application of the conductor's knowledge of his own instrument to control of an orchestra. Miss Posselt has never played so magnificently. She was convincingly at ease, sure and secure in every intricate demand, comfortingly true in intonation. There was a sweep and apparent unconcern with the notes per se which raised the performance to one of the most memorable ever heard on that stage. . . .

"Just as the first movement was coming to an end, Miss Posselt's A string snapped. She quickly and deftly handed her Guarnerius to George Zazofsky and took his Stradivarius with the loss of scarcely an instant or of an iota of composure. Both Krips and Zazofsky gallantly offered the lady their violins in her distress, but she, equally chivalrous and observant of protocol, did not disarm the concertmaster but left him equipped for his responsibilities and accepted the offer of his assistant. Zazofsky quickly replaced the broken string and the soloist's own instrument was ready for her at the beginning of the second movement."[242]

Milton Bass repeated the story of the broken string in his "Lively Arts" column the next day, using the occasion to meditate on the relative frequency of strings breaking during violin performances and then to recall the somewhat similar situation that had happened to Posselt in 1935:

"It seems that several years ago, while appearing as a soloist with the Boston Symphony, Miss Posselt had an unfortunate accident during the performance. Only this time it was the strings on her bow that came loose instead of the string on her violin. . . . But Galahad appeared in the person of the concertmaster, a gentleman by the name of Richard Burgin who had only been casually introduced to the guest artist. He leaped to the rescue, disentangled the hairs, saved the day and the concert was brought to a triumphant close. Miss Posselt felt that such a gallant gesture could be made by a man who was a concertmaster in all respects and so they were married. That is how the tale was told me, and if it isn't true, it ought to be."[243]

Thus was the Posselt-Burgin true romance inscribed into the Tanglewood Tales of the Boston Symphony Orchestra.

The performances of the Khachaturian in Symphony Hall at the end of October 1955, coupled with Mahler's First Symphony, marked joint and individual triumphs for the Burgins. Cyrus Durgin commented: "By the time the Boston Symphony was well into the opening movement of Mahler's First Symphony, it seemed that Richard Burgin had never conducted so superbly or that the orchestra had ever sounded better. When the concert had ended it had become fixed in my estimation as one of total and rare enjoyment. . . . Nor had Ruth Posselt as violin soloist ever within my memory exceeded her performance of the Khachaturian Concerto. Here is a work of difficulty, and also of great appeal. . . . Miss Posselt played it with authority and loving care, and she wholly deserved the large ovation she received – including a kiss of the hand from her husband on the stand."[244]

Harold Rogers, in *The Christian Science Monitor*, seconded and praised the Burgin-Posselt duo: "Richard Burgin and his wife, Ruth Posselt, took the honors yesterday afternoon in Symphony Hall – Miss Posselt for a spirited performance of the Khachaturian Violin Concerto, and Mr. Burgin for his superb reading of the Mahler First Symphony.

These artists are more than welcome when they appear with the Boston Symphony Orchestra. Miss Posselt brings fire to nearly everything she touches, and were it not for Mr. Burgin's love for and understanding of Mahler, Bostonians would starve for his magnificent music."[245]

Here, a brief digression on Burgin and Mahler. Upon Burgin's retirement as concertmaster in 1962, the critic Robert Sabin noted "his pioneer efforts to perform the works of Bruckner and Mahler, decades before they became the staples of orchestra programming they are today."[246] Over two decades, Burgin gave forty-eight performances of works by Mahler with the BSO, including Symphonies 1, 2, 3, 4, 5, 9, and 10 (Adagio); *Das Lied von der Erde*; and *Songs of a Wayfarer*. Burgin's introduction of Mahler began in January 1942 when he gave the first performance in Boston of Symphony No. 4 (the third and fourth movements). "I wanted to do the complete Fourth," he recalls in his *Memoralia*, "but the trustees said no. Mahler (in 1942) was taboo – people considered him long, tedious, and everything else wrong. I always liked Mahler very much; so I compromised and asked to do the last two movements of the Fourth. They agreed. Then, after the performance, we got letters asking, why don't we do the whole symphony? So I was allowed to do it two seasons later."[247]

In 1943, he introduced the first movement of Mahler's Third Symphony (on the same program that Posselt played the world premiere of the Dukelsky Violin Concerto); twenty years later, he did five performances of Symphony No. 3 in Boston, Brooklyn, and New York. "In Carnegie Hall yesterday afternoon Mr. Burgin led the orchestra in the gigantic Third Symphony by Gustav Mahler and received a magnificent ovation for his achievement. It was an altogether superb accomplishment for Mr. Burgin, a personal triumph that was seconded by the way his colleagues reacted to his bidding. . . . His feeling for the special language of Mahler, as he made abundantly clear, is as deep and sensible as that of any conductor around today."[248]

$$\text{♪♪♪}$$

Among the audience for the Khachaturian concerto and the Mahler First Symphony in Symphony Hall were the Ondříčeks. Gladys wrote to her sister: "*You were magnificent!* Richard's conducting was most impressive. He should really be the regular conductor. The program was unusually well-planned and we enjoyed the whole concert. One of the pupils told me she heard the broadcast and remarked about the 'bravos' (mostly Ondy's, I'm sure) sounding through the terrific applause."[249] The composer Gardner Read and his wife listened to both "*magnificent* performances" on their two FM radios, "turned top volume, as cruelly close as breathing," and "we reveled in your absolutely flawless control. And your superlative musicianship supplied an inspiration far more perceptive than the composer's. Bravo!"[250]

Posselt performed the Khachaturian concerto three more times under her husband's direction: with the Reading (Massachusetts) Symphony in 1963, the Florida State University (FSU) Chamber Orchestra in 1971, and the Atlanta Symphony in 1972. Perhaps because the piece suited her so well, she chose to do it with Arthur Fiedler and the Jacksonville Symphony Orchestra in 1975. Those two performances, in Jacksonville and Lakeland, Florida, were her last solo appearances with orchestra. She was sixty-three years old, but "her complete mastery of her instrument was made evident in the first few measures of the concerto, which throughout requires technical skill and musicianship of the highest caliber."[251] Lois Gosa, a violinist in the Jacksonville Symphony Orchestra (JSO), who studied with both Burgins when she was a student at FSU, recently recalled "the concert with your Mom and the JSO; the fun part for me was that

The Jacksonville Symphony Association and Willis Page, Music Director

invite you to enjoy

"AN EVENING WITH ARTHUR FIEDLER"

THURSDAY, FEBRUARY 27, 1975

CIVIC AUDITORIUM — 8:30 P.M.

Tickets: $4.75, $5.75, $6.75 and $8.00
(TAX INCLUDED)

ARTHUR FIEDLER

All seats reserved

World renowned ARTHUR FIEDLER conducting

The Jacksonville Symphony Orchestra

in a Gala Pops Concert of well-known favorites with guest artist Ruth Posselt, Violinist performing the Khatchaturian Violin Concerto

TICKETS AVAILABLE: HEMMING PARK, REGENCY SQUARE, CIVIC AUDITORIUM, and the JACKSONVILLE SYMPHONY OFFICE, OR USE COUPON FOR MAIL ORDER.

RUTH POSSELT

Ron (my ex) drove to Lakeland with your folks. Yes; the 4 of us in the car. It was all so colorful hearing your Mom talking about how she wanted 'tea and toast' before the concert. Your parents treated us to a good meal after the concert. (Italian I think.)"[252]

In the 1950s, or because of them, Posselt accepted, though not without regret and a hint of resentment, that her career as a concert violinist of national fame was over. She settled for the local and limited celebrity status granted her for the rest of her long life, as the wife of Richard Burgin and a "fine violinist in her own right." The number of her concert appearances each year was small, but when one adds numerous recitals, chamber music performances, recordings, and a significant amount of private teaching, at the New England Conservatory (from 1950), Wellesley College (from 1951), and the Berkshire Music Center (1952–1964), a diversified and active musical life emerges. I cannot really recall many days throughout my girlhood when I did not hear my mother playing the violin, either practicing or rehearsing or performing.

At the same time, Posselt was a full-time wife and very "present" mother to my brother and me. Every morning she made our breakfast and sent us off to school, and every evening she prepared dinner (from scratch) for the whole family. She was an excellent cook – her mother had taught her well – and she managed the house and kept the household accounts. In the late fifties and early sixties, she acted as an unofficial hostess of parties for BSO performers and visiting artists, especially those who came, after the Thaw, from the Soviet Union. She hosted a memorable party for the Soviet virtuoso Leonid Kogan and his wife in January 1958, at which Kogan somehow ended up in a bedroom playing solo Bach for the guests. "Your party for Mr. and Mrs. Kogan when they were here," wrote Todd Perry, general manager of the BSO, "was a very great help to us in doing the right thing by our distinguished visitor. We owe you a very great debt of gratitude for taking it on, and it would ease my conscience a bit if you would accept the enclosed check against the expenses of this. I know that you graciously declined this once before, but my conscience has really been bothering me, and you can satisfy your conscience if it bothers you by realizing that we should have had to do a good deal more officially than we did, at considerably more expense, and without one-half of the effectiveness of the result."[253]

November of 1958 brought what Posselt listed in her appointment book as the "Russian delegation" party for Georgii Zhukov (and his wife), who was in Boston working out a cultural exchange of American and Russian composers. That event took place the following year and brought to the Burgin home in Brookline the Russian composers Shostakovich, Kabalevsky, Amirov, and Khrennikov, and the Americans Herbert Lamb, Gardner Read, Walter Piston, Herbert Fromm, Irving Fine, and Leonard Bernstein. Posselt later recalled, "They had the time of their lives. Later in the evening Leonard Bernstein, Lukas Foss and Walter Piston took turns playing four-handed jazz. It was the best time the Russians had in the US."

Burgin's retirement from the concertmastership of the BSO at the end of the 1962 Tanglewood season brought great change in both his and his wife's lives. For Posselt, however, the change was more radical. Burgin had wanted to retire for several years and agreed to stay on because Munch asked him not to leave until he did. At the same time, since Burgin retained his position as associate conductor until 1967, his connection with the orchestra that he had worked with for forty-two years was not severed immediately. Finally, Burgin moved directly into a new position and career as Eminent Professor of Violin at Florida State University.

Posselt's final appearance as soloist with the Boston Symphony Orchestra in March 1964, under the new director, Erich Leinsdorf, constituted virtually her last appearance as soloist with a major U.S. orchestra. She went out with a bang, as the saying goes. The headlines proclaimed "Violinist Posselt Superb in Hindemith Concerto"; "Ruth Posselt Plays Brilliantly"; and "Thus spake Posselt."[254] Posselt was only fifty-two at the time, and had a lot more playing years ahead of her, but the number of her concert engagements was reduced after her association with the BSO ended. She became "an artist in academe," and initially not even a full-time one. To her credit, she plunged into her new career with energy, enthusiasm, and the same dedication to, and success in, achieving the highest performance standards that she had manifested all her life. Moreover, she developed musically in new directions, not only as a chamber musician, but also as an orchestral player. Nevertheless, a residue of sadness about what she considered the loss of the career she really loved took its toll. In a word, she "never really got Boston out of [her] system."[255]

CHAPTER SEVEN

An Artist in Academe: The Florida Years, 1965–1979

Although Miss Posselt shared the program, she also stole it with her superb musicianship and flair as a concert violinist. She physically throws herself into her playing with a manly depth of tone and strength.

— *St. Petersburg Times,* May 16, 1974

Posselt and Burgin moved to a new home in Tallahassee, Florida, in 1965. Posselt was no stranger to Florida. Members of her family lived there, she had occasionally vacationed there with Burgin both before and after their marriage, and she had played recitals and concerts in various Florida cities from 1937 on. She loved the climate and, especially, the beach. From earliest childhood, her best times and fondest personal memories were formed at the shore, somewhere: in Manomet, where she practiced with "Ondy" and for her dolls, and met her first love; in Bar Harbor and Hermon Pond, Maine, where she spent summers in private with her first husband; at St. Jean de Luz, where she loved swimming under Thibaud's watchful eye; in Redondo Beach, Florida, during her secret romance with Burgin; on family vacations, after the Tanglewood season, in Atlantic City, in Maine, on Cape Cod, and so on. Florida presented a very desirable locale for Posselt, but professionally, at least at first, it had downsides.

At the time Burgin was invited to FSU, its School of Music was beginning its rise to national prominence as an educational opportunity for young American musicians; in fact, Burgin was one of the "founding fathers" of the FSU School of Music. Posselt also contributed significantly to the venue's rise, but for several years, she was forced into an adjunct role that amounted to a whole new glass ceiling she had not previously come up against. She began working at FSU in 1964, but throughout the sixties, due to Florida's nepotism laws, she was a part-time employee, first a visiting artist in residence, then a part-time instructor. Although she was not officially on the teaching faculty until January 1972, whenever Burgin had to be away during the school year to fulfill his obligations as associate conductor of the BSO, Posselt would substitute-teach for him.

At the beginning of her Florida period, Posselt was back to being mainly the wife of Richard Burgin. The headline in *The Tallahassee Democrat* that announced the Burgins' first joint appearance in Florida says it all: "Richard Burgin, Wife to Appear as Soloists."[256]

However, the years Posselt spent in Florida were among the busiest of her long life in music, and once she finally was allowed a full faculty position, certainly they were the most financially remunerative. The majority of her concert appearances were connected with her academic appointments at FSU, but her musical activities were varied and not wholly confined to the university. As artist in residence and part-time instructor at FSU she formed and led the Florestan Quartet (1964–1972), which performed in various Florida music venues. Originally called the FSU Quartet in Residence, the Florestan was composed of School of Music faculty members: Ruth Posselt, first violin; Richard Burgin, second violin; Robert Sedore, viola; and Harry Dunscombe, cello. Posselt also gave recitals, at and outside the university, and served as concertmistress of the FSU Faculty Chamber Orchestra for seven years. In addition, she played in the Gulf Coast Symphony for two seasons and, in the late seventies, in the Opera Company of Boston Orchestra under Sarah Caldwell.

Once the Burgins moved to Tallahassee, they were empty-nesters; their daughter was a graduate student at Harvard University, and their son was an undergraduate at Brandeis and then a graduate student at Columbia. After Burgin's forced retirement due to his age in 1972, Posselt became professor of violin at FSU School of Music (she

QUARTET-IN-RESIDENCE — The Florida State University Quarter-in-Residence will perform tonight in Opperman Music Hall as 8:15 o'clock. From left are Mrs. Ruth Posselt, violin; Richard Burgin, violin; Harry Dunscombe, violoncello; and Robert Sedore, viola. Dr. Edward Kilenyi will perform on the piano during the second half of the program.

received tenure in 1975–76), a full-time, salaried employee for the first time in her life, and the chief wage earner in the family. Teaching became the main focus of her career.

Posselt had been teaching, however, since her girlhood, and for the same reasons as many musicians do initially: to help earn a living in music. Whatever praise, glory, and personal satisfaction her concert and recital performances brought her, the profit she actually realized from most of them was minimal (after expense deductions for commissions, publicity, circulars, advertisements, travel costs, gowns, hall rentals, and accompanists). In addition, teaching was both natural to and nurtured in Ruth. Both her parents and several maternal aunts, we recall, were music teachers, and three of her sisters made teaching their career and managed to be self-supporting. Posselt began teaching as a young teenager by giving lessons on the banjo, ukulele, and mandolin, all instruments her father taught her to play. As a young virtuoso, she occasionally gave lessons for Ondříček, and in the late forties she began teaching privately.

In addition to private lessons, Posselt taught in the academy from 1950, when she received her first appointment at the New England Conservatory of Music, where she taught until she left Boston. A year later, she joined the music faculty of Wellesley College, and in the summer of 1952, she joined the faculty of the Berkshire Music Center at Tanglewood in the Chamber Music Department as a teacher of violin sonata literature. She worked at the BMC every summer through 1964. For several summers, she served on the faculty of the American Federation of Musicians Congress of Strings at Saratoga Springs, New York, and Cincinnati, Ohio.

Posselt approached teaching as she did every aspect of her profession, with conscientiousness, enthusiasm, and the desire for her students to achieve the best possible results. She brought her well-honed performance skills into her teaching and aimed at helping her students be the best that each could be. She worked especially hard with her most gifted, "serious" students. Ann Casadaban, a former violinist in the New Orleans Symphony who was Posselt's student at FSU, remembers: "She was a devoted teacher to those she deemed worthy of her efforts. It took me a long time to realize her all-encompassing critiques were a sign that she felt I had potential! Ruth always stressed the importance of not practicing mistakes. She attributed her success in large part to her sister and first teacher Marjorie, who she said always practiced with her. She told me she never practiced for hours and hours on end, and said it wasn't necessary. As time has gone by, I realize that she was right; if your focus is good you can accomplish a lot in a short time. As a professional I think one must develop this skill, otherwise there is simply not enough time to do everything."[257]

Lois Gosa, violinist in the Jacksonville Symphony Orchestra, who knew and studied with both Burgins for many years, recalled in an email to me a particularly intense moment in a lesson with Posselt: "I studied *Baal Shem* First Movement, 'Vidui,' with your Mother. I found my part recently, and some of the pencil marks I'm sure were things she had told me. A triplet figure, 'Oh my dear.' I wish I could remember her words in reference to the deep tragic knowledge as the Jews of

Auschwitz were liberated; the looks of long suffering. That made a shift of a descending 5th more poignant."

Posselt gave as much of herself to her students who didn't aspire to be professional musicians as to those who went on to successful careers in music. One student from the first group, who studied with Posselt privately for ten years, from his junior year at Boston Latin School through his graduation from Harvard Medical School, is Dr. Michael Nieland, now retired, an eminent specialist in dermatopathology. Michael is still very active as a violinist, playing quartets and quintets with members of the Pittsburgh and Cleveland symphonies and in the past several years giving violin concerts in his home for friends and music lovers in the community. Since he knew Posselt as a student, and eventually as a friend for a long time, I asked him if he would be kind enough to share some memories of her for this book. Here is what he wrote: "During the ten years I studied with Ruth she provided me with a thorough grounding in the technique of violin playing which has enabled me to play almost anything I desired the rest of my life and for which I am truly grateful. Not that my lessons were all exercises and scales, etudes, and the usual short pieces. Musically, when I was more advanced, Ruth introduced me to Ives and Stravinsky and guided me through the concertos of Khachaturian and Szymanowski as well. I always looked forward to my lessons and to walking up the steps to her spacious home at 12 Salisbury Road in Brookline where she taught in a large room with a piano to the right of the doorway on her first floor. Ruth was always encouraging and inspirational and I was invariably dazzled by her recitals and appearances with the BSO in Boston and at Tanglewood whose programs I still keep.

"I treasure all my years and memories of Ruth. Even though she realized that my career path was not to be in music she never gave me anything less than her full attention and devotion. She and the violin have enriched my life immeasurably and I still hear her voice when I play and occasionally perform – 'Rhythm, Dear!'"

♬♬♬

Posselt's professionally oriented students continue to have active musical careers today. Some play or have played in orchestras such as the New York Philharmonic, Chicago Symphony, National Symphony Orchestra, Charlotte [North Carolina] Symphony, Jacksonville Symphony, Atlanta Symphony, and New Orleans Symphony; others have gone into teaching and have held positions in departments of music and conservatories across the country; still others have formed musical groups of their own. Those who became teachers have themselves brought up generations of violin students. The cycle of teaching and learning goes on and on, and no teacher can know where the seeds s/he has sown will blossom, and how. A case in point is Taiwanese master teacher Sylvia Shu-te Lee, who studied with Posselt at the New England Conservatory for seven years in the sixties, before returning to her homeland. There, "just about every successful violinist from Taiwan cites Sylvia Shu-te Lee as personal violin mentor in their biodata. The names read like a Who's Who list."[258] Posselt followed Sylvia's career with pride and interest, and was gratified to learn of her success when Lee returned in December 1989 to accept an award at the conservatory for her artistic education of young musicians.

Another of Posselt's gifted students at the New England Conservatory and the Berkshire Music Center, and in private, is Hiroko Abe Nakahara, who enjoyed success as a concert violinist in her native Japan, before her marriage. Over the years, she wrote many moving letters to Posselt, reporting on her life and professional development. These letters demonstrate that Posselt continued to play a collegial, mentoring role in some of her students' lives long after they left her tutelage, and that she was a role model, especially for aspiring women violinists. Writing of a successful concert in Tokyo, where she played the Khachaturian Violin Concerto, which she had studied with Posselt, Hiroko Abe recalled, "My thoughts went back [to] whenever I played in Boston, and you used to come to see me after the concert and hold me fast. I always felt relieved seeing you and what a great encouragement you gave me! . . . The more time passes, the more

I miss you. I can never express in words how grateful I am to you and how much I miss you now. I learned a great deal from you, not only music but also humanity. In accordance with all things which I learned from you, I continue to work hard and go my way steady. Please do not forsake me."[259]

Hiroko Nakahara, now a grandmother, lives with her husband on Long Island and is still actively involved in music making. She had a string quartet and a piano trio and performed for many years. Currently, she enjoys playing chamber music with her colleagues and she performs once in a while, but teaching, she avers, is now her great passion. Recently, she recalled to me her experience with Posselt:

"My life as a student in Boston and Tanglewood has been the highlight of my entire musical career. I was extremely lucky to be under the tutelage of Ms. Posselt during my time in Boston. I was also very lucky to have valuable lessons from Mr. Burgin. Ms. Posselt taught me not only the art of violin playing, but also the importance of stage presence. Even when I went back to Japan, she encouraged me to widen my repertoire and play in public as much as possible. When I was in Boston, Ms. Posselt always came to hear my concerts and brought chocolates during the intermission to energize me.

"Today I am still using the music which I studied with Ms. Posselt. She has an inimitable handwriting. In the second movement of the Fauré Sonata she wrote, capital letters, 'VULGAR.' I didn't understand the meaning of the word at the time, but I understood later what she meant. She didn't want me to play too proper, or too square in this movement.

"I've always admired her immensely as a great violinist, teacher, loving wife and a great mother. Even today it is a wonder how she played all these roles so perfectly. I still remember the delicious smell of roast lamb filling Ms. Posselt's Brookline home whenever I visited.

"Ms. Posselt always called me Koko, and now my grandchildren call me Coco."[260]

Finally, another of Posselt's students, Malcolm Brannen, a violinist and recently retired music educator, who began studying with her in Boston and then completed his education at FSU, where he studied with Burgin as well, recalled in print the benefits of their different approaches, and the "perils" of being caught in between:

"Ruth Posselt was a marvelous concert artist who started her career at a very young age. She had incredible musical ideas that she realized effortlessly in her playing. The bowings and fingerings that she recommended to her students, although sophisticated, were often very challenging. . . . Being exposed to her musicianship was an extraordinary education. . . . Posselt accepted me into her studio when I entered the 8th grade, and I worked primarily with her through high school. . . . I graduated from high school in 1964, . . . and I decided to pursue undergraduate studies at FSU.

"Continuing to hold the position of associate conductor with the BSO, Burgin was away periodically. At those times Posselt would teach his students.

"With regard to editing, Burgin was much more of a pragmatist. One particular amusing instance comes to mind. He was in Boston conducting the BSO, and I took a concerto into a lesson with Posselt. She edited the first movement and [her] suggested bowings and fingerings were difficult. The next week I played the movement for Burgin. 'We can't use these fingerings,' he said, and he re-edited the movement. The next week he was away again, and I played the work for Posselt, who promptly put the other markings back in. Being shy, I offered no clue as to why the changes had occurred. Once again, a week later, I played the movement for Burgin, who became rather agitated when he noticed that I had reverted to the former editing.

"He asked me, 'Where did you get these fingerings, and why aren't you using what I gave you?' I finally confessed that his wife had suggested them. He sighed and said, 'Now I understand! You have to realize that Miss Posselt is a phenomenal artist. If she hears something, she just makes it happen. For the rest of us mortal violinists, we must first achieve accuracy and clarity of notes and musical ideas. After this, we can branch out to more daring things. Put my edits in with hers and if you play this for her again, make her happy and attempt hers. But keep this conversation between you and me!'"[261]

In 1968, Posselt was incapacitated for ten months with a frozen shoulder. She wondered in despair if she would ever play the violin again. She recorded her slow, painful, but determined recovery in her diary. The entries (from fall 1968) read like the agonizing travail of a paralytic learning to walk again, step by step:

October: "Discouraged over shoulder progress, can't get out of miserable depression due to shoulder and inability to work"; "try violin, unable to reach D string without great painful effort and can't hold up high enough"; "practice 15 minutes, painful."

November: "Try A and E strings, 1st and 3rd position, cannot get elbow to right, unable to get left hand around to D string and G"; "try fiddle about 15–20 minutes, force self to put fingers on G-string, very painful, discouraged"; "discouraged over shoulder progress, feels like lead when I try to raise elbow to play. Pain!"; "practice violin short time on A and E strings, low positions, everything very stiff and pain. Frozen!"

December: "Decide to practice more, force arm a little, suffer for it later"; "cry over arm. Practice ½ hour"; "play violin easy for ½ hr. shoulder awful, poor progress, sad."

Perhaps the decision to practice more, an effort of will reminiscent of her mother's admonishment "to pick yourself up after a fall and *proceed*," was the turning point, for by the end of the year, Posselt, without noting the fact, was practicing on all strings, and at the beginning of the new year, she gave her first concert, with her quartet, in ten months. The two solo recitals she gave at FSU, in April and November 1969, were "triumphs." Her frozen shoulder had thawed, but for the last decade of her performing life, she was plagued by occupational pains in her neck, shoulder, back, and arm.

However, she was gratefully back in harness, as announced in a *St. Petersburg Times* article about the Burgins, "Return of the Traveling Musician," with a cartoon by Jack Barret: The article noted, "Miss Pos-

Times Art by Jack Barrett

selt, Burgin's vivacious, brown-eyed, bubbling partner, also . . . loves teaching, although her teaching is restricted to private lessons at home due to the nepotism ruling at the state university. . . . 'I love St. Petersburg and the beaches,' Miss Posselt said. 'You know, as a concert soloist, I'm really not experienced in the orchestral literature. But I love it. The music is challenging and it's such fun to work under Irwin Hoffman.'"[262]

From 1964 until her resignation from FSU in 1979, Posselt gave over a hundred concerts, especially in chamber music – with the Florestan Quartet, a new Bel Arte Trio, and other groups – but also as an orchestral musician and a recitalist and soloist with orchestra. Most of her solo appearances were with the FSU Chamber Orchestra, with which she performed the Bloch *Baal Shem* (1967); the Bach Brandenberg Concertos Nos. 4 and 5 (1968); Haydn's Sinfonia

Concertante (1969); and the concerti of Khachaturian (1971), Hindemith (1971), Bach (for violin and oboe, 1972), Mozart (Sinfonia Concertante, 1973), and Barber (1973). She also appeared during the Florida years as soloist with the State Symphony of Florida, the Fort Lauderdale Symphony, the Naumberg Symphony in New York, and the Atlanta and Jacksonville symphonies. She approached each and every concert with the same meticulous preparation, desire for perfection, and musicianship as she always had, regardless of the venue she played in. She still worried as much about her harmonics as about her health, in disregard of her husband's advice over twenty years earlier that she put her health first.

While at FSU, Posselt also maintained her dedication to performing works of contemporary composers, giving performances of Norman Dello Joio's Variations and Capriccio for Violin, considered one of his major works for the instrument; Efrem Zimbalist's Sonata for Violin and Piano; John Boda's Trio for Violin, Cello, and Piano and Sonatina for Violin and Harpsichord; Allen Sapp's Trio and second Violin Sonata; and Daniel Pinkham's *Cantilena.* She took advantage of the opportunity to introduce some of her favorite twentieth-century works to new audiences: the Martinů Duo for Violin and Cello, Ives's Second Sonata, Prokofiev's *Five Pieces for Violin,* and, of course, the Copland Sonata for Violin and Piano, which she chose for her valedictory recital at the university in May 1979.

Although Posselt continued to play the violin superbly, even in her own hypercritical judgment (as recorded in her diaries), those diaries, as well as some letters to me, reveal how much nervous strain preceded and accompanied some performances. To Posselt's chagrin, performing sometimes became more of a burden than a joy, and the best part of a concert invariably was after it was over. She carried out her teaching duties with enthusiasm and conscientiousness and received excellent teaching reviews. With the passing years, however, her work at FSU also became more burdensome than gratifying – often enough, and with reason, she felt overworked, underpaid, and most of all, unappreciated. It was with a sense of liberation, and very much with the encouragement of her husband, that she resigned in the spring of 1979, despite having received tenure and been granted a sabbatical. I shall let her tell this story, which she did for me and for others, with great gusto.

"After Richard retired, the Dean loaded the work on me, I was working fifty hours a week, I was a wreck. I had eighteen hours to teach every week, a seminar to give every two weeks, the faculty trio, plus I had to give a recital once a year and I was concertmaster for the faculty symphony. Eventually, I thought I just couldn't take it any more although they awarded me a sabbatical. I had a chance to play in the opera in Boston and it was during spring break – we had three weeks – and everybody leaves the school and I see a note in my box from the Dean saying, 'I'm sorry, I can't let you go this year, I need you badly to recruit some more students,' and I thought, 'The hell with you!' When I told him I had an engagement in Boston, he said, 'You never really did get Boston out of your system, did you?' And I said, 'No, I never did, and I hope I never will, and I'm going, it's an honor where I'm going to play, it's prestigious for the school. And I feel I should have had an assistant long ago to help with the administrative details.' And so I left his office, and I went home and thought for a minute and I sat down and wrote a note to him and said, 'As of June, I herewith return my sabbatical award and give you my resignation as professor of violin. Then I called up Richard in Boston. He said, 'Bravo!' He was so glad I was going to come."[263]

The seventies were the last decade of Posselt and Burgin's forty-year marriage. After Posselt left the university, they left Tallahassee and settled in Gulfport, moving for the last time, from their small bungalow there to a condominium in nearby Town Shores. Unfortunately, they had less than two years to spend together in retirement. On January 8, 1981, Richard Burgin suffered a cerebral hemorrhage while playing bridge in the Town Shores Clubhouse. A craniotomy was performed, but his brain was badly damaged. He lingered in a semiconscious state in the hospital until his death on April 29, 1981. Ruth Posselt lived as a widow in Gulfport for twenty-six years.

Living and Performing Loss

You are in the end . . . what you are.

– Goethe, Faust

During the first decade of widowhood, and after the shock of loss had subsided somewhat, Posselt kept up a fairly active life, doing a little teaching, playing some private recitals for friends, traveling up to Tanglewood in the summers, and successfully managing her finances. She maintained an active correspondence with her children, friends, and some of her former students. The following excerpts from some of her letters to me over a decade chart moments in the poignant story of her parting from her violin and her performing life.

Tues., Feb. 28, 1984: It is awful to have desires and ambitions and high hopes and spirit but a painful body that negates everything and refuses to cooperate. I guess one can only keep fighting until the spirit has gone.

Jan. 2, 1985: It was so beautiful yesterday again. 87 degrees and sunny and I was in pain and lonely, so I decided to force myself to go for a drive. I went to Passe-A-Grille Beach & saw so many landmarks on the way that made me feel worse! First, Pasadena Hospital – DeLuxe Nursing Home – Ted Peter's Smoked Fish (which Poppy loved) – the Beach itself (Pop always wanted to buy a little house there! Nothing for sale tho the past 15 yrs!) The air & beauty was magnificent, but didn't help me!

Nov. 25, 1985. I was able to practice an hour!

March 1, 1986. This is sort of a banner day for me because I practiced a good hour (with 3 intermissions) and played the Villa Lobos

"Fantaisie" with my old big style and my tone was brilliant and my fingers encompassed all the huge technical difficulties! It is an achievement for me because I had almost decided to take it off the program![264] I'm so self critical it's pitiful but probably it's all part of being a <u>real</u> artist and a perfectionist in order to achieve that status. – Unfortunately, I'm trying to maintain the status I had at my peak and with almost insurmountable physical ailments and pain.

Wed., Apr. 1st, 1987. I ache all over. Rehearsed with piano yesterday but we only got through ½ the program.[265] It is quite definite now that playing violin is very damaging to my cervical disks. I am in such pain it is hard to live with it until I lie flat – take aspirins and don't move my head. I guess I'm playing my swan song.

. . . There will be 31 people at my concert. I really don't know where I'll put them all! (Not to mention serve them various drinks and hors d'oeuvres afterwards!)

Sept. 23rd, '87. The days are too short and I always have the desire to take out my violin and practice a half hour! I really am deteriorating so much, but at least I want to get back into some shape! That keeps me going. – Mr. Kinberg called me a few days ago and wants me to try out a Guadagnini he has restored. I really want to do it for him, so I told him I've had a little setback physically and would call him in about two weeks. Now I'm trying to do just that so I had to start ½ an hour a day on the etudes and finger exercises. He's been very kind to me – did two slight repairs to my Guarneri for which I'm very grateful.

Sunday, Nov. 27th 1988. I'm glad Thanksgiving is over! Your phone call was a savior. It made me feel so close to you. – I was very busy last Wed. & Fri. teaching & coaching. When I'm through working, I'm completely exhausted. I can't walk and I try my best to hide my infirmities. I always used to play for my advanced pupils, but now that is impossible. I'm terribly out of shape and I know it's impossible to get back since many days go by without my touching the fiddle. I also have no desire when I'm in pain, realizing my neck will pain even worse. It's even hard to sit for any length of time because I have to bend my swollen knees. Such are the vicissitudes of old age. Gladys used to say it was "tragic," and she was so right.[266] No one can understand what it's like until you experience it.

Jan. 16, 1989. My concert for my student Ruby was a huge success. She played more beautifully than I expected and everyone was very excited. My buffet was delicious. There were 23 or 24 people. I was exhausted at the end and my poor legs so swollen I couldn't move afterwards! I won't give another soirée like that for a long time, if ever.

April 28, 1989. I saw Dr. Hobby on Tues. and he xrayed my cervical disks again and as I expected the arthritis has increased noticeably. Sometimes I can't turn my head to the right at all. I feel so badly about not practicing or attempting to play violin because it always worsens the pain.

June 11, 1990. Well, to finalize my day yesterday I took out my dear old Guarneri and moved my fingers for ½ hour! I certainly have deteriorated in that area! I feel guilty about it, too, but it does cause more pain in my neck. The thing that amazes me is that I am so alert mentally as regards notes, intonation, and music in general. That's why I feel so badly to allow myself to relinquish my stature as an artist.

Oct. 8, 1991. You did inspire me to practice a little again! I did ache but I think it helps [keep] my fingers from stiffening (and perhaps my morale, although it's too late for a comeback) at the expense of a sore neck and shoulder!

Starting in the mid-nineties, after three knee surgeries, Posselt began a long, slow physical and mental decline. Not wanting to admit to a hearing impairment, nor willing to be seen in a wheelchair, she increasingly withdrew into the seclusion of her home, her recliner, and her recollections of her performing life. That life, it seemed, had become fixed in the shape of her hands – the fingers of her left hand were locked in the position they had assumed on the fingerboard for eighty years, and her right hand always looked as if she were holding a bow. And she was quick to respond to her memory of who she knew she was - Ruth Posselt, the great violinist. I recall on one visit, after I had taken up the violin again at the age of sixty, I mustered the courage to play for her. When I took out my fiddle and approached her, she seemed to think I was a student who had come for a lesson. After I played a few bars, she stopped me, having noticed that I was not bowing correctly, and said, "Who is your teacher? You're not bowing right. You need to bow this way, with your wrist, like this." And she proceeded to draw several perfect bows in the air. Then she said encouragingly, "Try it again." I tried to imitate her as best I could, and she said, "Yes, that's better," but she turned to her beloved nurse, Rosina Persad, and whispered, "Very mediocre."

After a series of small strokes, she changed markedly. "When I returned to work for Ruth in September 2003," Rosina recalled after my mother's death, "it was sad to see the change in her from being very talkative, demanding, and always having the last word, to a calmer, more quiet person. She remained alert to herself and her profession, always remembered being a violinist and all the places she played, was able to recall the names of her sisters, brother, and spoke with great pride of her children and all their accomplishments. There were days that she was confused about her surroundings; sometimes she thought we were traveling on a train or a ship and even in her car, and some days she thought we were at my house, yet there were many days that she was able to carry on a perfect conversation. She always talked with so much love for her husband and her mother. Ruth always thought of her appearance, whether her make-up was okay, or her hair was done right, or if she smelled good. She was interested in me and my family, always asked if I was married and if I was happy. Every day that I was there, Ruth would say, 'I love you, do you love me?' Sometimes when I told her I loved her, she would say, 'I know you do.' She started calling me 'Mommy'; she enjoyed it when I gave her a back rub, played with her hair, or just held her hand, especially when she was having a bad day. Several times, she was admitted to the hospital, but she always came back. She had a strong will and often said, 'I don't want to die.'"

In January 2007, when I saw my mother for the last time, I noticed she was very different, almost not with us. She barely recognized me and was in her own world, often humming and making sounds to herself. Rosina was with her to the very end: "I took her to the hospital just after I came in on February 19th. Her vital signs were very weak and she was unresponsive. Ruth passed away very peacefully at 12:25 p.m. with me still holding on to those tiny hands that had played all those wonderful notes."

Ruth Posselt was interred in the double crypt she had bought for Richard Burgin and herself in Abbey Court, Woodlawn Gardens Cemetery, St. Petersburg, Florida. A small group gathered with my brother and me to listen to her last recorded performance, of Prokofiev's *Five Melodies* and Arbos's *Tango*.

Housatonic, Massachusetts, March 2016

Koussevitzky, Posselt, Munch, February 1951. *Photo by John Brook.*

The Bel Arte Trio, Ruth Posselt, Samuel Mayes, and Joseph de Pasquale, rehearses at Tanglewood, July 7, 1952.

Charles Munch, inscribed "For Ruth Posselt, the marvelous musician and violinist and most charming woman, with all my admiration," Charles Munch, 1951.

Flyer for the fifties.

Posselt and Burgin take their bows after performing the Bach Double Concerto, Tanglewood, July 5, 1952. *Photo by Will Plouffe Studio.*

The Bel Arte Trio in the mid-1950s: Joseph de Pasquale, Ruth Posselt, and Martin Hoherman.

Ruth Posselt, shaking the hand of an unidentified woman, and Joseph de Pasquale, after a performance of the Mozart Symphonia Concertante, Theater Concert Hall, Tanglewood, July 11, 1958.

Ruth Posselt, Olga Koussevitzky, Leonard Bernstein before the Dallapiccola premiere, *Tartiniana,* March 29, 1953.

The Posselt-Philipp Guarnerius. Photograph from the Bein & Fushi inc. 2015 Calendar, November-December: A violin by Giuseppe Guarneri del Gesu, Cremona, 1732. "Posselt, Philipp."

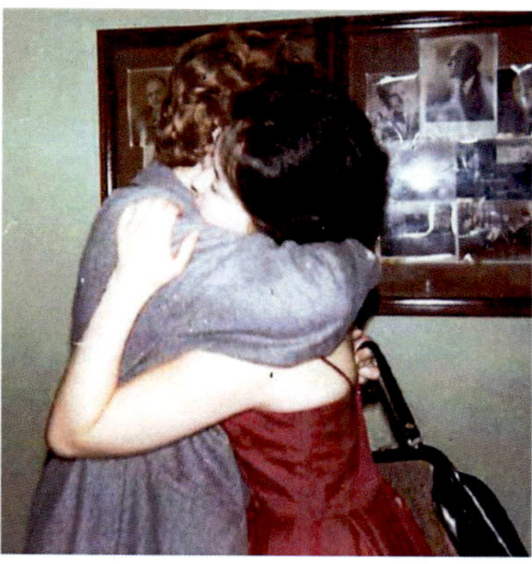

Posselt's final performance with the BSO, March 1964.

Ruth Posselt and Hiroko Abe, 1964.

Luise Vosgerchian and Ruth Posselt, 1956.

Posselt teaching a chamber music class at Tanglewood. *Whitestone Photo.*

The two R's at their son's graduation from Brandeis University, June 1968.

RUTH POSSELT

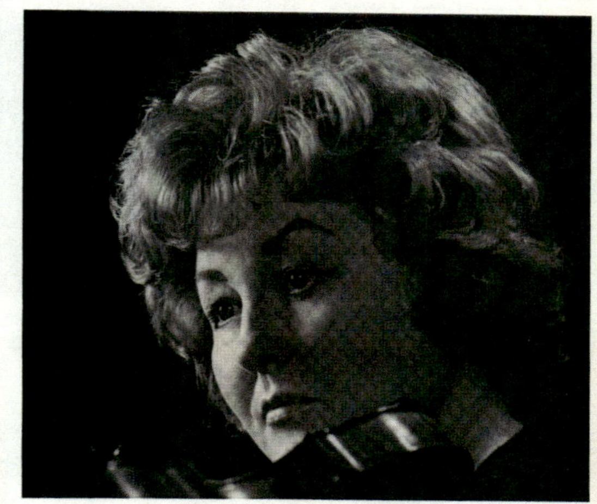

Flyer for the Sixties.

Ann Taylor Casadaban, violinist, composer and former student of Ruth Posselt at FSU.

Ruth at the Memorial service for Richard Burgin, Symphony Hall, Boston, May 29, 1981.

Rosina Persad, PN. Westminster Communities of Florida Employee of the Year 2014.

"Those tiny hands that played so many wonderful notes":
Diana and Ruth, January 11, 2006.

Notes

Preface

1 Ann Taylor Casadaban, violinist, composer, teacher, and former student of Ruth Posselt's at Florida State University School of Music, email communication to the author. Serge Koussevitzky's words, as reported in a letter from Richard Burgin to Ruth Posselt, November 17, 1938. Ruth Posselt Archive. Jonathan Woolf, Review of WHRA CD, November 29, 2011, http://www.musicweb-international.com/classrev/2008/June08/posselt_WHRA6016.htm.

2 Most sources give Posselt's year of birth as 1914. In fact, she was born in 1911.

3 *The Art of the Violin,* a film written and directed by Bruno Monsaingeon, Kultur D4639.

4 See Lucy Green, *Music, Gender, Education* (Cambridge: Cambridge University Press, 1997).

5 Nancy B. Reich, "European Composers and Musicians, ca. 1800–1890," in *Women & Music. A History,* ed. Karin Pendle (Bloomington: Indiana University Press, 2001).

6 Letter from Haensel and Jones to Ruth Posselt, October 13, 1937. Ruth Posselt Archive.

7 *Denver Post,* January 10, 1931. Ruth Posselt Archive.

8 *Boston Traveler,* March 23, 1933. Ruth Posselt Archive.

9 *Washington Daily News,* January 24, 1938. Ruth Posselt Archive.

10 *Cincinnati Enquirer,* December 2,1939. Ruth Posselt Archive

11 *Houston Post*, February 13, 1945. Ruth Posselt Archive.

12 Clipping of a review titled "Ruth Posselt in Violin Debut," April 14, 1930, in a Baltimore newspaper. Ruth Posselt Archive.

13 *Knickerbocker News,* Albany, NY, August 18, 1941.Ruth Posselt Archive.

14 *Fort Lauderdale [FL] Herald,* 1942.

15 This performance is now available on YouTube with an accompanying photo montage at https://www.youtube.com/watch?v=z7tvdbiwlbs&list=PLMTc64NR DY5U7ewKxNknaSJOzEifLsqOc.

Chapter 1: A Wonder-Child's Normal American Girlhood: 1914–1925

16 Letter from Ida L. Posselt to Ruth Posselt, September 5, 1946. Ruth Posselt Archive.

17 Letter from Marjorie Posselt to Ruth Posselt, September, 1953. Ruth Posselt Archive.

18 *Medford Mercury* [?], May 19, 1918. Ruth Posselt Archive.

19 Letter from Marjorie Posselt to Ruth Posselt, August 1943. Ruth Posselt Archive.

20 Quoted in *Boston Sunday Advertiser*, "Ruth Posselt Back in Boston," February 17, 1935. Ruth Posselt Archive.

21 Clipping from a Boston newspaper, May 1918. Ruth Posselt Archive.

22 Letter of Marjorie Posselt from Bad Elster to "Dearest sweetest honeybunch Ruthie," August 29, 1922. Ruth Posselt Archive.

23 Quoted language from the flyer for the program. Ruth Posselt Archive.

24 Ida Posselt conveyed all this information for the public in an extensive interview for *The Boston Sunday Globe*, March 18, 1923. Ruth Posselt Archive.

25 Max Smith, "Girl of Ten Makes Violin Fairly Sing in Amazing Concert," *New York American*, March 7, 1923. Ruth Posselt Archive.

26 *Boston Sunday Globe*, March 18, 1923. Ruth Posselt Archive.

27 "Medford Girl Violinist Read Music at 4 Years," *Boston Traveler*, April 1923. Ruth Posselt Archive.

28 *Boston Globe*, April 16, 1923. Ruth Posselt Archive.

29 Ruth Posselt's School Notebooks. Ruth Posselt Archive.

30 Joseph Horowitz, *Classical Music in America: A History of Its Rise and Fall* (New York: W. W. Norton, 2005), p. 265.

31 While vividly recalling playing for Heifetz, the "offer" he made her, and the terrible row this caused in her family, Posselt herself was not precise on when this audition took place, and how exactly it came about. She was firm, however, about her being 12 years old at the time and about playing the Rondo Capriccioso that Heifetz had

just played. These details are consonant with the February 1924 recital program Heifetz played in Symphony Hall. Posselt told this story in a long taped conversation about Richard Burgin that she had with Bob Ripley at her home in Gulfport, Fla., in September 1994. Mr. Ripley graciously made a copy for me. It will henceforth be cited here as "Interview with Bob Ripley," September 1994. Tape recording transcribed and edited by Diana Burgin. Ruth Posselt Archive.

Chapter 2: A Struggling Young Artist: 1926–1931

32 Phrase used by Charles Watkins, president of the Harvard Club, in a letter to Ruth Posselt, February 4, 1949. Watkins added in closing, "Please give my best regards to your distinguished husband and remember that I feel that you are quite as distinguished as he is, and don't let him lord it over you." Ruth Posselt Archive.

33 Tape of an interview with Borgeson, WFSU (?) Tallahassee, Florida, April 14, 1969. Ruth Posselt Archive.

34 Beneath the photos of Posselt and Ondříček the caption reads: "Miss Ruth Posselt, famed Medford violinist, and her teacher and brother-in-law, Boston's famed maestro, Emanuel Ondricek." Ruth Posselt Archive.

35 "Ruth Posselt Masters Violin at Aeolian Hall," *New York Herald*, November 9, 1926. Ruth Posselt Archive,

36 *Boston Traveler,* November 11, 1926. Ruth Posselt Archive.

37 Clipping from a Boston newspaper, December 6, 1926, "Girl Violinist in Fine Recital. Ruth Posselt Shows Feeling and Technique." Ruth Posselt Archive.

38 "Ruth Posselt in Violin Recital. Medford Girl Plays with Phenomenal Skill," *Boston Globe*, December 6, 1926. Ruth Posselt Archive.

39 Posselt's verbal communication to the author (May 1981).

40 Letter from Ruth Posselt to Arthur Newcomb, November 4, 1927. Ruth Posselt Archive.

41 Review in *Boston Globe*, January 30, 1928. Ruth Posselt Archive.

42 Letter from Ruth Posselt to Arthur Newcomb, March 22, 1928. Ruth Posselt Archive.

43 Letter from Ruth Posselt to Arthur Newcomb, December 23, 1927. Posselt did have "bad tonsils" and a chronic sinus condition, and suffered from frequent sore throats.

44 Letter from Ruth Posselt to Arthur Newcomb, March 23, 1928. Ruth Posselt Archive.

45 Letter from Ruth Posselt to Arthur Newcomb, March 28, 1928. Ruth Posselt Archive.

46 Letter from Ida Posselt to Ruth Posselt, March 1953. Ruth Posselt Archive.

47 *New York Telegram,* December 3, 1928. Ruth Posselt Archive.

48 Copy of letter from Ruth Posselt to Max Smith, January 8, 1929. Copy provided me by the Max Smith Archives at the Music Library, Yale University.

49 Letter from Kenneth Teele to Ruth Posselt, June 25, 1928. Ruth Posselt Archive.

50 Information about Olga Samaroff from *Virtuoso. The Olga Samaroff Story*, DVD, Vivace I Productions, Tiburon, California.

51 Brochure for the Schubert Memorial, 1929. Ruth Posselt Archive.

52 "Medford Entry in Quest," *Boston Evening American*, April 2, 1929. Ruth Posselt Archive.

53 Reported by Ruth Posselt in a letter to Arthur Newcomb, April 22, 1929. Ruth Posselt Archive.

54 *Medford Mercury* May 15 1929. Ruth Posselt Archive.

55 Letter from Ruth Posselt to Arthur Newcomb, April 24, 1929. Ruth Posselt Archive.

56 Letter from Ruth Posselt to Arthur Newcomb, May 15, 1929. Ruth Posselt Archive.

57 H. J. Henderson, *New York Evening Sun*, December 5, 1929, and Olin Downes, *New York Times,* December 5, 1929. Clippings in the Ruth Posselt Archive.

58 *Rocky Mountain News*, Denver, Colorado, January 10, 1931.

59 Letter from Victor Argenzio to Ruth Posselt, October 28, 1973. Ruth Posselt Archive.

60 Letter from May Fiske Hoffman to Ruth Posselt, March 27, 1951. Hoffman was concert chairman and president of the Massachusetts Federation of Music Clubs. Ruth Posselt Archive.

61 Warren Storey Smith, "Ruth Posselt Recital," *Boston Post*, March 10, 1932. Ruth Posselt Archive.

62 Copy of letter from Ruth Posselt to Max Smith, April 27, 1932. Copy provided me by the Max Smith Archives at the Music Library, Yale University.

Chapter Three: An American Virtuosa in Europe: 1932–1935

63 Information about Jacques Thibaud from Henry Roth, *Violin Virtuosos from Paganini to the 21st Century* (Los Angeles: California Classics Books, 1997), pp. 49-59.

64 Albert Spalding, *Rise to Follow*, quoted in Roth, *Violin Virtuosos,* p. 50.

65 Christian Goubault, *Jacques Thibaud – Violoniste français* (Paris: Champion, 1988), p. 105 (translation mine).

66 Undated note in French from Jacques Thibaud to Viola T. Fuller, probably from the summer of 1932. Thibaud's glowing words eventually found their way into the Boston press. Thibaud must have given his assessment to Ruth who copied it on the back of one of her letters to Arthur, which is where I came across it. Ruth Posselt Archive.

67 Letter from Ruth Posselt to Arthur Newcomb, July 7, 1932. Ruth Posselt Archive.

68 Quoted in Frederick Herman Martens, *Violin Mastery: Talks with Master Violinists and Teachers* (New York: Frederick A. Stokes Co., 1919), p. 111.

69 Ibid.

70 Letter from Ruth Posselt to Arthur Newcomb, July 7, 1932. Ruth Posselt Archive.

71 Letter from Jacques Thibaud to Ruth Posselt, November 14, 1932; original in French (translation mine). Ruth Posselt Archive.

72 Ironically, when Posselt debuted in Paris with the Paganini Concerto at Thibaud's insistence, one critic wrote: "the nicest compliment that can be given her is to say that she made the [Paganini concerto] sound like important music." When she played the Tchaikovsky (a concerto Thibaud detested) in Paris with the maestro Paul Paray three weeks later, there were no snide remarks about the intrinsic value of the piece that this time, she chose. Maybe because she did choose it.

73 Letter from Ruth Posselt to Ida Posselt, November 7, 1932. Ruth Posselt Archive.

74 *Boston Traveler*, "Medford Girl Violinist Astounds Critics Abroad," February 18, 1933. Ruth Posselt Archive

75 Ibid.

76 *Boston Traveler*, March 23, 1933. Ruth Posselt Archive.

77 Dwight Shepler, "Ruth Posselt Takes Salt with Her Flattery," *Boston Herald*, January 1934. Emphasis added. The original portrait is in the Ruth Posselt Archive.

78 *Rotterdam Courant*, January 29, 1934. Ruth Posselt Archive.

79 By "some small criticisms" Ida meant "such great reviews."

80 Letter from Jacques Thibaud to Ruth Posselt, February 21, 1934, original in French (translation mine). Ruth Posselt Archive.

81 "Ruth Posselt Performs 'Tour de Cadenza,'" Press Material on Ruth Posselt, Violinist. National Concert and Artists Corporation. Typescript of press releases for local managers. Ruth Posselt Archive.

82 "Ruth Posselt, la soliste brilliante," *De Telegraaf*, March 2, 1934, original in French (translation mine). Ruth Posselt Archive.

83 Letter from Jacques Thibaud to Ruth Posselt, May 14, 1934, original in French (translation mine). Ruth Posselt Archive.

84 Information paraphrased from two unpublished letters of July 11 and 25, 1934, from Alexander Merovitch to Ruth Posselt. Ruth Posselt Archive.

85 Letter from Jacques Thibaud to Ruth Posselt, August 16, 1934, original in French (translation mine). Ruth Posselt Archive.

86 L. D. Zimont (1909–1986), *Memuary (Memoirs),* chapter 33: "Institut." http://luzim.narod.ru/memuary/ZiLDm33.html. Published on the Zimont-Luchinskii family site, March 6, 2007. In Russian (translation mine). My thanks to Svetlana Sivak for finding this reminiscence for me.

87 In relating this to Bob Ripley (see note 31 above), Posselt did not mention the name of the American friend in Moscow. I suspect it was Arthur, her husband.

88 Cited by Galina Kopytova, *Yasha Heifetz v Rossii (Jascha Heifetz in Russia),* p. 548. (Translation mine – DLB).

89 *Boston Globe*, March 10, 1935.

90 "Medford Girl Fiddles for 5000 Soviet Troops," *Boston Daily Record*, February 14, 1935.

91 "Almost Froze to Death, but She Liked Russia," *Boston Sunday Globe*, March 10, 1935.

92 This orchestra, Nemgosfilarmonia (Acronym for German State Philharmonic), was founded in the Autonomous Socialist Republic of Volga Germans in 1934,

and based in Engels, which had a large population of Germans, dating from the 18th century. The German Philharmonic was disbanded in 1937, re-established the following year and went out of existence in 1941 at the start of World War II. "In 1934, many leading soloists appeared under A.I. Klimov, the orchestra's first music director, including Lev Oborin, Boris Fishman, David Oistrakh, Genrikh Neigauz, Ruth Posseit [*sic!*]," and others. Posselt appears to be the only foreign-born soloist listed in the online article, "Filarmoniia nemetskaia gosudarstvennaia" (German State Philharmonic), at <u>http://rusdeutsch-panorama.ru/jencik_statja.php?mode=view&site_id=34&own_menu_id=3364</u>

93 "Ruth Posselt, Violinist, Gives Town Hall Recital," *New York Tribune,* February 4, 1935.

94 "Ruth Posselt Wins Applause at Town Hall Violin Recital," *New York World-Telegram*, February 5, 1935.

95 Clipping from a Boston newspaper, March 3, 1935. Ruth Posselt Archive.

96 *Journal-Transcript,* Franklin, N.H., March 21, 1935.

97 *Boston Sunday Post,* March 3, 1935. Ruth was actually twenty-three at the time of this interview.

Chapter Four: The Love of Two R's: 1935–1940

98 "Ruth Posselt Borrows Suit in White House," *Boston Globe*, December 20, 1937.

99 *Boston Globe,* March 15, 1935.

100 *Journal-Transcript* (Franklin, N.H.), March 21, 1935. Posselt had played a recital in Phenix Hall, Concord, N.H as a youngster, on November 1, 1923. The program included pieces by Saltarella, Wieniawski, Sarasate, Rimsky-Korsakov and Rehfield, but nothing by Beethoven.

101 Gary Graffman, *I Really Should Be Practicing* (New York: Avon Books, 1981), pp. 10, 35.

102 "Interview with Bob Ripley," September 1994. Tape recording transcribed and edited by Diana Burgin. Ruth Posselt Archive.

103 Warren Storey Smith, *Boston Post,* March 26, 1935.

104 In a letter of November 27 from Mounds Park Hospital in St. Paul, Minnesota, Merovitch wrote "Ruthotshka" and asked her to visit him. Ruth Posselt Archive.

105 *Chicago Herald Examiner*, November 29, 1935.

106 "Woman Violinist Declares Men Spoil Feminine Stage Careers," *Richmond Post Dispatch*, January 6, 1936.

107 Ayke Agus, *Heifetz As I Knew Him* (Pompton Plain, N.J.: Amadeus Press, 2005).

108 Moses Smith, *Boston Evening Transcript*, October 31, 1936.

109 William Chase, "Ruth Posselt Scores at Concert," *Boston Traveler*, October 31, 1936.

110 C. W. D[urgin], *Boston Globe*, October 31, 1936.

111 Ruth Masters, "Posselt with the Symphony," *Boston Sunday Advertiser*, November 1, 1936.

112 Koussevitzky spoke these words to Mr. Smith, dean of the music faculty at Yale University, after a BSO concert in New Haven on November 16, 1938. He later put his assessment in writing in a letter.

113 Charles Munch had already begun his tenure as music director of the BSO in the fall 1950. Koussevitzky directed the BSO with Posselt as his soloist for the last time at Tanglewood on July 16, 1950. She played the Bach E Major Concerto.

114 *New York Sun*, February 20, 1937.

115 Letter from Jacques Thibaud to Ruth Posselt, May 5, 1937, original in French (translation mine). Ruth Posselt Archive.

116 Letter from Ruth Posselt to Richard Burgin, June 17, 1937. Ruth Posselt Archive.

117 Henry Roth, *Violin Virtuosos from Paganini to the 21st Century* (Los Angeles: California Classics Books, 1997), p. 188.

118 Elena Ostleitner, "Erica Morini," *Jewish Women: A Comprehensive Historical Encyclopedia.* http://jwa.org/encyclopedia/article/morini-erica.

119 Letter from Haensel & Jones, October 13, 1937. Ruth Posselt Archive.

120 The policeman was obviously more familiar with Edgar Bergen, the famous ventriloquist, one of whose famous dummies was Charlie McCarthy, than with Richard Burgin, concertmaster of the BSO. Burgin pronounced his surname with a hard *g*, in the Russian pronunciation.

121 Letter from Richard Burgin to Ruth Posselt, December 6, 1937, Ruth Posselt Archive.

122 Eleanor Roosevelt, "My Day," *New York World-Telegram*, December 16, 1937.

123 Letter from Richard Burgin to Ruth Posselt, December 14, 1937. Ruth Posselt Archive.

124 *Boston Globe,* December 20, 1937.

125 Information about the Hill concerto from John N. Burk, "Violin Concerto, Op. 38," *Concert Bulletin of the Boston Symphony Orchestra,* Fifty-Eighth Season, 1938–1939, pp. 267–68.

126 The world premiere of the Hill Violin Concerto has been digitally remastered and is included in the 3-CD set, "Ruth Posselt American Violinist Historic Performances," WHRA-6016 (West Hill Radio Archives, 2007).

127 Cyrus Durgin, *Boston Globe*, November 12, 1938.

128 *Boston Herald,* November 13, 1938.

129 Alexander Williams, "Weekend Concerts," *Boston Herald,* November 13, 1938.

130 Postcard from Ruth Posselt to Richard Burgin, December 31, 1938.

131 Letter from Richard Burgin to Ruth Posselt, postmarked December 28, 1938, 1:30 p.m.

132 Glenn Dillard Gunn, "Ruth Posselt Acclaimed as Violin Soloist," *Times-Herald* (Washington, D.C.), March 13, 1939.

133 Letter from E. B. Hill to Ruth Posselt, April 24, 1951. Ruth Posselt Archive.

134 According to the divorce law at the time, a divorced woman would officially retain her husband's name unless the courts granted her permission to revert to her maiden name.

135 Letter from Richard Burgin to Ruth Posselt, August 4, 1939. Ruth Posselt Archive. Burgin's plan exists in a 7-page carbon –copy of a typescript, entitled "The Berkshire Institute of Music. Plan of Organization." (Submitted by Richard Burgin). The manuscript has four sections: I – The purpose of the institute; II – Requirements for admission; III - Practical and theoretical studies; IV - Sample program covering two weeks of the Institute's activity. It would seem that this Plan of Organization represents Burgin's idea for setting up the Academy that he spoke of in his 1939 letter to Posselt, and convinced Koussevitzky to accept.

136 It is now a well-known fact that Koussevitzky learned what he conducted not from studying the score but from listening to the music performed. When he

first came to Boston, he hired Nicholas Slonimsky to play the piano scores of every piece he conducted.

137 Olin Downes, "American Music Applauded Again," *New York Times,* November 26, 1939. Ruth Posselt Archive

138 Ann Taylor Casadaban, email to the author, February 28, 2016.

139 Information on Bosmans is paraphrased and quoted from Helen Metzelaar, Bosmans, Henriette, Oxford Music Online. URL: http://www.oxfordmusiconline. com:80/subscriber/article/grove/music/03662, p. 1.

140 "Leon Barzin Conducts Hartford Orchestra and Ruth Posselt Is Violin Soloist," *Hartford Daily Courant*, November 15, 1939.

141 Quoted in Carol J. Oja, "Reappraising Walter Piston," http://www.newmusicbox. org/articles/reappraising-walter-piston/. [The online article isn't paginated.]

142 Ibid.

143 Ruth Posselt, radio interview with Mr. An Borgeson, Assistant Program Director at WFSU-FM, Tallahassee, Fla., 1969. Transcription by author. Ruth Posselt Archive.

144 Letter from Walter Piston to Ruth Posselt, September 17, 1939. Ruth Posselt Archive.

145 *Medford Mercury*, March 4, 1940. Ruth Posselt Archive.

146 Program of the Fifth Concert of the Season 1939–40 by the National Orchestral Association, Carnegie Hall, Monday evening, March 18, 1940, at 8:45 o'clock. Ruth Posselt Archive.

147 Ruth Posselt, 1940 Diary, entry for March 18, 1940. Ruth Posselt Archive.

148 R.C.B, "Carnegie Concert," *New York World-Telegram*, March 19, 1940.

149 Letter from Ruth Posselt to Richard Burgin, March 9, 1940. Ruth Posselt Archive.

150 Oja, "Reappraising Walter Piston."

151 Ibid.

152 Alexander Williams, "Ruth Posselt, Violinist, Soloist with Symphony – Richard Burgin Directs," *The Boston Herald*, February 1, 1941.

153 Cyrus Durgin, "Symphony Hall," *Boston Globe*, February 1, 1941.

154 Warren Storey Smith, "Posselt with Symphony. Wife Soloist as Richard Burgin Conducts," *Boston Post*, February 1, 1941.

155 Richard Burgin, *Memoralia*, edited by Diana Burgin. Available in English at www.dianaburgin.com.

156 Due to the outbreak of war in Europe, the world premiere actually took place in March 1940.

157 Excerpts from Ruth Posselt's unpublished 1940 Diary, edited and shaped into a continuous narrative by DLB.

158 *New York Herald Tribune*, July 31, 1956.

159 Letter from Ida Posselt to Ruth Posselt, July 7, 1940. Ruth Posselt Archive.

Chapter Five: Posselt at Her Peak: 1940–1951

160 Ruth Posselt, 1940 Diary, Ruth Posselt Archive.

161 Lillian Tyler Plogstedt, *Cincinnati Post*, October 19, 1940. Ruth Posselt Archive.

162 *Musical America*, "Posselt Offers Hindemith Work," November 10, 1940.

163 Letter of Gertrude Hindemith to Ruth Posselt, February 15, 1952 (emphasis in original). Ruth Posselt Archive.

164 *New York Herald Tribune*, January 11, 1941. Ruth Posselt Archive.

165 *New York Times*, January 10, 1941. Ruth Posselt Archive.

166 Comment made by Richard Burgin in a letter to Ruth Posselt of September 18, 1956, where he said how happy he was she had been able to hear the tape of her performance of the Hindemith at Tanglewood.

167 *Christian Science Monitor*, March 21, 1964. Ruth Posselt Archive.

168 *Boston Globe*, March 21, 1964. Ruth Posselt Archive.

169 Flyer in Ruth Posselt Archive.

170 Francis D. Perkins, "Music Festival in Berkshires Ends Eighth Year," *New York Tribune*, August 18, 1941. Ruth Posselt Archive.

171 Letter of Samuel Barber to Ruth Posselt, August 1940. Ruth Posselt Archive.

172 *Fort Lauderdale Herald*, March 3, 1942.

173 Edmund Wilson. *The Forties*. New York: Farrar, Straus and Giroux, 1983, p. 25.

174 Letter from Ruth Posselt to Richard Burgin of December 5, 1948. The letter was returned to sender. Ruth Posselt Archive.

175 Excerpted and edited from "Interview with Bob Ripley," September 1994. Tape recording transcribed and edited by Diana Burgin. Ruth Posselt Archive.

176 Robert Taylor, "Burgin Receives Rising Ovation," *Boston Herald*, April 14, 1962, and Cyrus Durgin, "Burgin Leads Symphony, Ruth Posselt Is Soloist," *Boston Globe*, April 14, 1962. P.S. If I may add my voice as a member of the audience, they *were* superb. [DLB]

177 Ann Taylor Casadaban, "Scattered memories of Ruth Posselt," June 2010, email communication to the author.

178 "Ruth Posselt in Concert at Woolsey Hall," New Haven, Conn., April 6, 1942.

179 New Haven Symphony Orchestra Program, Season 1941–42 – Seventh Concert, April 6, 1942. Author not indicated. Ruth Posselt Archive.

180 "Miss Posselt Scores," *New Haven Register,* April 7, 1942.

181 Vernon Duke, *Passport to Paris* (Boston: Little, Brown, 1955), p. 398.

182 Ibid.

183 The full score of the violin concerto was not completed until after the first performance in March 1943.

184 Duke, *Passport to Paris,* p. 399. Emphasis in original.

185 Dukelsky's own words in a letter to Ruth Posselt of July 1943. Ruth Posselt Archive.

186 Duke, *Passport to Paris*, p. 399.

187 Ruth Posselt, 1942 Diary. Ruth Posselt Archive.

188 A digitally remastered recording of the first performance, with accompanying video, is available on YouTube, https://www.youtube.com/watch?v=z7tvdbiwlbs.

189 Doris Reno, "Miss Posselt Mixes Career, Motherhood," *Miami Herald*, June 1953.

190 Letter of Richard Burgin to Ruth Posselt, December 10, 1942. Ruth Posselt Archive.

191 Letter of Ruth Posselt to Richard Burgin, January 6, 1943. Ruth Posselt Archive.

192 Quoted in the Program Note, Philharmonic Symphony Society of New York, One Hundred Second Season, 1943–44, Program for Wednesday Evening and Friday Afternoon, January 5, 7, 1944. Ruth Posselt Archive.

193 "Ruth Posselt Discusses Work She Will Play with Symphony," *Christian Science Monitor*, March 18, 1943.

194 Duke, *Passport to Paris,* p. 417.

195 My thanks to Ann Casadaban for pointing out these difficulties to me.

196 *Boston Daily Globe*, March 20, 1943.

197 Letter from Ida Posselt to Ruth Posselt, March 29, 1943. Ruth Posselt Archive.

198 Copy of a letter of Bruno Zirato to Arthur Rodzinski, June 14, 1943, provided me by Professor Simon and the Bohuslav Martinu Institute.

199 Copy of a letter of Arthur Rodzinski to Bruno Zirato, June 16, 1943, re scheduling of Ruth Posselt's playing Martinu [Concerto da Camera] with New York Philharmonic, provided me by Professor Simon and the Bohuslav Martinu Institute. Emphasis added.

200 Letter from Vernon Duke to Ruth Posselt, July 26, 1943. Emphasis in original. Ruth Posselt Archive.

201 Letter from Bruno Zirato to Arthur Rodzinski, August 30, 1943. Clearly, the Philharmonic had decided not to cut Martinů out entirely, and would perform his Second Symphony instead of his Concerto da Camera.

202 Letter from H. W. Heinsheimer, Boosey & Hawkes, to Ruth Posselt, August 30, 1943. Ruth Posselt Archive.

203 Letter from Bohuslav Martinu to Ruth Posselt, September 2, 1943. Ruth Posselt Archive.

204 Vernon Duke, *Passport to Paris*, p. 421.

205 Olin Downes, "Miss Posselt Heard," *New York Times*, January 6, 1944.

206 Musical Events, *The New Yorker*, January 1944.

207 Letter from Richard Burgin to Ruth Posselt, early January 1944. Ruth Posselt Archive.

208 Virgil Thomson, "A Serious Evening," *New York Herald Tribune*, January 18, 1944.

209 This recording can now be heard on YouTube at https://www.youtube.com/watch?v=8sXJu7CxBC0.

210 "Ruth Posselt," *Boston Herald*, January 31, 1944.

211 G. Y. Loveridge, *Berkshire Eagle*, August 5, 1944. Sketch by Carl Meier.

212 Letter from Marjorie Posselt to Ruth Posselt, August 26, 1944.

213 Isaac Stern (with Chaim Potok), *My First 79 Years* New York: Alfred A. Knopf, 1999), p. 32.

214 Letter from Marks Levine to Ruth Posselt, September 7, 1945. Ruth Posselt Archive.

215 Letter from Richard Burgin to Ruth Posselt, December 4, 1947.

216 *Boston Globe*, March 15, 1948.Ruth Posselt Archive.

217 Letter from Mildred Shaw to Ruth Posselt, March 13, 1948. Emphasis added. Ruth Posselt Archive.

218 Copy of a letter from David Libidins to Aaron Richmond, December 8, 1948. Ruth Posselt Archive.

219 Letter from Ida Posselt to Ruth Posselt, August 15, 1949. Ruth Posselt Archive.

Chapter Six: Nerves, Nostrums, and New Musical Outlets: 1951–1964

220 Henry Roth comments: "Menuhin had a critical breakdown-one from which he… never fully recovered! … [He] had to contend with the most onerous rival of all-Yehudi Menuhin and his early reputation. He did survive the pressure of his violinistic competitors if audience attendance, size of fees, and box office clout are any barometer, though his violinistic potential, in the opinion of many firsthand observers, has never been completely fulfilled." *Violin Virtuosos From Paganini to the 21ˢᵗ Century*, p. 162.

221 *Pittsburgh Sun-Telegraph*, December 30, 1943. Ruth Posselt Archive.

222 *Jascha Heifetz: God's Fiddler*, a film by Peter Rosen. Kultur D4729.

223 Draft of a letter from Ruth Posselt to Richard Burgin, January 8, 1945, Indianapolis. Ruth Posselt Archive.

224 Letter from Richard Burgin to Ruth Posselt, January 8, 1945. Ruth Posselt Archive.

225 Letter from Richard Burgin to Ruth Posselt, January 5, 1945. Ruth Posselt Archive.

226 See Lucy Green, "The Solo Instrumentalist in Classical Music," in *Music, Gender, Education* (Cambridge: Cambridge University Press, 1997).

227 Rudolph Elie, *Boston Herald*, February 3, 1951. Ruth Posselt Archive.

228 Barbara L. Kelly, Rivier, Jean. Oxford Music Online, URL: http://www.oxford-musiconline.com:80/subscriber/article/grove/music/23541, p.1.

229 Posselt's remarks quoted from a Boston newspaper article, February 1[?], 1951. Ruth Posselt Archive.

230 "Rivier's Violin Concerto Presented – Ruth Posselt is Soloist," *New York Times*, February 18, 1951. Ruth Posselt Archive

231 Jerome Bohm, *New York Herald Tribune*, February 18, 1951. Ruth Posselt Archive.

232 All three reviews appeared in their respective newspapers on February 3, 1951.

233 *Boston Globe*, April 19, 1951. Ruth Posselt Archive.

234 Milt Sosin, *Miami Daily News*, June 25, 1953. Ruth Posselt Archive.

235 John Wm. Riley, "Early Music Society Concert in Cambridge," *Boston Daily Globe*, December 1, 1953. Ruth Posselt Archive.

236 Information about Erwin Bodky and CSEM from Helen Slosberg, Mary Ullman, and Isabel Whiting, eds. *Erwin Bodky: A Memorial Tribute* (Waltham, Mass.: Brandeis University, 1965).

237 "Early Music in Cambridge," *Christian Science Monitor*, December 2, 1952. Ruth Posselt Archive.

238 Olin Downes, "New Music Heard under Bernstein," *New York Times*, March 30, 1953. Ruth Posselt Archive.

239 Letter from Luigi Dallapiccola to Ruth Posselt, May 31, 1956; original in French. Ruth Posselt Archive.

240 The photo appeared in *The Berkshire Eagle*, July 31, 1954.

241 *New York Times,* August 2, 1954. Ruth Posselt Archive.

242 *Berkshire Eagle*, August 2, 1954. Ruth Posselt Archive.

243 Milton Bass, *Berkshire Eagle*, August 3, 1954. Ruth Posselt Archive.

244 The gesture of Burgin kissing Posselt's hand, recalls the newlyweds' second joint appearance with the BSO in 1941. *Boston Daily Globe*, October 29, 1955.

245 *Christian Science Monitor*, October 20, 1955. Ruth Posselt Archive.

246 Robert Sabin, "Richard Burgin: Veteran in Two Careers," *Musical America*, March 1962.

247 Richard Burgin, *Memoralia*, English version, at www.dianaburgin.com.

248 *New York Times*, January 29, 1962. Ruth Posselt Archive.

249 Letter from Gladys Ondříček to Ruth Posselt, October 31, 1955. Ruth Posselt Archive.

250 Letter from Mrs. Gardner Read to Ruth Posselt, October 29, 1955. Ruth Posselt Archive.

251 *Florida Times-Union*, Jacksonville, Fla., February 28, 1975. Ruth Posselt Archive.

252 Lois Gosa, email to the author, March 1, 2016.

253 Letter from Thomas Perry to Ruth Posselt, February 10, 1958. Ruth Posselt Archive.

254 Quotes are from, respectively, *Boston Herald*; *Boston Globe*; and *Christian Science Monitor*.All three appeared on March 21, 1964.

255 Spoken by the dean of the FSU School of Music during a conversation with Posselt in March 1979.

Chapter Seven: An Artist in Academe: The Florida Years, 1965–1979

256 *The Tallahassee Democrat*, October 29, 1963. Ruth Posselt Archive.

257 Ann Taylor Casadaban, email communication to the author, June 2010.

258 Nancy T. Lu, "Taiwan's Finest Violinists Plan to Honor Beloved Teacher Sylvia Shu-Te Lee on Her 80th Birthday," Living and Loving Art, June 8, 2009. http://worldofnancylublog.blogspot.com/2009/06/taiwans-finest-violinists-to-honor.html.

259 Letter from Hiroko Abe to Ruth Posselt, June 14, 1967. Ruth Posselt Archive.

260 Email from Hiroko Nakahara to the author, February 29, 2016.

261 Malcolm Brannen, "The Art of Editing – Musical Ownership," *American String Teacher*, May 2005, Vol. 55, Issue 2, p. 104.

262 *St. Petersburg Times*, August 9, 1970. Ruth Posselt Archive.

263 Ruth Posselt, "Interview with Bob Ripley," September 1994. Tape recording transcribed and edited by Diana Burgin. Ruth Posselt Archive.

Postlude: Living and Performing Los

264 Posselt gave a private recital in Gulfport, Fla., on April 13, 1986.

265 Posselt's last live performance, a recital with pianist Margaret Sullivan, at her home in Gulfport, Fla., on April 12, 1987.

266 Gladys Ondříček died in a Brookline nursing home in October 1982, and after Naomi Posselt Breault succumbed to a heart condition about a year later, Ruth became the last surviving Posselt of 60 Sheridan Avenue, Medford. (Marjorie had passed in 1978 and Grace in 1980).

List of Illustrations

36. Recital program in Kharkov, USSR, December 19, 1934.

37. "In remembrance from Moskow," sketch by an unknown member of the audience at Posselt's recital in Moscow on New Year's Day, 1935.

38. "Producer of Child Prodigies": Emanuel Ondricek and his star pupil, Ruth Posselt.

Chapter Four – The Love of Two R's: 1935–1940

39. The headline in *The Boston Globe* read "Miss Posselt Crowned 'Queen of America on the Violin.'"

40. Richard Burgin in the 1930s. Photo by Roberts Studio, Boston.

41. Ruth and her dog, Peke. Photo by Juan Sanroma, Boston. Published in *The Boston Herald,* September 27, 1936.

42. Posselt in The Hague, March 1937.

43. Program of Posselt's concert with the Czech Philharmonic, Prague, March 20, 1937.

44. Richard Burgin in 1920. Inscribed to "Ruth Posselt with admiration and love. Jan. 25, 1937, Boston." Photo by Bachrach, 1920.

45. *The Boston Globe*, December 20, 1937.

46. Ruth and Richard at the Towers' camp in New Hampshire, summer 1938.

47. Swedish conductor Georg Schnéevoigt, inscribed "To Miss Ruth Posselt in kind remembrance from Georg Schnéevoigt, 1939 Helsingfors 5th of February."

48. Happiness: Posselt frolics in the waves at Manomet, July 27, 1939.

49. Ruth, Ida, and Richard's shadow, Manomet, July 1939.

50. Henriëtte Bosmans, inscribed "To my genial colleague Ruth Posselt, very thankfully for all musical collaboration and friendly assistance, Henriëtte Bosmans, March, 1940." Photo by Groot, Amsterdam.

51. First page of the manuscript of the Piston Concerto No. 1 for Violin. Ruth Posselt Archive.

52. " 'Well Done, my Dear': Richard Burgin, concertmaster of the Boston Symphony Orchestra, who turned conductor last night as his wife, Ruth Posselt, played a violin solo in two compositions, kisses her hand following the performance." February 1, 1941. Whitestone Photo.

53. Paul Hindemith playing the rebec.

54. *The Boston Globe* on July 5, 1940: "Famed Violinist a Bride."

55. The Burgins' wedding breakfast, July 14, 1940.

Chapter Five – Posselt at Her Peak: 1940–1951

56. The Towers (Stanley, Mary, and Barbara) and the Burgins (Ruth and Richard), Tanglewood, 1940.

57. "It was good wasn't it?" Posselt and Burgin take their bows after the Hindemith at Tanglewood, July 29, 1956.

58. Tanglewood premiere of the Barber Violin Concerto, August 1941. Left to right: Richard Burgin, clapping, Ruth Posselt, Samuel Barber, and Serge Koussevitzky on the podium.

59. Koussevitzky and Posselt after the premiere of the Barber Violin Concerto in New York.

60. Vladimir Dukelsky, inscribed "To Ruth Posselt, with whom it has been a joy to collaborate, with my true admiration and my friendship, Vladimir Dukelsky, February 10, 1940." Photo by Laskin, St. Louis.

61. Unidentified man, Ruth Posselt, and Bohuslav Martinů, Tanglewood, 1942.

62. Ruth and baby Diana, early fall, 1943.

63. Performance with the Springfield Symphony Orchestra, May 7, 1944.

64. Posselt Playing the Mozart D Major Violin Concerto at Tanglewood. Sketch by Carl Meier.

65. Flyer, "Ruth Posselt, One of the Greatest Violinists of Our Time," October 1944.

66. Igor Stravinsky, inscribed "To Ruth Posselt, the beautiful virtuoso, Warmest wishes, I. Stravinsky, 1946."

67. Ruth Posselt receiving flowers after her performance of the Lalo Symphonie Espagnole with the Springfield Symphony, October 22, 1947.

68. The Burgins, early July 1947. Ruth is holding her son. Photo by Mitchell Studio, Pittsfield, Mass.

69. After the Hindemith at Tanglewood. Left to right: Richard Burgin, Ruth Posselt, and Leonard Bernstein, July 1947.

Chapter Six – Nerves, Nostrums, and New Musical Outlets: 1952–1964

Bibliography

Books and DVDs

Agus, Ayke. *Heifetz as I Knew Him*. Pompton Plain, N.J.: Amadeus Press, 2005.

Axelrod, Herbert, and Todd Axelrod. *Heifetz*. 3rd rev. ed. Neptune City, N.J.: Paganiniana Publications, 1990.

Bazzana, Kevin. *Lost Genius. The Curious and Tragic Story of an Extraordinary Musical Prodigy*. Boston: Da Capo Press, 2007.

Bowers, Jane, and Judith Tick, eds. *Women Making Music. The Western Art Tradition, 1150–1950*. Urbana: University of Illinois Press, 1987.

Burton, Humphrey. *Yehudi Menuhin*. Boston: Northeastern University Press, 2001.

Campbell, Margaret. *The Great Violinists*. New York: Doubleday, 1981.

Cook, Susan, and Judy Tsou, eds. *Cecilia Reclaimed. Feminist Perspectives on Gender and Music*. Urbana: University of Illinois Press, 1994.

Crawford, Richard. *A History of America's Musical Life*. New York: W. W. Norton, 2001.

Doring, Ernest N.. *The Guadagnini Family Violin Makers*. Mineola, N.Y.: Dover Publications, 2012.

Duke, Vernon. *Passport to Paris*. Boston: Little, Brown, 1955.

Goubault, Christian. *Jacques Thibaud (1880–1933): Violoniste français*. Paris: Librairie Honore Champion, 1988.

Green, Lucy. *Music, Gender, Education*. Cambridge: Cambridge University Press, 1997.

Hetherington, John. *Melba: A Biography*. Melbourne: Melbourne University Press, 1967.

Jusefovich, Viktor. *David Oistrakh: Conversations with Igor Oistrakh*. London: Cassell, 1977.

Kloss, Sherry. *Jascha Heifetz Through My Eyes*. Muncie, Ind.: Ball State University/Music, 2000.

Kopytova, Galina. *Yasha Heifetz v Rossii (Jascha Heifetz in Russia)*. Saint Petersburg: Izd. Kompozitor, 2004.

Leichtentritt, Hugo. *Serge Koussevitzky. The Boston Symphony Orchestra and the New American Music*. Cambridge, Mass.: Harvard University Press, 1946.

Martens, Frederick Herman. *Violin Mastery: Talks with Master Violinists and Teachers*. New York: Frederick A. Stokes Company, 1919.

Menuhin, Yehudi. *Unfinished Journey*. New York: Fromm International, 1999.

Milstein, Nathan, and Solomon Volkov. *From Russia to the West: The Musical Memoirs and Reminiscences of Nathan Milstein*. New York: Henry Holt, 1990.

Neuls-Bates, Carol, ed. *Women in Music: An Anthology of Source Readings from the Middle Ages to the Present*. Boston: Northeastern University Press, 1996.

Pendle, Karin, ed. *Women & Music: A History*. Bloomington: Indiana University Press, 2001.

Rolfe, Lionel Menuhin. *The Menuhins: A Family Odyssey*. San Francisco: Panjandrum/Aris Books, 1978.

Rosen, Peter, dir. *Jascha Heifetz: God's Fiddler*. New Jersey: Kultur Video, 2011. DVD.

Roth, Henry. *Violin Virtuosos from Paganini to the 21st Century*. Los Angeles: California Classics Books, 1997.

Schoenbaum, David. *The Violin: A Social History of the World's Most Versatile Instrument*. New York: W. W. Norton, 2013.

Slosberg, Helen, Mary Ullman, and Isabel Whiting, eds. *Erwin Bodky: A Memorial Tribute*. Waltham, Mass.: Brandeis University, 1965.

Stern, Isaac, and Chaim Potok. *My First 79 Years*. New York: Alfred A. Knopf, 1999.

Virtuoso: The Olga Samaroff Story. Narrated by Frederica von Stade. Director: Donna Kline. Tiburon, Calif.: Vivace 1 Productions, 2009. DVD.

Unpublished Sources: The Ruth Posselt Archive

The Ruth Posselt Archive is currently housed at the author's home in Housatonic, Massachusetts. Parts of it can be browsed online at www.dianaburgin.com. For inquiries: Diana.Burgin@umb.edu.

1. Flyers and Pictures, 1922–2007

2. Ruth's Story in Her Own Words (a chronological compilation of Posselt's writings in diaries, appointment books, letters, interviews, quoted words in articles, anecdotes, press releases, etc.)

3. Letters from Ruth's Family (mother, siblings, in-laws, first husband)

4. The Love of Two R's: Richard Burgin & Ruth Posselt in Concerts, Letters, Memories & Diaries, 1935–1981

5. Letters to Ruth Posselt from Musicians and Managers

6. Photographs of a Lifetime, 1913–2007

7. Forty Years Making Music Together – The Richard Burgin–Ruth Posselt Double Concerto

8. Queen of the Violin and Queen of Pulchritude: Gendered and Nationalist Perceptions of Ruth Posselt

9. Performing Premieres: Timeline of Premier Performances, 1933–1979 (Dates and commentary in the history of each work from composition to repeat performances.)

10. Scrapbooks and School Notebooks of Ruth Posselt

11. Reviews of Posselt Performances 1926-1978

12. Performing Life. Programs by Ruth Posselt, Volume 1: 1918-1946; Volume 2: 1947-1987

Discography

Commercial Recordings

1. Albinoni: Trio Sonata for 2 Violins & Continuo w. Richard Burgin, violin, Cambridge Society for Early Music.	Unicorn 1030 Kapp 9024
2. Arbos: Tango, Op. 6 No. 3, w. Allan Sly, piano.	Academy ALP-304 WHRA - CD 6016
3. Bach: Sonata in G Major for Flute, Violin & Continuo w. Philip Kaplan, flute; Erwin Bodky, harpsichord; Samuel Mayes, cello.	Allegro AL 89 Allegro-Elite 4004
4. Barber: Violin Concerto Op. 14 w. Richard Burgin cond. Boston Symphony Orchestra. Live. April 13, 1962 (Stereo).	WHRA - CD 6016
5. Barber: Violin Concerto Op. 14 (rev. version) w. Serge Koussevitzky cond. Boston Symphony Orchestra. Live. January 7, 1949.	WHRA - CD 6039
6. Beethoven: Trio in G Major, Op. 1, No. 2; Trio in D Major, Op. 70, No. 1 "Ghost" w. Samuel Mayes, cello; Abba Bogin, piano.	Allegro-Elite 3026
7. Beethoven: Trio No. 1 in G Major, Op. 9; Trio No. 2 in D Major, Op. 9 w. Samuel Mayes, cello; Joseph De Pasquale, viola.	Brunswick AXTL 1056 Decca DL-9635
8. Bloch: *Baal Shem* w. Richard Burgin cond. Florida State Chamber Orchestra. Live. Oct. 17, 1967.	WHRA - CD 6016
9. Brahms: Piano Quartet in G Minor, Opus 25 w. Bel Arte Trio, Ralph Berkowitz, piano.	The Sinequan (doxepin HCl) Collector's Series SPS HK-3272
10. Dall' Abaco: Sonata in C for 2 Violins & Continuo, w. Richard Burgin, violin, Cambridge Society for Early Music.	Kapp 9024 Unicorn 1030
11. Dallapiccola: Tartiniana for Violin w. Columbia Symphony, Leonard Bernstein cond.	Columbia ML-4996 (CD) Sony SMK-60125
12. Fauré: Sonata for Violin & Piano, Op. 108.	Festival 70-203

13. Fibich: Poem (Arr. Kubelik), w. Gladys Posselt, piano.	Vic. 4184 (78 RPM)
14. Haydn: Duet for Violin & cello in D Major with Samuel Mayes, cello.	Festival 70-203
15. Hill: Concerto for Violin, Op. 38 Premiere Performance: Serge Koussevitzky, cond. Boston Symphony Orchestra. Live. Nov. 11, 1938.	WHRA- CD 6016
16. Hindemith: Violin Sonata in E Major. w. Allan Sly, piano.	Academy ALP-304 WHRA- CD 6016
17. Hindemith: Violin Concerto w. Russell Stanger cond. Harvard-Radcliffe Orchestra. Live. March 25, 1951.	WHRA- CD 6016
18. Khachaturian: Violin Concerto in D Minor w. Richard Burgin cond. Boston Symphony Orchestra. Live. Oct. 28, 1955.	WHRA- CD 6016
19. Martinů: Duo for Violin & cello w. Samuel Mayes, cello.	Festival 70-203
20. Mozart: Trio in B-flat, K. 502; Trio in E Major, K. 542 w. Samuel Mayes, cello; Abba Bogin, piano.	Allegro-Elite 3014
21. Mozart: Divertimento in E-flat, K. 563 w. Samuel Mayes, cello; Joseph De Pasquale, viola.	Decca DL-9659
22. Prokofiev: *Five Melodies,* Op. 35. w. Allan Sly, piano.	Academy ALP-304 (CD) WHRA - 6016
23. Stich (Gen'l Punto): Quartet in F for Horn & Strings.	Boston B-209
24. Tchaikovsky: Violin Concerto in D Major w. Richard Burgin cond. Springfield Symphony Orchestra. Live. May 7, 1944.	WHRA-CD 6016
25. Torelli: Concerto in D for Violin, Strings & Continuo.	Unicorn 1030
26. Veracini: Sonata for Violin & Continuo in B, Op. 1 No. 3.	Unicorn 1030 Kapp 9024
27. Villa-Lobos: Premiere Sonate Fantaisie, w. Allan Sly, piano.	Academy ALP-304 (CD) WHRA 6016
28. Vivaldi: Concerto in A Major for Violin & Strings & Continuo.	Unicorn 1030
29. Wieniawski: Sielanka (La Champêtre) w. Gladys Posselt, piano.	Vic. 4184 (78 RPM)

Noncommercial Recordings

Unless otherwise noted, these CDs were made by Nathan Brown of Albuquerque, New Mexico, and were digitally remastered from tapes of radio broadcasts in his personal collection, and in some cases from private tapes and recordings in Ruth Posselt's personal archive.

Concertos and Sonatas

BACH: Brandenburg Concerto No. 4 w/FSU Chamber Orchestra, Richard Burgin, conducting, Oct. 30, 1970.

BACH: Concerto in D Minor for Violin & Oboe w/ Ralph Gomberg, BSO, Munch, conducting, July 5, 1959.

BARBER: Violin Concerto
    (a) with BSO, Koussevitsky, Jan. 7, 1949
    (b) with BSO, Burgin, Apr. 13, 1962
    (c) with FSU Chamber Orchestra, Spurgeon, May 7, 1973

BARTOK: Sonata No. 2: Rehearsal with John Boda, piano, undated but probably Feb. 1971.

BLOCH: Baal Shem
    (a) Rehearsal, with BSO, Munch, Mar. 24, 1951
    (b) with FSU Chamber Orchestra, Burgin, Oct. 17, 1967

COPLAND: Sonata for violin and piano: Ruth Posselt, violin; Aaron Copland, piano. February 20, 1944. Recorded off the air from WNYC. Remastered by Ward Marston, August 2012. (Available on YouTube)

DUKELSKY: Violin Concerto w/BSO, Burgin, Mar. 20, 1943. Remastered by Ward Marston, 2012. (Available on YouTube)

FROMM: Sonata in G w/Boykan, piano (1951?)

HILL: Violin Concerto, with BSO, Koussevitsky, Nov. 12, 1938 (premiere)

HINDEMITH: Violin Concerto
    (a) with Harvard-Radcliffe Orchestra, Stanger, Mar. 25, 1951
    (b) with NEC Orchestra, Dixon, 1960
    (c) with BSO, Leinsdorf, Mar. 20, 1964

KHACHATURIAN: Violin Concerto with BSO, Burgin, Oct. 28, 1955

LALO: Symphonie Espagnole
    (a) with BSO, Szell, Jan. 19, 1945
    (b) with BSO, Munch, Dec. 11, 1953 (played I.M. Jacques Thibaud)

MOZART: Serenade No. 9, K.250 "Haffner" with FSU Chamber Orchestra, Burgin, Feb. 17, 1970.

MOZART: Sinfonia Concertante in E-flat, K. 364, all with Joseph de Pasquale, viola.
    (a) with BSO, Munch, Oct. 25, 1957
    (b) with BSO, Munch, July 11, 1958
    (c) with BSO, Munch, July 14, 1962

MOZART: Violin Concerto in D Major, w. Koussevitzky & BSO, recorded from radio broadcast, August 5, 1944, Tanglewood.

RAVEL: Sonata for violin & cello with Samuel Mayes, cello. (inc.) May be test for Allegro LP never issued.

TCHAIKOVSKY: Violin Concerto w/Springfield Symphony, Burgin, May 7, 1944.

Chamber Music and Recitals

FSU Quartet in Residence, Nov. 24, 1964: HAYDN: Quartet in D, Op. 64, No. 5; BRAHMS: Piano Quartet in G, Op. 25.

FSU Quartet in Residence, Oct. 19, 1965: BEETHOVEN: Quartet in C, Op. 18, No. 4. MARTINU: Duo for violin and cello; BRAHMS: Piano Quartet in G, Op. 25.

FSU Recital with Nigel Cox & Harold Gray, pianos, Apr. 23, 1969: CORELLI-POSSELT: Suite; IVES: Sonata No. 2; BARTOK: Roumanian Dances; BACH: Sonata in A; BLOCH: Nigun; short pieces by DEBUSSY, BENNETT, COPLAND.

FSU Faculty Recital, Nov. 4, 1969 with Harold Gray, piano and organ; VITALI: Chaconne; LEKEU: Sonata; HINDEMITH: Sonata in E; PROKOFIEFF: Melodies; short pieces by KABALEVSKY, DE FALLA, LEVY.

Florestan Quartet, Mar. 13, 1970: BORODIN: Quartet in D; HINDEMITH: Quartet No. 3; DVORAK: Pianoforte Quartet.

Florestan Quartet, Dec. 2, 1970: BEETHOVEN: Septet (excerpt); BEETHOVEN: Opus 130 (incomplete)

FSU Recital with John Boda, piano, Feb. 21, 1971: BARTOK: Contrasts; Sonata No. 2

Florestan Quartet Recital, Mar. 2, 1971 with John Boda, piano: BRAHMS: Trio, Op. 8; MARTINU: Duo for Violin and Cello; PROKOFIEV: Quartet No. 2

Florestan Quartet, Nov. 23, 1971: BRAHMS: Clarinet Quintet w/ Schmidt; HAYDN: Quartet in E; SHOSTAKOVICH: Quartet, Op. 49

Florida State Trio (Ruth Posselt, Harry Dunscombe, John Boda) at Troy State, Alabama, May 28, 1973: TCHAIKOVSKY: Piano Trio, Op. 50

Recital in Gulfport, Fla with Margaret Douglas, piano, Apr. 12, 1987: DES-PLANES-NACHEZ: Intrada; CORELLI-POSSELT: Suite; DEBUSSY: Golliwog's Cake Walk; Beau Soir; MASSENET: Meditation from "Thais"; BLOCH: Nigun; RACHMANINOV: Vocalise; KABALEVSKY: Improvisation.